AN OUTLINE OF PHILOSOPHY

Philosophy, Russell argues in *An Outline of Philosophy*, is concerned with the universe as a whole. Man demands consideration solely as the instrument by which we acquire knowledge of the universe. In the first part of this book Russell illuminates the ways in which we are capable of knowledge and discovering natural laws with a discussion of perception, memory, learning in infants and animals and linguistic ability. He moves on to a study of the physical world and then to a discussion of man as he sees himself. Finally Russell considers some of the great philosophers of the past and what Philosophy has to say about man's place in the universe. Throughout the book Russell attempts to reveal the sort of world in which, according to modern science, we really live, and just how it differs from the world in which we seem to live. He makes clear the effect of modern scientific advance which has transformed our concept of the world: in this book the new world is presented with great clarity.

BY BERTRAND RUSSELL

An Outline of Philosophy

BERTRAND RUSSELL

with an introduction by
John G. Slater

London and New York

First published in Great Britain 1927 by George Allen & Unwin
First published in paperback 1979 by Unwin Hyman Ltd

Reprinted 1993
by Routledge
11 New Fetter Lane, London EC4P 4EE
29 West 35th Street. New York, NY 10001

Revised edition 1995
Reprinted in 1996

© 1927, 1989 Unwin Hyman Limited
Introduction © 1995 John G. Slater

Typeset in Plantin by Solidus (Bristol) Limited
Printed in Great Britain by Cox & Wyman Ltd, Reading, Berkshire

British Library Cataloguing in Publication Data
A catalogue record for this book is available from the Library of Congress

ISBN 0-415-14030-7 (hbk)
ISBN 0-415-14117-6 (pbk)

Contents

Introduction

Russell wrote *An Outline of Philosophy* (*Philosophy* in the USA) between 1 April and 1 July 1927. The idea for the book originated with W. W. Norton, an American publisher who was eager to add Russell to his stable of authors. To advance his case, Norton wrote to Stanley Unwin, who had been Russell's principal British publisher ever since he dared to publish Russell's controversial book, *Principles of Social Reconstruction* (*Why Men Fight* in the USA) in 1916, after other publishers had turned it down because of Russell's anti-war activities; in his letter, dated 19 July 1926, Norton sought to persuade Unwin that Russell would be better served by a single American publisher instead of the many he then had. At that time Russell had books with half a dozen American publishers. In addition to offering to work hard to sell his books, Norton made him a very attractive offer for his next one: 'If Mr. Russell has any general work in philosophy which he is considering or possibly has in preparation, we should be very glad to guarantee him the sum of $5,000.00 as royalties, and we should be willing to make a substantial advance against this sum.' Unwin, who found Norton's argument for a single American publisher convincing, communicated the proposal to Russell on 29 July. Russell responded two days later; he was prepared to accept Norton's offer if Unwin was satisfied with the financial arrangements. He went on to say that he was in the process of finishing the first draft of *The Analysis of Matter*, which he had placed with Kegan Paul (a very sore point with Unwin), and planned to complete the revision of it at Christmas-time. 'When this book is off my mind, I should like to do a book treating of philosophy in general. It is not clear to me how "popular" he wants me to be; does he want the book to be easier than *The Analysis of Mind*?'

Russell was not involved in the negotiations again until the autumn. Unwin, who functioned as his literary agent, had meanwhile settled the finances with Norton. On 14 October Russell told Unwin that he could write the book during the summer of 1927 with delivery in September. This quick schedule was possible because Russell was just then starting his delivery of a course of twenty lectures on 'Mind and Matter', under the auspices of the new British Institute for Philosophical Studies; during the previous year he had offered a similar course on the 'Problems of Philosophy' for the same Institute. 'The lectures that I am giving', he wrote to Unwin, 'would form a framework for the book, but the whole would have to be written out afresh.' The syllabuses for these lecture courses have been published in Appendix III of *Essays on Language, Mind and Matter, 1919–1926*, which is Volume 9 of *The Collected Papers of Bertrand Russell*. The finished book does not follow either syllabus, although nearly all of the topics covered in his lectures are discussed in the book. The fact that he had so recently developed these courses makes it clear why he so quickly agreed to Norton's proposal for a general book in philosophy. Russell was always ready to rework such popular material if it increased his income.

On 22 October 1926 Unwin sent Russell a signed contract for the book, specifying that a manuscript of about 100,000 words was to be delivered to him on or before 31 October 1927. Russell was to receive an advance against royalties of £200 – about one-fifth Norton's guarantee. Unwin, who was still smarting over Russell's failure to offer him *The Analysis of Matter*, was happy to have a new Russell title for his 1927 list. Even though the contract had been signed, there was still a question about the level at which the book should be pitched. Russell broached this question in a letter to Unwin on 17 November:

> Would you mind giving me your idea as to its scope? Should it attempt to deal popularly with all philosophy, or with the problem of Mind and Matter? Should the level of popularity be that of *The Problems of Philosophy* (Home University Library), or that of *Our Knowledge of the External World*, or that of *The Analysis of Mind*? I want to be thinking it over during the winter, though I can't begin writing till April.
>
> I should myself prefer *Mind and Matter*. Have you any views as to title?

Unwin advised him that the American market would prefer a book which dealt popularly with all of philosophy, and which was no more demanding on the general reader than *The Problems of Philosophy*. Personally, he would choose 'the book that you yourself preferred to write, because the more you enjoyed writing it the more people would enjoy reading it', but he doubted that such a book would prove popular enough for the United States market.

By the end of March 1927 Norton was becoming edgy by Russell's failure to supply him with any information about the proposed book, so he wrote to Unwin to urge him to remind Russell of his contractual obligations. Norton complained that they did not even have a title for advertising purposes, and stated that he would be satisfied with *Philosophy*, since books with titles of one word sold very well in America. About a week later Russell sent Unwin a short description of the book and a proposed table of contents, but he warned Unwin that the contents might be altered when he got down to writing the book. We gather that he proposed *An Outline of Philosophy* as the title: 'I don't care what title is chosen. If Mr. Norton wants *Philosophy*, well and good. But I slightly prefer the title I have suggested.' In a later letter he informed Unwin that he had met with Norton and they had agreed that the American edition should be called *Philosophy*. 'I gathered that in England you were going to stick to *An Outline of Philosophy* but I see the shorter title in your list of announcements. I don't care much either way, though, for England, I have a *slight* preference of the longer title. But it is not strong enough to outweigh any contrary feeling on your part.'

Russell presumably began writing the book shortly after he sent Unwin a description of it, for on 3 June he wrote to Unwin again: 'I am getting on faster than I expected with the *Outline of Philosophy* and hope to finish it by the end of this month, so that I can let you have it by July 15 about.' The book was finished well before the end of June, because on 2 July Russell told Unwin that he had three-quarters of the typescript in hand. 'I can certainly let you have the two typescripts of my book before July 9. I had hoped to be able to send them today but the typist has been slow.' While he was proof-reading it he had qualms about its suitability for the American market: 'I feel some anxiety lest the book should not satisfy Mr. Norton; he may think it not easy enough for his public. Will you please tell him that, if so, I can modify any parts that he objects to? Often more diffuseness is enough to make a book easy.' Two days later he sent Unwin the typescripts; he estimated its length at 105,000 words. Norton made no demands for alterations.

As has been noted, the scope of the book was determined by the perceived demands of the American reading public. Russell agreed to discuss a wide range of philosophical topics, including, and here his customary reluctance shows itself, those collectively called 'ethics'. In his opening paragraph to the chapter on ethics he gives the reader to understand that he is discussing the subject only because a treatment of it is expected in a book on philosophy generally. Even though he would have preferred to omit this chapter, he nevertheless used it to make two significant points. The first is to inform his readers that, partly due to Santayana's criticism, he has abandoned his earlier ethical position, which he had taken over from G. E. Moore. He no longer believed that *good* is a unique indefinable quality which some states of mind and some actions have and others lack. Actually, he had announced his rejection of the Moorian position, without crediting Santayana, in 1914, in 'Scientific Method in Philosophy' (included in *Mysticism and Logic*), where he made this startling statement: 'Ethics is in origin the art of recommending to others the sacrifices required for cooperation with oneself.' In that essay he did not develop an alternative theory. But given the nature of this book, he felt obliged to supply one, and the one he favours is emotivism. In this ethic 'good and bad are derivative from desire' (184); he then goes on to offer a preliminary analysis of what is meant by this statement. Had Norton not wanted a general work in philosophy, it seems unlikely that Russell would have recorded his ideas about the emotive meaning of ethical terms, ideas which were developed by others into a full-blown rival to Moore's position.

But Norton's expressed desires determined the content of the book in a more significant way. In his original letter to Unwin he remarked that it was his 'conviction that Mr. Russell is the one scholar today who should undertake a revision of philosophy in terms of modern science'. Norton also mentioned that John B. Watson, the behaviourist psychologist, was one of his authors. Now Russell had, nearly a decade earlier, developed a great respect for Watson's work, because it seemed to open the way to analysing mental phenomena using only physical events as data, a goal which fit nicely with the direction of Russell's own thinking on the nature of mind. Early in 1919 Russell wrote to Watson to this effect. Unfortunately his letters to Watson seem not to have survived, although Watson's have. Watson's reply, on 21 February 1919, contains a remark that seems to have made a strong impression on Russell. Watson remarked that he was 'writing a book on objective psychology', and a little later spelled out what he meant by this phrase: 'with no disrespect to philosophy at all, I am trying to get psychology just as far away from philosophy as are chemistry and physics – which of course is not so far as the average run of chemists and physicists think it is. I am hoping that when I succeed in getting out a systematic presentation the philosophers will take it up and show whether the system is possible.' This is just what Russell proceeds to do in *An Outline of Philosophy*.

A central theme of the book is to develop a behaviouristic definition of knowledge and then to apply it to various problems in an attempt to determine its limitations. As the reader will learn, Russell does uncover the point at which 'behaviourism *as a final philosophy* breaks down' (102). Introspection, which behaviourism rejects, is necessary, Russell argues, even in science. But although he finds behaviourism inadequate, he still thinks it valuable as a working hypothesis. Early in his discussion of truth and falsehood, he remarks that these predicates are supposed, by extension, to apply to beliefs, but 'let us first consider the truth and falsehood of statements, following our practice of going as far as we can with the behaviourists before falling back on introspection' (204).

The role played by behaviourism ('the new psychology' as the American blurb has it) in this book will hardly surprise those who are acquainted with Russell's philosophical development. From the time he read William James's *Essays in Radical Empiricism* in 1912 until he began work on *The Analysis of Mind* (1921) Russell thought about, but resisted accepting, James's contention that matter and mind were simply different organizations of the same basic stuff. James called it 'experience'; Russell, after adopting the Jamesian position in 1918, preferred 'events' as the designator of the neutral building blocks. Prior to espousing James's position, Russell had called his philosophy 'logical atomism', afterwards he shifted to the name 'neutral monism', perhaps because it had a more traditional ring about it. Neutral monism was, of course, not incompatible with logical atomism; indeed, Russell gradually developed the one out of the other. His earlier name for his philosophical position did strongly suggest the method of logical analysis, which remained, for the rest of his life, Russell's choice of method in philosophy. It is the method used in this book, and neutral monism, Russell informs us, is 'the view advocated in the present volume' (168).

This book is probably best known in philosophic circles as the place where Russell made his devastating judgment of Kant's place in philosophy. 'Kant has the reputation of being the greatest of modern philosophers, but to my mind he was a mere misfortune' (64). In his *Five Types of Ethical Theory* (1930), C. D. Broad questioned Russell's judgment of Kant's place in the philosophical pantheon on the ground that 'it seems a pity to apply to him an epithet which should obviously be reserved for Hegel' (10). At another place, and to the dismay of psychologists of all schools, Russell suggests that the design of many psychological experiments fails the test of objectivity: 'Animals studied by Americans rush about frantically, with an incredible display of hustle and pep, and at last achieve the desired result by chance. Animals observed by Germans sit still and think, and at last evolve the solution out of their inner consciousness. To the plain man, such as the present writer, this situation is discouraging' (23). Russell's wry description of himself as 'the plain man' is delicious. Finally, he irritated nearly the whole corps of academic philosophers by asserting that our thoughts are in our heads (108ff.). As he later (in *Portraits from Memory*) mischievously put it: 'I horrified all the philosophers by saying that their thoughts were in their heads. With one voice they assured me that they had no thoughts in their heads whatever, but politeness forbids me to accept this assurance' (163). Russell loved to tweak the establishment's nose, and especially that of the philosophical establishment.

John G. Slater
University of Toronto

Chapter 1

Philosophic Doubts

Perhaps it might be expected that I should begin with a definition of 'philosophy', but, rightly or wrongly, I do not propose to do so. The definition of 'philosophy' will vary according to the philosophy we adopt; all that we can say to begin with is that there are certain problems, which certain people find interesting, and which do not, at least at present, belong to any of the special sciences. These problems are all such as to raise doubts concerning what commonly passes for knowledge; and if the doubts are to be answered, it can only be by means of a special study, to which we give the name 'philosophy'. Therefore the first step in defining 'philosophy' is the indication of these problems and doubts, which is also the first step in the actual study of philosophy. There are some among the traditional problems of philosophy that do not seem to me to lend themselves to intellectual treatment, because they transcend our cognitive powers; such problems I shall not deal with. There are others, however, as to which, even if a final solution is not possible at present, yet much can be done to show the direction in which a solution is to be sought, and the *kind* of solution that may in time prove possible.

Philosophy arises from an unusually obstinate attempt to arrive at real knowledge. What passes for knowledge in ordinary life suffers from three defects: it is cocksure, vague, and self-contradictory. The first step towards philosophy consists in becoming aware of these defects, not in order to rest content with a lazy scepticism, but in order to substitute an amended kind of knowledge which shall be tentative, precise, and self-consistent. There is of course another quality which we wish our knowledge to possess, namely, comprehensiveness: we wish the area of our knowledge to be as wide as possible. But this is the business of science rather than of philosophy. A man does not necessarily become a better philosopher through knowing more scientific facts; it is principles and methods and general conceptions that he should learn from science if philosophy is what interests him. The philosopher's work is, so to speak, at the second remove from crude fact. Science tries to collect facts into bundles by means of scientific laws; these laws, rather than the original facts, are the raw material of philosophy. Philosophy involves a criticism of scientific knowledge, not from a point of view ultimately different from that of science, but from a point of view less concerned with details and more concerned with the harmony of the whole body of special sciences.

The special sciences have all grown up by the use of notions derived from common sense, such as things and their qualities, space, time, and causation. Science itself has shown that none of these common-sense notions will quite serve for the explanation of the world; but it is hardly the province of any special science to undertake the necessary reconstruction of fundamentals. This must be the business of philosophy. I want to say, to begin with, that I believe it to be a business of very great importance. I believe that the philosophical errors in common-sense beliefs not only produce confusion in science, but also do harm in ethics and politics, in social institutions, and in the conduct of everyday life. It will be no part of my business, in this volume, to point out these practical effects of a bad philosophy: my business will be purely intellectual. But if I am right, the intellectual adventures which lie before us have effects in many directions which seem, at first sight, quite remote from our theme. The effect of our passions upon our beliefs forms a favourite subject of modern psychologists; but the converse effect, that of our beliefs upon our passions, also exists, though it is not such as an old-fashioned intellectualist psychology would have supposed. Although I shall not discuss it, we shall do well to bear it in mind, in order to realise that our discussions may have bearings upon matters lying outside the sphere of pure intellect.

I mentioned a moment ago three defects in common beliefs, namely, that they are cocksure, vague, and self-contradictory. It is the business of philosophy to correct these defects so far as it can, without throwing over knowledge altogether. To be a good philosopher, a man must have a strong desire to know, combined with great caution in believing that he knows; he must also have logical acumen and the habit of exact thinking. All these, of course, are a matter of degree. Vagueness, in particular, belongs, in some degree, to all human thinking; we can diminish it indefinitely, but we can never abolish it wholly. Philosophy, accordingly, is a continuing activity, not something in which we can achieve final perfection once for all. In this respect, philosophy has suffered from its association with theology. Theological dogmas are fixed, and are regarded by the orthodox as incapable of improvement. Philosophers have too often tried to produce similarly final systems:

they have not been content with the gradual approximations that satisfied men of science. In this they seem to me to have been mistaken. Philosophy should be piecemeal and provisional like science; final truth belongs to heaven, not to this world.

The three defects which I have mentioned are interconnected, and by becoming aware of any one we may be led to recognise the other two. I will illustrate all three by a few examples.

Let us take first the belief in common objects, such as tables and chairs and trees. We all feel quite sure about these in ordinary life, and yet our reasons for confidence are really very inadequate. Naïve common sense supposes that they are what they appear to be, but that is impossible, since they do not appear exactly alike to any two simultaneous observers; at least, it is impossible if the object is a single thing, the same for all observers. If we are going to admit that the object is not what we see, we can no longer feel the same assurance that there is an object; this is the first intrusion of doubt. However, we shall speedily recover from this set-back, and say that of course the object is 'really' what physics says it is[1]. Now physics says that a table or a chair is 'really' an incredibly vast system of electrons and protons in rapid motion, with empty space in between. This is all very well. But the physicist, like the ordinary man, is dependent upon his senses for the existence of the physical world. If you go up to him solemnly and say, 'Would you be so kind as to tell me, as a physicist, what a chair really is?' you will get a learned answer. But if you say, without preamble, 'Is there a chair there?' he will say, 'Of course there is; can't you see it?' To this you ought to reply in the negative. You ought to say, 'No, I see certain patches of colour, but I don't see any electrons or protons, and you tell me that they are what a chair consists of.' He may reply: 'Yes, but a large number of electrons and protons close together look like a patch of colour.' 'What do you mean by "look like"?' you will then ask. He is ready with an answer. He means that light-waves start from the electrons and protons (or, more probably, are reflected by them from a source of light), reach the eye, have a series of effects upon the rods and cones, the optic nerve, and the brain, and finally produce a sensation. But he has never seen an eye or an optic nerve or a brain any more than he has seen a chair: he has only seen patches of colour which, he says, are what eyes 'look like'. That is

---

[1] I am not thinking here of the elementary physics to be found in a school text-book; I am thinking of modern theoretical physics, more particularly as regards the structure of atoms, as to which I shall have more to say in later chapters.

to say, he thinks that the sensation you have when (as you think) you see a chair, has a series of causes, physical and psychological, but all of them, on his own showing, lie essentially and forever outside experience. Nevertheless, he pretends to base his science upon observation. Obviously there is here a problem for the logician, a problem belonging not to physics, but to quite another kind of study. This is a first example of the way in which the pursuit of precision destroys certainty.

The physicist believes that he infers his electrons and protons from what he perceives. But the inference is never clearly set forth in a logical chain, and, if it were, it might not look sufficiently plausible to warrant much confidence. In actual fact, the whole development from common-sense objects to electrons and protons has been governed by certain beliefs, seldom conscious, but existing in every natural man. These beliefs are not unalterable, but they grow and develop like a tree. We start by thinking that a chair is as it appears to be, and is still there when we are not looking. But we find, by a little reflection, that these two beliefs are incompatible. If the chair is to persist independently of being seen by us, it must be something other than the patch of colour we see, because this is found to depend upon conditions extraneous to the chair, such as how the light falls, whether we are wearing blue spectacles, and so on. This forces the man of science to regard the 'real' chair as the cause (or an indispensable part of the cause) of our sensations when we see the chair. Thus we are committed to causation as an *a priori* belief without which we should have no reason for supposing that there is a 'real' chair at all. Also, for the sake of permanence we bring in the notion of substance: the 'real' chair is a substance, or collection of substances, possessed of permanence and the power to cause sensations. This metaphysical belief has operated, more or less unconsciously, in the inference from sensations to electrons and protons. The philosopher must drag such beliefs into the light of day, and see whether they still survive. Often it will be found that they die on exposure.

Let us now take up another point. The evidence for a physical law, or for any scientific law, always involves both memory and testimony. We have to rely both upon what we remember to have observed on former occasions, and on what others say they have observed. In the very beginnings of science, it may have been possible sometimes to dispense with testimony; but very soon every scientific investigation began to be built upon previously ascertained results, and thus to depend upon what others had recorded. In fact, without the corroboration of testimony we should hardly have had much confidence in the existence of physical objects. Sometimes people suffer from hallucinations, that is to say, they think they perceive physical objects, but are not confirmed in this belief by the testimony of others. In such cases, we decide that they are mistaken. It is the similarity between the perceptions of different people in similar situations that makes us feel confident of the external causation of our perceptions; but for this, whatever naïve beliefs we might have had in physical objects would have been dissipated long ago. Thus memory and testimony are essential to science. Nevertheless, each of these is open to criticism by the sceptic. Even if we succeed, more or less, in meeting his criticism, we shall, if we are rational, be left with a less complete confidence in our original beliefs than we had before. Once more, we shall become less cocksure as we become more accurate.

Both memory and testimony lead us into the sphere of psychology. I shall not at this stage discuss either beyond the point at which it is clear that there are genuine philosophical problems to be solved. I shall begin with memory.

Memory is a word which has a variety of meanings. The kind that I am concerned with at the moment is the recollection of past occurrences. This is so notoriously fallible that every experimenter makes a record of the result of his experiment at the earliest possible moment: he considers the inference from written words to past events less likely to be mistaken than the direct beliefs which constitute memory. But some time, though perhaps only a few seconds, must elapse between the observation and the making of the record, unless the record is so fragmentary that memory is needed to interpret it. Thus we do not escape from the need of trusting memory to some degree. Moreover, without memory we should not think of interpreting records as applying to the past, because we should not know that there was any past. Now, apart from arguments as to the proved fallibility of memory, there is one awkward consideration which the sceptic may urge. Remembering, which occurs now, cannot possibly – he may say – prove that what is remembered occurred at some other time, because the world might have sprung into being five minutes ago, exactly as it then was, full of acts of remembering which were entirely misleading. Opponents of Darwin, such as Edmund Gosse's father, urged a very similar argument against evolution. The world, they said, was created in 4004 BC, complete with fossils, which were inserted to try our faith. The world was created suddenly, but was made such as it would have been if it had evolved. There is no logical impossibility about this view. And similarly there is no logical impossibility in the view that the world was created five minutes ago, complete with memories and records. This may seem an improbable hypothesis, but it is not logically refutable.

Apart from this argument, which may be thought fantastic, there are reasons of detail for being more or less distrustful of memory. It is obvious that no *direct* confirmation of a belief about a past occurrence is possible, because we cannot make the past recur. We can find confirmation of an indirect kind in the revelations of others and in contemporary records. The latter, as we have seen, involve some degree of memory, but they may involve very little, for instance when a shorthand report of a conversation or speech has been made at the time. But even then, we do not escape wholly from the need of memory extending over a longer stretch of time. Suppose a wholly imaginary conversation were produced for some criminal purpose, we should depend upon the memories of witnesses to establish its fictitious character in a law-court. And all memory which extends over a long period of time is very apt to be mistaken; this is shown by the errors invariably found in autobiographies. Any man who comes across letters which he wrote many years ago can verify the manner in which his memory has falsified past events. For these reasons, the fact that we cannot free ourselves from dependence upon memory in building up knowledge is, *prima facie,* a reason for regarding what passes for knowledge as not quite certain. The whole of this subject of memory will be considered more carefully in later chapters.

Testimony raises even more awkward problems. What makes them so awkward is the fact that testimony is involved in building up our knowledge of physics, and that, conversely, physics is required in establishing the trustworthiness of testimony. Moreover, testimony raises all the problems connected with the relation of mind and matter. Some eminent philosophers, e.g. Leibniz, have constructed systems according to which there would be no such thing as testimony, and yet have accepted as true many things which cannot be known without it. I do not think philosophy has quite done justice to this problem, but a few words will, I think, show its gravity.

For our purposes, we may define testimony as noises heard, or shapes seen, analogous to those which we should make if we wished to convey an assertion, and believed by the hearer or seer to be due to someone else's desire to convey an assertion. Let us take a concrete instance : I ask a policeman the way, and he says, 'Fourth to the right, third to the left'. That is to say, I hear these sounds, and perhaps I see what I interpret as his lips moving. I assume that he has a mind more or less like my own, and has uttered these sounds with the same intention as I should have had if I had uttered them, namely to convey information. In ordinary life, all this is not, in any proper sense, an inference; it is a belief which arises in us on the appropriate occasion. But if we are challenged, we have to substitute inference for spontaneous belief, and the more the inference is examined the more shaky it looks.

The inference that has to be made has two steps, one physical and one psychological. The physical inference is of the sort we considered a moment ago, in which we pass from a sensation to a physical occurrence. We hear noises, and think they proceed from the policeman's body. We see moving shapes, and interpret them as physical motions of his lips. This inference, as we saw earlier, is in part justified by testimony; yet now we find that it has to be made before we can have reason to believe that there is any such thing as testimony. And this inference is certainly sometimes mistaken. Lunatics hear voices which other people do not hear; instead of crediting them with abnormally acute hearing, we lock them up. But if we sometimes hear sentences which have not proceeded from a body, why should this not always be the case? Perhaps our imagination has conjured up all the things that we think others have said to us. But this is part of the general problem of inferring physical objects from sensations, which, difficult as it is, is not the most difficult part of the logical puzzles concerning testimony. The most difficult part is the inference from the policeman's body to his mind. I do not mean any special insult to policemen; I would say the same of politicians and even of philosophers.

The inference to the policeman's mind certainly *may* be wrong. It is clear that a maker of waxworks could make a life-like policeman and put a gramophone inside him, which would cause him periodically to tell visitors the way to the most interesting part of the exhibition at the entrance to which he would stand. They would have just the sort of evidence of his being alive that is found convincing in the case of other policemen. Descartes believed that animals have no minds, but are merely complicated automata. Eighteenth-century materialists extended this doctrine to men. But I am not now concerned with materialism; my problem is a different one. Even a materialist must admit that, when he talks, he means to convey something, that is to say, he uses words as signs, not as mere noises. It may be difficult to decide exactly what is meant by this statement, but it is clear that it means something, and that it is true of one's own remarks. The question is: Are we sure that it is true of the remarks we hear, as well as of those we make? Or are the remarks we hear perhaps just like other noises, merely meaningless disturbances of the air? The chief argument against this is analogy: the remarks we hear are so like those we make that we think they must have similar causes. But although we cannot dispense with analogy as a form of inference, it is by no means demonstrative, and not infrequently leads us astray. We are therefore left, once more, with a *prima facie* reason for uncertainty and doubt.

This question of what we mean ourselves when we speak brings me to another problem, that of introspection. Many philosophers have held that introspection gave the most indubitable of all knowledge; others have held that there is no such thing as introspection. Descartes, after trying to doubt everything, arrived at 'I think, therefore I am', as a basis for the rest of knowledge. Dr. John B. Watson the behaviourist holds, on the contrary, that we do not think, but only talk. Dr. Watson, in real life, gives as much evidence of thinking as anyone does, so, if *he* is not convinced that he thinks, we are all in a bad way. At any rate, the mere existence of such an opinion as his, on the part of a competent philosopher, must suffice to show that introspection is not so certain as some people have thought. But let us examine this question a little more closely.

The difference between introspection and what we call perception of external objects seems to me to be connected, not with what is primary in our knowledge, but with what is inferred. We think, at one time, that we are seeing a chair; at another, that we are thinking about philosophy. The first we call perception of an external object; the second we call introspection. Now we have already found reason to doubt external perception, in the full-blooded sense in which common sense accepts it. I shall consider later what there is that is indubitable and primitive in perception; for the moment, I shall anticipate by saying that what is indubitable in 'seeing a chair' is the occurrence of a certain pattern of colours. But this occurrence, we shall find, is connected with me just as much as with the chair; no one except myself can see exactly the pattern that I see. There is thus something subjective and private about what we take to be external perception, but this is concealed by precarious extensions into the physical world. I think introspection, on the contrary, involves precarious extensions into the mental world: shorn of these, it is not very different from external perception shorn of its extensions. To make this clear, I shall try to show what we know to be occurring when, as we say, we think about philosophy.

Suppose, as the result of introspection, you arrive at a belief which you express in the words: 'I am now believing that mind is different from matter'. What do you know, apart from inferences, in such a case? First of all, you must cut out the word 'I': the person who believes is an inference, not part of what you know immediately. In the second place, you must be careful about the word 'believing'. I am not now concerned with what this word should mean in logic or theory of knowledge; I am concerned with what it can mean when used to describe a direct experience. In such a case, it would seem that it can only describe a certain kind of feeling. And as for the proposition you think you are believing, namely, 'mind is different from matter', it is very difficult to say what is really occurring when you think you believe it. It may be mere words, pronounced, visualised, or in auditory or motor images. It may be images of what the words 'mean', but in that case it will not be at all an accurate representation of the logical content of the proposition. You may have an image of a statue of Newton 'voyaging through strange seas of thought alone', and another image of a stone rolling downhill, combined with the words 'how different!' Or you may think of the difference between composing a lecture and eating your dinner. It is only when you come to expressing your thought in words that you approach logical precision.

Both in introspection and in external perception, we try to express what we know in WORDS.

We come here, as in the question of testimony, upon the social aspect of knowledge. The purpose of words is to give the same kind of publicity to thought as is claimed for physical objects. A number of people can hear a spoken word or see a written word, because each is a physical occurrence. If I say to you, 'mind is different from matter', there may be only a very slight resemblance between the thought that I am trying to express and the thought which is aroused in you, but these two thoughts have just this in common, that they can be expressed by the same words. Similarly, there may be great differences between what you and I see when, as we say, we look at the same chair; nevertheless we can both express our perceptions by the same words.

A thought and a perception are thus not so very different in their own nature. If physics is true, they are different in their correlations: when I see a chair, others have more or less similar perceptions, and it is thought that these are all connected with light-waves coming from the chair, whereas, when I think a thought, others may not be thinking anything similar. But this applies also to feeling a toothache, which would not usually be regarded as a case of introspection. On the whole, therefore, there seems no reason to regard introspection as a different *kind* of knowledge from external perception. But this whole question will concern us again at a later stage.

As for the *trustworthiness* of introspection, there is again a complete parallelism with the case of external perception. The actual datum, in each case, is unimpeachable, but the extensions which we make instinctively are questionable. Instead of saying, 'I am believing that mind is different from matter', you ought to say, 'certain images are occurring in a certain relation to each other, accompanied by a certain feeling'. No words exist for describing the actual occurrence in all its particularity; all words, even proper names, are general, with the possible exception of 'this', which is ambiguous. When you translate the occurrence into words, you are making generalisations and inferences, just as you are when you say 'there is a chair'. There is really no vital difference between the two cases. In each case, what is really a datum is unutterable, and what can be put into words involves inferences which may be mistaken.

When I say that 'inferences' are involved, I am saying something not quite accurate unless carefully interpreted. In 'seeing a chair', for instance, we do not first apprehend a coloured pattern, and then proceed to infer a chair: belief in the chair arises spontaneously when we see the coloured pattern. But this belief has causes not only in the present physical stimulus, but also partly in past experience, partly in reflexes. In animals, reflexes play a very large part; in human beings, experience is more important. The infant learns slowly to correlate touch and sight, and to expect others to see what he sees. The habits which are thus formed are essential to our adult notion of an object such as a chair. The perception of a chair by means of sight has a physical stimulus which affects only sight directly, but stimulates ideas of solidity and so on through early experience. The inference might be called 'physiological'. An inference of this sort is evidence of past correlations, for instance between touch and sight, but may be mistaken in the present instance; you may, for example, mistake a reflection in a large mirror for another room. Similarly in dreams we make mistaken physiological inferences. We cannot therefore feel certainty in regard to things which are in this sense inferred, because, when we try to accept as many of them as possible, we are nevertheless compelled to reject some for the sake of self-consistency.

We arrived a moment ago at what we called 'physiological inference' as an essential ingredient in the common-sense notion of a physical object . Physiological inference, in its simplest form, means this: given a stimulus S, to which, by a reflex, we react by a bodily movement R, and a stimulus S′ with a reaction R′, if the two stimuli are frequently experienced together, S will in time produce R′[1]. That is to say, the body will act as if S′ were present. Physiological inference is important in theory of knowledge, and I shall have much to say about it at a later stage. For the present, I have mentioned it partly to prevent it from being confused with logical inference, and partly in order to introduce the problem of *induction*, about which we must say a few preliminary words at this stage.

Induction raises perhaps the most difficult problem in the whole theory of knowledge. Every scientific law is established by its means, and yet it is difficult to see why we should believe it to be a valid logical process. Induction, in its bare essence, consists of the argument that, because A and B have been often found together and never found apart, therefore, when A is found again, B will probably also be found. This exists first as a 'physiological inference', and as such is practised by animals. When we first begin to reflect, we find ourselves making inductions in the physiological sense, for instance, expecting the food we see to have a certain kind of taste. Often we only become aware of this expectation through having it disappointed, for instance if we take salt thinking it is sugar. When mankind took to science, they tried to formulate logical principles justifying this kind of inference. I shall discuss these attempts in later chapters; for the present, I will only say that they seem to me very unsuccessful. I am convinced that induction must have validity of some kind in some degree, but the problem of showing how or why it can be valid remains unsolved. Until it is solved, the rational man will doubt whether his food will nourish him, and whether the sun will rise tomorrow. I am not a rational man in this sense, but for the moment I shall pretend to be. And even if we cannot be completely rational, we should probably all be the better for becoming somewhat more rational than we are. At the lowest estimate, it will be an interesting adventure to see whither reason will lead us.

The problems we have been raising are none of them new, but they suffice to show that our everyday views of the world and of our relations to it are unsatisfactory. We have been asking whether we know this or that, but we have not yet asked what 'knowing' is. Perhaps we shall find that we have had wrong ideas as to knowing, and that our difficulties grow less when we have more correct ideas on this point.

[1]E.g. if you hear a sharp noise and see a bright light simultaneously often, in time the noise without the light will cause your pupils to contract.

I think we shall do well to begin our philosophical journey by an attempt to understand knowing considered as part of the relation of man to his environment, forgetting, for the moment, the fundamental doubts with which we have been concerned. Perhaps modern science may enable us to see philosophical problems in a new light. In that hope, let us examine the relation of man to his environment with a view to arriving at a scientific view as to what constitutes knowledge.

PART I MAN FROM WITHOUT

Chapter 2

Man and his Environment

If our scientific knowledge were full and complete, we should understand ourselves and the world and our relation to the world. As it is, our understanding of all three is fragmentary. For the present, it is the third question, that of our relation to the world, that I wish to consider, because this brings us nearest to the problems of philosophy. We shall find that it will lead us back to the other two questions, as to the world and as to ourselves, but that we shall understand both these better if we have considered first how the world acts upon us and how we act upon the world.

There are a number of sciences which deal with Man. We may deal with him in natural history, as one among the animals, having a certain place in evolution, and related to other animals in ascertainable ways. We may deal with him in physiology, as a structure capable of performing certain functions, and reacting to the environment in ways of which some, at least, can be explained by chemistry. We may study him in sociology, as a unit in various organisms, such as the family and the state. And we may study him, in psychology, as he appears to himself. This last gives what we may call an internal view of man, as opposed to the other three, which give an external view. That is to say, in psychology we use data which can only be obtained when the observer and the observed are the same person, whereas in the other ways of studying Man all our data can be obtained by observing other people. There are different ways of interpreting this distinction, and different views of its importance, but there can be no doubt that there is such a distinction. We can remember our own dreams, whereas we cannot know the dreams of others unless they tell us about them. We know when we have toothache, when our food tastes too salt, when we are remembering some past occurrence, and so on. All these events in our lives other people cannot know in the same direct way. In this sense, we all have an inner life, open to our own inspection but to no one else's. This is no doubt the source of the traditional distinction of mind and body: the body was supposed to be that part of us which others could observe, and the mind that part which was private to ourselves. The importance of the distinction has been called in question in recent times, and I do not myself believe that it has any fundamental philosophical significance. But historically it has played a dominant part in determining the conceptions from which men set out when they began to philosophise, and on this account, if on no other, it deserves to be borne in mind.

Knowledge, traditionally, has been viewed from within, as something which we observe in ourselves rather than as something which we can see others displaying. When I say that it has been so viewed, I mean that this has been the practice of philosophers; in ordinary life, people have been more objective. In ordinary life, knowledge is something which can be tested by examinations, that is to say, it consists in a certain kind of response to a certain kind of stimulus. This objective way of viewing knowledge is, to my mind, much more fruitful than the way which has been customary in philosophy. I mean that, if we wish to give a definition of 'knowing', we ought to define it as a manner of reacting to the environment, not as involving something (a 'state of mind') which only the person who has the knowledge can observe. It is because I hold this view that I think it best to begin with Man and his environment, rather than with those matters in which the observer and the observed must be the same person. Knowing, as I view it, is a characteristic which may be displayed in our reactions to our environment; it is therefore necessary first of all to consider the nature of these reactions as they appear in science.

Let us take some everyday situation. Suppose you are watching a race, and at the appropriate moment you say, 'They're off'. This exclamation is a reaction to the environment, and is taken to show knowledge if it is made at the same time as others make it. Now let us consider what has been really happening, according to science. The complication of what has happened is almost incredible. It may conveniently be divided into four stages: first, what happened in the outside world between the runners and your eyes; secondly, what happened in your body from your eyes to your brain; thirdly, what happened in your brain; fourthly, what happened in your body from your brain to the movements of your throat and tongue which constituted your exclamation. Of these four stages, the first belongs to physics, and is dealt with in the main by the theory of light; the second and fourth belong to physiology; the third, though it should theoretically also belong to physiology, belongs in fact rather to psychology, owing to our lack of knowledge as to the brain. The third stage embodies the results of experience and learning. It is responsible for the fact that you speak, which an animal would not do, and that you speak English, which a Frenchman would not do. This immensely complicated occurrence is, nevertheless, about the simplest example of knowledge that could possibly be given.

For the moment, let us leave on one side the part of this process which happens in the outside world and belongs to physics. I shall have much to say about it later, but what has to be said is not altogether easy, and we will take less abstruse matters first. I will merely observe that the event which we are said to perceive, namely, the runners starting, is separated by a longer or shorter chain of events from the event which happens at the surface of our eyes. It is this last that is what is called the 'stimulus'. Thus the event that we are said to perceive when we see is not the stimulus, but an anterior event related to it in a way that requires investigation. The same applies to hearing and smell, but not to touch or to perception of states of our own body. In these cases, the first of the above four stages is absent. It is clear that, in the case of sight, hearing and smell, there must be a certain relation between the stimulus and the event said to be perceived, but we will not now consider what this relation must be. We will consider, rather, the second, third, and fourth stages in an act of perceptive knowledge. This is the more legitimate as these stages always exist, whereas the first is confined to certain senses.

The second stage is that which proceeds from the sense-organ to the brain. It is not necessary for our purposes to consider exactly what goes on during this journey. A purely physical event – the stimulus – happens at the boundary of the body, and has a series of effects which travel along the afferent nerves to the brain. If the stimulus is light, it must fall on the eye to produce the characteristic effects; no doubt light falling on other parts of the body has effects, but they are not those that distinguish vision. Similarly, if the stimulus is sound, it must fall on the ear. A sense-organ, like a photographic plate, is responsive to stimuli of a certain sort: light falling on the eye has effects which are different for different wave-lengths, intensities, and directions. When the events in the eye due to incident light have taken place, they are followed by events in the optic nerve, leading at last to some occurrence in the brain – an occurrence which varies with the stimulus. The occurrence in the brain must be different for different stimuli in all cases where we can *perceive* differences. Red and yellow, for instance, are distinguishable in perception; therefore the occurrences along the optic nerve and in the brain must have a different character when caused by red light from what they have when caused by yellow light. But when two shades of colour are so similar that they can only be distinguished by delicate instruments, not by perception, we cannot be sure that they cause occurrences of different characters in the optic nerve and brain.

When the disturbance has reached the brain, it may or may not cause a characteristic set of events in the brain. If it does not, we shall not be what is called 'conscious' of it. For to be 'conscious' of seeing yellow, whatever else it may be, must certainly involve some kind of cerebral reaction to the message brought by the optic nerve. It may be assumed that the great majority of messages brought to the brain by the afferent nerves never secure any attention at all – they are like letters to a government office which remain unanswered. The things in the margin of the field of vision, unless they are in some way interesting, are usually unnoticed; if they are noticed, they are brought into the centre of the field of vision unless we make a deliberate effort to prevent this from occurring. These things are visible, in the sense that we could be aware of them if we chose, without any change in our physical environment or in our sense-organs; that is to say, only a cerebral change is required to enable them to cause a reaction. But usually they do not provoke any reaction; life would be altogether too wearing if we had to be always reacting to everything in the field of vision. Where there is no reaction, the second stage completes the process, and the third and fourth stages do not arise. In that case, there has been nothing that could be called 'perception' connected with the stimulus in question.

To us, however, the interesting case is that in which the process continues. In this case there is first a process in the brain, of which the nature is as yet conjectural, which travels from the centre appropriate to the sense in question to a motor centre. From there there is a process which travels along an efferent nerve, and finally results in a muscular event causing some bodily movement. In our illustration of the man watching the beginning of a race, a process travels from the part of the brain concerned with sight to the part concerned with speech; this is what we called the third stage. Then a process travels along the efferent nerves and brings about the movements which constitute saying 'They're off'; this is what we called the fourth stage.

Unless all four stages exist, there is nothing that can be called 'knowledge'. And even when they are all present, various further conditions must be satisfied if there is to be 'knowledge'. But these observations are premature, and we must return to the analysis of our third and fourth stages.

The third stage is of two sorts, according as we are concerned with a reflex or with a 'learned reaction', as Dr. Watson calls it. In the case of a reflex, if it is complete at birth, a new-born infant or animal has a brain so constituted that, without the need of any previous experience, there is a connection between a certain process in the afferent nerves and a certain other process in the efferent nerves. A good example of a reflex is sneezing. A certain kind of tickling in the nose produces a fairly violent movement having a very definite character, and this connection exists already in the youngest infants. Learned reactions, on the other hand, are such as only occur because of the effect of previous occurrences in the brain. One might illustrate by an analogy which, however, would be misleading if pressed. Imagine a desert in which no rain has ever fallen, and suppose that at last a thunderstorm occurs in it; then the course taken by the water will correspond to a reflex. But if rain continues to fall frequently, it will form watercourses and river valleys; when this has occurred, the water runs away along pre-formed channels, which are attributable to the past 'experience' of the region. This corresponds to 'learned reactions'. One of the most notable examples of learned reactions is speech: we speak because we have learned a certain language, not because our brain had originally any tendency to react in just that way. Perhaps all knowledge, certainly nearly all, is dependent upon learned reactions, i.e. upon connections in the brain which are not part of man's congenital equipment but are the result of events which have happened to him.

To distinguish between learned and unlearned responses is not always an easy task. It cannot be assumed that responses which are absent during the first weeks of life are all learned. To take the most obvious instance: sexual responses change their character to a greater or less extent at puberty, as a result of changes in the ductless glands, not as a result of experience. But this instance does not stand alone: as the body grows and develops, new modes of response come into play, modified, no doubt, by experience, but not wholly due to it.

For example: a new-born baby cannot run, and therefore does not run away from what is terrifying, as an older child does. The older child has learned to run, but has not necessarily learned to run *away*; the stimulus in learning to run may have never been a terrifying object. It would therefore be a fallacy to suppose that we can distinguish between learned and unlearned responses by observing what a new-born infant does, since reflexes may come into play at a later stage. Conversely, some things which a child does at birth may have been learned, when they are such as it could have done in the womb – for example, a certain amount of kicking and stretching. The whole distinction between learned and unlearned responses, therefore, is not so definite as we could wish. At the two extremes we get clear cases, such as sneezing on the one hand and speaking on the other; but there are intermediate forms of behaviour which are more difficult to classify.

This is not denied even by those who attach most importance to the distinction between learned and unlearned responses. In Dr. Watson's *Behaviourism* (p. 103), there is a 'Summary of Unlearned Equipment', which ends with the following paragraph:

'Other activities appear at a later stage – such as blinking, reaching, handling, handedness, crawling, standing, sitting-up, walking, running, jumping. *In the great majority of these later activities it is difficult to say how much of the act as a whole is due to training or conditioning. A considerable part is unquestionably due to the growth changes in structure, and the remainder is due to training and conditioning.*' (Watson's italics.)

It is not possible to make a logically sharp distinction in this matter; in certain cases we have to be satisfied with something less exact. For example, we might say that those developments which are merely due to normal growth are to count as unlearned, while those which depend upon special circumstances in the individual biography are to count as learned. But take, say, muscular development: this will not take place normally unless the muscles are used, and if they are used they are bound to learn some of the skill which is appropriate to them. And some things which must certainly count as learned, such as focussing with the eyes, depend upon circumstances which are normal and must be present in the case of every child that is not blind. The whole distinction, therefore, is one of degree rather than of kind; nevertheless it is valuable.

The value of the distinction between learned and unlearned reactions is connected with the laws of learning, to which we shall come in the next chapter. Experience modifies behaviour according to certain laws, and we may say that a learned reaction is one in the formation of which these laws have played a part. For example: children are frightened of loud noises from birth, but are not at first frightened of dogs; after they have heard a dog barking loudly, they may become frightened of dogs, which is a learned reaction. If we knew enough about the brain, we could make the distinction precise, by saying that learned reactions are those depending upon modifications of the brain other than mere growth. But as it is, we have to judge by observations of bodily behaviour, and the accompanying modifications in the brain are assumed on a basis of theory rather than actually observed.

The essential points, for our purposes, are comparatively simple. Man or any other animal, at birth, is such as to respond to certain stimuli in certain specific ways, i.e. by certain kinds of bodily movements; as he grows, these ways of responding change, partly as the mere result of developing structure, partly in consequence of events in his biography. The latter influence proceeds according to certain laws, which we shall consider, since they have much to do with the genesis of 'knowledge'.

But – the indignant reader may be exclaiming – knowing something is not a bodily movement, but a state of mind, and yet you talk to us about sneezing and such matters. I must ask the indignant reader's patience. He 'knows' that he has states of mind, and that his knowing is itself a state of mind. I do not deny that he has states of mind, but I ask two questions: First, what sort of thing are they? Secondly, what evidence can he give me that he knows about them? The first question he may find very difficult; and if he wants, in his answer, to show that states of mind are something of a sort totally different from bodily movements, he will have to tell me also what bodily movements are, which will plunge him into the most abstruse parts of physics. All this I propose to consider later on, and then I hope the indignant reader will be appeased. As to the second question, namely, what evidence of his knowledge another man can give me, it is clear that he must depend upon speech or writing, i.e. in either case upon bodily movements. Therefore whatever knowledge may be to the knower, as a social phenomenon it is something displayed in bodily movements. For the present I am deliberately postponing the question of what knowledge is to the knower, and confining myself to what it is for the external observer. And for him, necessarily, it is something shown by bodily movements made in answer to stimuli – more specifically, to examination questions. What else it may be I shall consider at a later stage.

However we may subsequently add to our present account by considering how knowledge appears to the knower, that will not invalidate anything that we may arrive at by considering how knowledge appears to the external observer. And there is something which it is important to realise, namely, that we are concerned with a process in which the environment first acts upon a man, and then he reacts upon the environment. This process has to be considered as a whole if we are to discuss what knowledge is. The older view would have been that the effect of the environment upon us might constitute a certain kind of knowledge (perception), while our reaction to the environment constituted volition. These were, in each case, 'mental' occurrences, and their connection with nerves and brain remained entirely mysterious. I think the mystery can be eliminated, and the subject removed from the realm of guesswork, by starting with the whole cycle from stimulus to bodily movement. In this way, knowing becomes something active, not something contemplative. Knowing and willing, in fact, are merely aspects of the one cycle, which must be considered in its entirety if it is to be rightly understood.

A few words must be said about the human body as a mechanism. It is an inconceivably complicated mechanism, and some men of science think that it is not explicable in terms of physics and chemistry but is regulated by some 'vital principle' which makes its laws different from those of dead matter. These men are called 'vitalists'. I do not myself see any reason to accept their view, but at the same time our knowledge is not sufficient to enable us to reject it definitely. What we can say is that their case is not proved, and that the opposite view is, scientifically, a more fruitful working hypothesis. It is better to look for physical and chemical explanations where we can, since we know of many processes in the human body which can be accounted for in this way, and of none which *certainly* cannot. To invoke a 'vital principle' is to give an excuse for laziness, when perhaps more diligent research would have enabled us to do without it. I shall therefore assume, as a working hypothesis, that the human body acts according to the same laws of physics and chemistry as those which govern dead matter, and that it differs from dead matter, not by its laws, but by the extraordinary complexity of its structure.

The movements of the human body may, none the less, be divided into two classes, which we may call respectively 'mechanical' and 'vital'. As an example of the former, I should give the movement of a man falling from a cliff into the sea. To explain this, in its broad features, it is not necessary to take account of the fact that the man is alive; his centre of gravity moves exactly as that of a stone would move. But when a man climbs up a cliff, he does something that dead matter of the same shape and weight would never do; this is a 'vital' movement. There is in the human body a lot of stored chemical energy in more or less unstable equilibrium; a very small stimulus can release this energy, and cause a considerable amount of bodily movement. The situation is analogous to that of a large rock delicately balanced on the top of a conical mountain: a tiny shove may send it thundering down into the valley, in one direction or another according to the direction of the shove. So if you say to a man 'Your house is on fire', he will start running; although the stimulus contained very little energy, his expenditure of energy may be tremendous. He increases the available energy by panting, which makes his body burn up faster and increases the energy due to combustion; this is just like opening the draught in a furnace. 'Vital' movements are those that use up this energy which is in unstable equilibrium. It is they alone that concern the biochemist, the physiologist, and the psychologist. The others, being just like the movements of dead matter, may be ignored when we are specially concerned with the study of Man.

Vital movements have a stimulus which may be inside or outside the body, or both at once. Hunger is a stimulus inside the body, but hunger combined with the sight of good food is a double stimulus, both internal and external. The effect of a stimulus may be, in theory, according to the laws of physics and chemistry, but in most cases this is, at present, no more than a pious opinion. What we know from observation is that behaviour is modified by experience, that is to say, that if similar stimuli are repeated at intervals they produce gradually changing reactions. When a bus conductor says 'Fares, please,' a very young child has no reaction, an older child gradually learns to look for pennies, and, if a male, ultimately acquires the power of producing the requisite sum on demand without conscious effort. The way in which our reactions change with experience is a distinctive characteristic of animals; moreover it is more marked in the higher than in the lower animals, and most marked of all in Man. It is a matter intimately connected with 'intelligence', and must be investigated before we can understand what constitutes knowledge from the standpoint of the external observer; we shall be concerned with it at length in the next chapter.

Speaking broadly, the actions of all living things are such as tend to biological survival, i.e. to the leaving of a numerous progeny. But when we descend to the lowest organisms, which have hardly anything that can be called individuality, and reproduce themselves by fission, it is possible to take a simpler view. Living matter, within limits, has the chemical peculiarity of being self-perpetuating, and of conferring its own chemical composition upon other matter composed of the right elements. One spore falling into a stagnant pond may produce millions of minute vegetable organisms; these, in turn, enable one small animal to have myriads of descendants living on the small plants; these, in turn, provide life for larger animals, newts, tadpoles, fishes, etc. In the end there is enormously more protoplasm in that region than there was to begin with. This is no doubt explicable as a result of the chemical constitution of living matter. But this purely chemical self-preservation and collective growth is at the bottom of everything else that characterises the behaviour of living things. Every living thing is a sort of imperialist, seeking to transform as much as possible of its environment into itself and its seed. The distinction between self and posterity is one which does not exist in a developed form in asexual unicellular organisms; many things, even in human life, can only be completely understood by forgetting it. We may regard the whole of evolution as flowing from this 'chemical imperialism' of living matter. Of this, Man is only the last example (so far). He transforms the surface of the globe by irrigation, cultivation, mining, quarrying, making canals and railways, breeding certain animals, and destroying others; and when we ask ourselves, from the standpoint of an outside observer, what is the end achieved by all these activities, we find that it can be summed up in one very simple formula: to transform as much as possible of the matter on the earth's surface into human bodies. Domestication of animals, agriculture, commerce, industrialism have been stages in this process. When we compare the human population of the globe with that of other large animals and also with that of former times, we see that 'chemical imperialism' has been, in fact, the main end to which human intelligence has been devoted. Perhaps intelligence is reaching the point where it can conceive worthier ends, concerned with the quality rather than the quantity of human life. But as yet such intelligence is confined to minorities, and does not control the great movements of human affairs. Whether this will ever be changed I do not venture to predict. And in pursuing the simple purpose of maximising the amount of human life, we have at any rate the consolation of feeling at one with the whole movement of living things from their earliest origin on this planet.

Chapter 3

The Process of Learning in Animals and Infants

In the present chapter I wish to consider the processes by which, and the laws according to which, an animal's original repertoire of reflexes is changed into a quite different set of habits as a result of events that happen to it. A dog learns to follow his master in preference to anyone else; a horse learns to know his own stall in the stable; a cow learns to come to the cow-shed at milking time. All these are acquired habits, not reflexes; they depend upon the circumstances of the animals concerned, not merely upon the congenital characteristics of the species. When I speak of an animal 'learning' something, I shall include all cases of acquired habits, whether or not they are useful to the animal. I have known horses in Italy 'learn' to drink wine, which I cannot believe to have been a desirable habit. A dog may 'learn' to fly at a man who has ill-treated it, and may do so with such regularity and ferocity as to lead to its being killed. I do not use learning in any sense involving praise, but merely to denote modification of behaviour as the result of experience.

The manner in which animals learn has been much studied in recent years, with a great deal of patient observation and experiment. Certain results have been obtained as regards the kinds of problems that have been investigated, but on general principles there is still much controversy. One may say broadly that all the animals that have been carefully observed have behaved so as to confirm the philosophy in which the observer believed before his observations began. Nay, more, they have all displayed the national characteristics of the observer. Animals studied by Americans rush about frantically, with an incredible display of hustle and pep, and at last achieve the desired result by chance. Animals observed by Germans sit still and think, and at last evolve the solution out of their inner consciousness. To the plain man, such as the present writer, this situation is discouraging. I observe, however, that the type of problem which a man naturally sets to an animal depends upon his own philosophy, and that this probably accounts for the differences in the results. The animal responds to one type of problem in one way and to another in another; therefore the results obtained by different investigators, though different, are not incompatible. But it remains necessary to remember that no one investigator is to be trusted to give a survey of the whole field.

The matters with which we shall be concerned in this chapter belong to behaviourist psychology, and in part to pure physiology. Nevertheless, they seem to me vital to a proper understanding of philosophy, since they are necessary for an objective study of knowledge and inference. I mean by an 'objective' study one in which the observer and the observed need not be the same person; when they must be identical, I call the study 'subjective'. For the present we are concerned with what is required for understanding 'knowledge' as an objective phenomenon. We shall take up the question of the subjective study of knowledge at a later stage.

The scientific study of learning in animals is a very recent growth; it may almost be regarded as beginning with Thorndike's *Animal Intelligence,* which was published in 1911. Thorndike invented the method which has been adopted by practically all subsequent American investigators. In this method an animal is separated from food, which he can see or smell, by an obstacle which he may overcome by chance. A cat, say, is put in a cage having a door with a handle which he may by chance push open with his nose. At first the cat makes entirely random movements, until he gets his result by a mere fluke. On the second occasion, in the same cage, he still makes some random movements, but not so many as on the first occasion. On the third occasion he does still better, and before long he makes no useless movements. Nowadays it has become customary to employ rats instead of cats, and to put them in a model of the Hampton Court maze rather than in a cage. They take all sorts of wrong turnings at first, but after a time they learn to run straight out without making any mistake. Dr. Watson gives averages for nineteen rats, each of which was put into the maze repeatedly, with food outside where the rat could smell it. In all the experiments care was taken to make sure that the animal was very hungry. Dr. Watson says: 'The first trial required on the average over seventeen minutes. During this time the rat was running around the maze, into blind alleys, running back to the starting point, starting for the food again, biting at the wires around him, scratching himself, smelling this spot and that on the floor. Finally he got to the food. He was allowed only a bite. Again he was put back into the maze. The taste of the food made him almost frantic in his activity. He dashed about more rapidly. The average time for the group on the second trial is only a little over seven minutes; on the fourth trial not quite three minutes; from this point to the twenty-third trial the improvement is very gradual.' On the thirtieth trial the time required, on the average, was about thirty seconds[1]. This set of experiments may be taken as typical of the whole group of studies to which it belongs.

Thorndike, as a result of experiments with cages and mazes, formulated two 'provisional laws', which are as follows:

'The Law of Effect is that: Of several responses made to the same situation, those which are accompanied or closely followed by satisfaction to the animal will, other things being equal, be more firmly connected with the situation, so that, when it recurs, they will be more likely to recur; those which are accompanied or closely followed by dissatisfaction to the animal will, other things being equal, have their connections with that situation weakened, so that, when it recurs, they will be less likely to recur. The greater the satisfaction or discomfort, the greater the strengthening or weakening of the bond.'

'The Law of Exercise is that: Any response to a situation will, other things being equal, be more strongly connected with the situation in proportion to the number of times it has been connected with that situation and to the average vigour and duration of the connections.'

We may sum up these two laws, roughly, in the two statements: First, an animal tends to repeat what has brought it pleasure; second, an animal tends to repeat what it has often done before. Neither of these laws is at all surprising, but, as we shall see, there are difficulties in the theory that they are adequate to account for the process of learning in animals.

Before going further there is a theoretical point to be cleared up. Thorndike, in his first law, speaks of satisfaction and discomfort, which are terms belonging to subjective psychology. We cannot observe whether an animal *feels* satisfaction or *feels* discomfort; we can only observe that it behaves in ways that we have become accustomed to interpret as signs of these feelings. Thorndike's law, as it stands, does not belong to objective psychology, and is not capable of being experimentally tested. This, however, is not so serious an objection as it looks. Instead of speaking of a result that brings satisfaction, we can merely enumerate the results which, in fact, have the character

[1]Watson, *Behaviourism*, pp. 169–70.

which Thorndike mentions, namely, that the animal tends to behave so as to make them recur. The rat in the maze behaves so as to get the cheese, and when an act has led him to the cheese once, he tends to repeat it. We may say that this is what we mean when we say that the cheese 'gives satisfaction', or that the rat 'desires' the cheese. That is to say, we may use Thorndike's 'Law of Effect' to give us an objective definition of desire, satisfaction, and discomfort. The law should then say: there are situations such that animals tend to repeat acts which have led to them; these are the situations which the animal is said to 'desire' and in which it is said to 'find satisfaction'. This objection to Thorndike's first law is, therefore, not very serious, and need not further trouble us.

Dr. Watson considers one principle alone sufficient to account for all animal and human learning, namely, the principle of 'learned reactions'. This principle may be stated as follows:

When the body of an animal or human being has been exposed sufficiently often to two roughly simultaneous stimuli, the earlier of them alone tends to call out the response previously called out by the other.

Although I do not agree with Dr. Watson in thinking this principle alone sufficient, I do agree that it is a principle of very great importance. It is the modern form of the principle of 'association'. The 'association of ideas' has played a great part in philosophy, particularly in British philosophy. But it now appears that this is a consequence of a wider and more primitive principle, namely, the association of bodily processes. It is this wider principle that is asserted above. Let us see what is the nature of the evidence in its favour.

Our principle becomes verifiable over a much larger field than the older principle owing to the fact that it is movements, not 'ideas', that are to be associated. Where animals are concerned, ideas are hypothetical, but movements can be observed; even with men, many movements are involuntary and unconscious. Yet animal movements and unconscious involuntary human movements are just as much subject to the law of association as the most conscious ideas. Take, e.g., the following example (Watson, p. 33). The pupil of the eye expands in darkness and contracts in bright light; this is an involuntary and unconscious action of which we only become aware by observing others. Now take some person and repeatedly expose him to bright light at the same moment that you ring an electric bell. After a time the electric bell alone will cause his pupils to contract. As far as can be discovered, all muscles behave in this way. So do glands where they can be tested. It is said that a brass band can be reduced to silence by sucking a lemon in front of it, owing to the effect upon the salivary glands of its members; I confess that I have never verified this statement. But you will find the exact scientific analogue for dogs in Watson, p. 26. You arrange a tube in a dog's mouth so that saliva drops out at a measurable rate. When you give the dog food it stimulates the flow of saliva. At the same moment you touch his left thigh. After a certain length of time the touch on the left thigh will produce just as much saliva without the food as with it. The same sort of thing applies to emotions, which depend upon the ductless glands. Children at birth are afraid of loud noises, but not of animals. Watson took a child eleven months old, who was fond of a certain white rat; twice at the moment when the child touched the rat, a sudden noise was made just behind the child's head. This was enough to cause fear of the rat on subsequent occasions, no doubt owing to the fact that the adrenal gland was now stimulated by the substitute stimulus, just like the salivary glands in the dog or the trumpet player. The above illustrations show that 'ideas' are not the essential units in association. It seems that not merely is 'mind' irrelevant, but even the brain is less important than was formerly supposed. At any rate, what is known experimentally is that the glands and muscles (both striped and unstriped) of the higher animals exhibit the law of transfer of response, i.e. when two stimuli have often been applied together, one will ultimately call out the response which formerly the other called out. This law is one of the chief bases of habit. It is also obviously essential to our understanding of language: the sight of a dog calls up the word 'dog', and the word 'dog' calls up some of the responses appropriate to a real dog.

There is, however, another element in learning, besides mere habit. This is the element dealt with by Thorndike's 'Law of Effect'. Animals tend to repeat acts which have pleasant consequences, and to avoid such as have unpleasant consequences. But, as we saw a moment ago, 'pleasant' and 'unpleasant' are words which we cannot verify by objective observation. What we can verify by observation is that an animal seeks situations which in fact have had certain results, and avoids situations which in fact have had certain other results. Moreover, broadly speaking, the animal seeks results which tend to survival of itself or its offspring, and avoids results which tend in the opposite direction. This, however, is not invariable. Moths seek flames and men seek drink, though neither is biologically useful. It is only approximately, in situations long common, that animals are so adjusted to their environment as to act in a way which is advantageous from a biological standpoint. In fact, biological utility must never be employed as an explanation, but only noticed as a frequent characteristic, of the ways in which animals behave.

Dr. Watson is of the opinion that Thorndike's 'Law of Effect' is unnecessary. He first suggests that only two factors are called for in the explanation of habit, namely, *frequency* and *recency*. Frequency is covered by Thorndike's 'Law of Exercise', but recency, which is almost certainly a genuine factor, is not covered by Thorndike's two laws. That is to say, when a number of random movements have finally resulted in success, the more recent of these movements are likely to be repeated earlier, on a second trial, than the earlier ones. But Dr. Watson finally abandons this method of dealing with habit-formation in favour of the one law of 'conditioned reflexes' or 'learned reactions'. He says (*Behaviourism*, p. 166):

'Only a few psychologists have been interested in the problem. Most of the psychologists, it is to be regretted, have even failed to see that there is a problem. They believe habit formation is implanted by kind fairies. For example, Thorndike speaks of pleasure stamping in the successful movement and displeasure stamping out the unsuccessful movements. Most of the psychologists talk, too, quite volubly about the formation of new pathways in the brain, as though there were a group of tiny servants of Vulcan there who run through the nervous system with hammer and chisel digging new trenches and deepening old ones. I am not sure that the problem when phrased in this way is a soluble one. I feel that there must come some simpler way of envisaging the whole process of habit formation or else it may remain insoluble. Since the advent of the conditioned reflex hypothesis in psychology with all of the simplifications (and I am often fearful that it may be an over-simplification!) I have had my own laryngeal processes [i.e. what others call "thoughts"] stimulated to work upon this problem from another angle.'

I agree with Dr. Watson that the explanations of habit-formation which are usually given are very inadequate, and that few psychologists have realised either the importance or the difficulty of the problem. I agree also that a great many cases are covered by his formula of the conditioned reflex. He relates a case of a child which once touched a hot radiator, and afterwards avoided it for two years. He adds: 'If we should keep our old habit terminology, we should have in this example a habit formed by a single trial. There can be then in this case no "stamping in of the successful movement" and no "stamping out of the unsuccessful movement".' On the basis of such examples, he believes that the whole of habit-formation can be derived from the principle of the conditioned reflex, which he formulates as follows (p. 168):

Stimulus X will not now call out reaction R; stimulus Y will call out reaction R (unconditioned reflex); but when stimulus X is presented first and then Y (which does call out R) shortly thereafter, X will thereafter call out R. In other words, stimulus X becomes ever thereafter substituted for Y.

This law is so simple, so important, and so widely true that there is a danger lest its scope should be exaggerated, just as, in the eighteenth century, physicists tried to explain everything by means of gravitation. But when considered as covering all the ground, it seems to me to suffer from two opposite defects. In the first place, there are cases where no habit is set up, although by the law it should be. In the second place, there are habits which, so far as we can see at present, have a different genesis.

To take the first point first: the word 'pepper' does not make people sneeze, though according to the law it should[1]. Words which describe succulent foods will make the mouth water; voluptuous words will have some of the effect that would be produced by the situations they suggest; but no words will produce sneezes or the reactions appropriate to tickling. In the diagram given by Dr. Watson (p. 106), there are four reflexes which appear to be not sources of conditioned reflexes, namely sneezing, hiccoughing, blinking, and the Babinski reflex; of these, however, blinking, it is suggested (p. 99), may be really itself a conditioned reflex. There may be some quite straightforward explanation of the fact that some reactions can be produced by substitute stimuli while others cannot, but none is offered. Therefore the law of the conditioned reflex, as formulated, is too wide, and it is not clear what is the principle according to which its scope should be restricted.

The second objection to Dr. Watson's law of habit, if valid, is more important than the first; but its validity is more open to question. It is contended that the acts by which solutions of problems are obtained are, in cases of a certain kind, not random acts leading to success by mere chance, but acts proceeding from 'insight', involving a 'mental' solution of the problem as a preliminary to the physical solution. This

[1] Dr. Watson apparently entertains hopes of teaching babies to sneeze when they see the pepper box, but he has not yet done so. See *Behaviourism*, p. 90.

is especially the view of those who advocate *Gestaltpsychologie* or the psychology of configuration. We may take, as typical of their attitude on the subject of learning, Köhler's *Mentality of Apes*. Köhler went to Tenerife with certain chimpanzees in the year 1913; owing to the war he was compelled to remain with them until 1917, so that his opportunities for study were extensive. He complains of the maze and cage problems set by American investigators that they are such as *cannot* be solved by intelligence. Sir Isaac Newton himself could not have got out of the Hampton Court maze by any method except trial and error. Köhler, on the other hand, set his apes problems which could be solved by what he calls 'insight'. He would hang up a banana[1] out of reach, and leave boxes in the neighbourhood so that by standing on the boxes the chimpanzees could reach the fruit. Sometimes they had to pile three or even four boxes on top of each other before they could achieve success. Then he would put the banana outside the bars of the cage, leaving a stick inside, and the ape would get the banana by reaching for it with the stick. On one occasion, one of them, named Sultan, had two bamboo sticks, each too short to reach the banana; after vain efforts followed by a period of silent thought, he fitted the smaller into the hollow of the other, and so manufactured one stick which was long enough. It seems, however, from the account, that he first fitted the two together more or less accidently, and only then realised that he had found a solution. Nevertheless, his behaviour when he had once realised that one stick could be made by joining the two was scarcely Watsonian: there was no longer anything tentative, but a definite triumph, first in anticipation and then in action. He was so pleased with his new trick that he drew a number of bananas into his cage before eating any of them. He behaved, in fact, as capitalists have behaved with machinery.

Köhler says: 'We can, from our own experience, distinguish sharply between the kind of conduct which, from the very beginning, arises out of a consideration of the characteristics of a situation, and one that does not. Only in the former case do we speak of insight, and only that behaviour of animals definitely appears to us intelligent which takes account from the beginning of the lie of the land, and proceeds to deal with it in a smooth continuous course. Hence follows this characteristic: *to set up as the criterion of insight, the appearance of a complete solution with reference to the whole lay-out of the field.*'

[1]Called by Köhler 'the objective', because the word 'banana' is too humble for a learned work. The pictures disclose the fact that 'the objective' was a mere banana.

Genuine solutions of problems, Köhler says, do not improve by repetition; they are perfect on the first occasion, and, if anything, grow worse by repetition, when the excitement of discovery has worn off. The whole account that Köhler gives of the efforts of his chimpanzees makes a totally different impression from that of the rats in mazes, and one is forced to conclude that the American work is somewhat vitiated by confining itself to one type of problem, and drawing from that one type conclusions which it believes to be applicable to all problems of animal learning. It seems that there are two ways of learning, one by experience, and the other by what Köhler calls 'insight'. Learning by experience is possible to most vertebrates, though rarely, so far as is known, to invertebrates. Learning by 'insight', on the contrary, is not known to exist in any animals lower than the anthropoid apes, though it would be extremely rash to assert that it will not be revealed by further observations on dogs or rats. Unfortunately, some animals – for instance, elephants – may be extremely intelligent, but the practical difficulty and expense of experimentation with them is so great that we are not likely to know much about them for some time to come. However, the real problem is already sufficiently definite in Köhler's book: it is the analysis of 'insight' as opposed to the method of the conditioned reflex.

Let us first be clear as to the nature of the problem, when described solely in terms of behaviour. A hungry monkey, if sufficiently near to a banana, will perform acts such as, in circumstances to which it has been accustomed, have previously enabled it to obtain bananas. This fits well with either Watson or Thorndike, so far. But if these familiar acts fail, the animal will, if it has been long without food, is in good health, and is not too tired, proceed to other acts which have never hitherto produced bananas. One may suppose, if one wishes to follow Watson, that these new acts are composed of a number of parts, each of which, on some former occasion, has occurred in a series which ended with the obtaining of the banana. Or one may suppose – as I think Thorndike does – that the acts of the baffled animal are random acts, so that the solution emerges by pure chance. But even in the first hypothesis, the element of chance is considerable. Let us suppose that the acts A, B, C, D, E have each, on a former occasion, been part of a series ending with success, but that now for the first time it is necessary to perform them all, and in the right order. It is obvious that, if they are only combined by chance, the animal will be lucky if it performs them all in the right order before dying of hunger. But Köhler maintains that to anyone watching his chimpanzees it was obvious they did not obtain 'a composition of the solutions out of chance parts'. He says (pp. 199–200):

'It is certainly not a characteristic of the chimpanzee, when he is brought into an experimental situation, to make any chance movements, out of which, among other things, a non-genuine solution could arise. He is very seldom seen to attempt anything which would have to be considered accidental in relation to the situation (excepting, of course, if his interest is turned away from the objective to other things). As long as his efforts are directed to the objective, all distinguishable stages of his behaviour (as with human beings in similar situations) tend to appear as complete attempts at solutions, *none* of which appears as the produce of accidentally arrayed parts. This is true, most of all, of the solution which is finally successful. Certainly it often follows upon a period of perplexity or quiet (often a period of survey), but in real and convincing cases the solution never appears in a disorder of blind impulses. It is one continuous smooth action, which can be resolved into its parts *only by the imagination* of the onlooker; in reality they do *not* appear independently. But that in so many "genuine" cases as have been described, these solutions as wholes should have arisen from mere chance, is an entirely inadmissible supposition.'

Thus we may take it as an observed fact that, so far as overt behaviour is concerned, there are two objections to the type of theory with which we began, when considered as covering the whole field. The first objection is that in cases of a certain kind, the solution appears sooner than it should according to the doctrine of chances; the second is that it appears as a whole, i.e. that the animal, after a period of quiescence, suddenly goes through the right series of actions smoothly, and without hesitation.

Where human beings are concerned, it is difficult to obtain such good data as in the case of animals. Human mothers will not allow their children to be starved, and then shut up in a room containing a banana which can only be reached by putting a chair on the table and a footstool on the chair, and then climbing up without breaking any bones. Nor will they permit them to be put into the middle of a Hampton Court maze, with their dinner getting cold outside. Perhaps in time the State will perform these experiments with the children of political prisoners, but as yet, perhaps fortunately, the authorities are not sufficiently interested in science. One can observe, however, that human learning seems to be of both sorts, namely, that described by Watson and that described by Köhler. I am persuaded that speech is learnt by the Watsonian method, so long as it is confined to single words: often the trial and error, in later stages, proceeds *sotto voce*, but it takes place overtly at first, and in some children until their speech is quite correct. The speaking of sentences, however, is already more difficult to explain without bringing in the apprehension of wholes which is the thing upon which *Gestaltpsychologie* lays stress. In the later stages of learning, the sort of sudden illumination which came to Köhler's chimpanzees is a phenomenon with which every serious student must be familiar. One day, after a period of groping bewilderment, the schoolboy knows what algebra is all about. In writing a book, my own experience – which I know is fairly common, though by no means universal – is that for a time I fumble and hesitate, and then suddenly I see the book as a whole, and have only to write it down as if I were copying a completed manuscript.

If these phenomena are to be brought within the scope of behaviourist psychology, it must be by means of 'implicit' behaviour. Watson makes much use of this in the form of talking to oneself, but in apes it cannot take quite this form. And it is necessary to have some theory to explain the success of 'implicit' behaviour, whether we call it 'thought' or not. Perhaps such a theory can be constructed on Watson's lines, but it has certainly not yet been constructed. Until the behaviourists have satisfactorily explained the kind of discovery which appears in Köhler's observations, we cannot say that their thesis is proved. This is a matter which will occupy us again at a later stage; for the present let us preserve an open mind.

Chapter 4

Language

The subject of language is one which has not been studied with sufficient care in traditional philosophy. It was taken for granted that words exist to express 'thoughts', and generally also that 'thoughts' have 'objects' which are what the words 'mean'. It was thought that, by means of language, we could deal directly with what it 'means', and that we need not analyse with any care either of the two supposed properties of words, namely that of 'expressing' thoughts and that of 'meaning' things. Often when philosophers intended to be considering the objects meant by words they were in fact considering only the words, and when they were considering words they made the mistake of supposing, more or less unconsciously, that a word is a single entity, not, as it really is, a set of more or less similar events. The failure to consider language explicitly has been a cause of much that was bad in traditional philosophy. I think myself that 'meaning' can only be understood if we treat language as a bodily habit, which is learnt just as we learn football or bicycling. The only satisfactory way to treat language, to my mind, is to treat it in this way, as Dr. Watson does. Indeed, I should regard the theory of language as one of the strongest points in favour of behaviourism.

Man has various advantages over the beasts, for example, fire, clothing, agriculture, and tools – not the possession of domestic animals, for ants have them. But more important than any of these is language. It is not known how or when language arose, nor why chimpanzees do not speak. I doubt if it is even known whether writing or speech is the older form of language. The pictures made in caves by the Cro-Magnon men may have been intended to convey a meaning, and may have been a form of writing. It is known that writing developed out of pictures, for that happened in historical times; but it is not known to what extent pictures had been used in prehistoric times as a means of giving information or commands. As for spoken language, it differs from the cries of animals in being not merely an expression of emotion. Animals have cries of fear, cries expressing pleasure in the discovery of food, and so on, and by means of these cries they influence each other's actions. But they do not appear to have any means of expressing anything except emotions, and then only emotions which they are actually feeling. There is no evidence that they possess anything analogous to narrative. We may say, therefore, without exaggeration, that language is a human prerogative, and probably the chief habit in which we are superior to the 'dumb' animals.

There are three matters to be considered in beginning the study of language. First: what words are, regarded as physical occurrences; secondly, what are the circumstances that lead us to use a given word; thirdly, what are the effects of our hearing or seeing a given word. But as regards the second and third of these questions, we shall find ourselves led on from words to sentences and thus confronted with fresh problems, perhaps demanding rather the methods of *Gestaltpsychologie*.

Ordinary words are of four kinds: spoken, heard, written, and read. It is of course largely a matter of convention that we do not use words of other kinds. There is the deaf-and-dumb language; a Frenchman's shrug of the shoulders is a word; in fact, any kind of externally perceptible bodily movement may become a word, if social usage so ordains. But the convention which has given the supremacy to speaking is one which has a good ground, since there is no other way of producing a number of perceptibly different bodily movements so quickly or with so little muscular effort. Public speaking would be very tedious if statesmen had to use the deaf-and-dumb language, and very exhausting if all words involved as much muscular effort as a shrug of the shoulders. I shall ignore all forms of language except speaking, hearing, writing, and reading, since the others are relatively unimportant and raise no special psychological problems.

A spoken word consists of a series of movements in the larynx and the mouth, combined with breath. Two closely similar series of such movements may be instances of the same word, though they may also not be, since two words with different meanings may sound alike; but two such series which are not closely similar cannot be instances of the same word. (I am confining myself to one language.) Thus a single spoken word, say 'dog', is a certain set of closely similar series of bodily movements, the set having as many members as there are occasions when the word 'dog' is pronounced. The degree of similarity required in order that the occurrence should be an instance of the word 'dog' cannot be specified exactly. Some people say 'dawg', and this must certainly be admitted. A German might say "tok", and then we should begin to be doubtful. In marginal cases, we cannot be sure whether a word has been pronounced or not. A spoken word is a form of bodily behaviour without sharp boundaries, like jumping or hopping or running. Is a man running or walking? In a walking-race the umpire may have great difficulty in deciding. Similarly there may be cases where it cannot be decided whether a man has said 'dog' or 'dock'. A spoken word is thus at once general and somewhat vague.

We usually take for granted the relation between a word spoken and a word heard. 'Can you hear what I say?' we ask, and the person addressed says 'yes'. This is of course a delusion, a part of the naïve realism of our unreflective outlook on the world. We never hear what is said; we hear something having a complicated causal connection with what is said. There is first the purely physical process of sound-waves from the mouth of the speaker to the ear of the hearer, then a complicated process in the ear and nerves, and then an event in the brain, which is related to our hearing of the sound in a manner to be investigated later, but is at any rate simultaneous with our hearing of the sound. This gives the physical causal connection between the word spoken and the word heard. There is, however, also another connection of a more psychological sort. When a man utters a word, he also hears it himself, so that the word spoken and the word heard become intimately associated for anyone who knows how to speak. And a man who knows how to speak can also utter any word he hears in his own language, so that the association works equally well both ways. It is because of the intimacy of this association that the plain man identifies the word spoken with the word heard, although in fact the two are separated by a wide gulf.

In order that speech may serve its purpose, it is not necessary, as it is not possible, that heard and spoken words should be identical, but it is necessary that when a man utters different words the heard words should be different, and when he utters the same word on two occasions the heard word should be approximately the same on the two occasions. The first of these depends upon the sensitiveness of the ear and its distance from the speaker; we cannot distinguish between two rather similar words if we are too far off from the man who utters them. The second condition depends upon uniformity in the physical conditions, and is realised in all ordinary circumstances. But if the speaker were surrounded by instruments which were resonant to certain notes but not to certain others, some tones of voice might carry and others might be lost. In that case, if he uttered the same word with two different intonations, the hearer might be quite unable to recognise the sameness.

Thus the efficacy of speech depends upon a number of physical conditions. These, however, we will take for granted, in order to come as soon as possible to the more psychological parts of our topic.

Written words differ from spoken words in being material structures. A spoken word is a process in the physical world, having an essential time-order; a written word is a series of pieces of matter, having an essential space-order. As to what we mean by 'matter', that is a question with which we shall have to deal at length at a later stage. For the present it is enough to observe that the material structures which constitute written words, unlike the processes that constitute spoken words, are capable of enduring for a long time – sometimes for thousands of years. Moreover, they are not confined to one neighbourhood, but can be made to travel about the world. These are the two great advantages of writing over speech. This, at least, has been the case until recently. But with the coming of radio writing has begun to lose its pre-eminence: one man can now speak to multitudes spread over a whole country. Even in the matter of permanence, speech may become the equal of writing. Perhaps, instead of legal documents, we shall have gramophone records, with voice signatures by the parties to the contract. Perhaps, as in Wells's *When the Sleeper Awakes,* books will no longer be printed but merely arranged for the gramophone. In that case the need for writing may almost cease to exist. However, let us return from these speculations to the world of the present day.

The word read, as opposed to the written or printed word, is just as evanescent as the word spoken or heard. Whenever a written word, exposed to light, is in a suitable spatial relation to a normal eye, it produces a certain complicated effect upon the eye; the part of this process which occurs outside the eye is investigated by the science of light, whereas the part that occurs in the eye belongs to physiological optics. There is then a further process, first in the optic nerve and afterwards in the brain; the process in the brain is simultaneous with vision. What further relation it has to vision is a question as to which there has been much philosophical controversy; we shall return to it at a later stage. The essence of the matter, as regards the causal efficacy of writing, is that the act of writing produces quasi-permanent material structures which throughout the whole of their duration, produce closely similar results upon all suitably placed normal eyes; and as in the case of speaking, different written words lead to different read words, and the same word written twice leads to the same read word – again with obvious limitations.

So much for the physical side of language, which is often unduly neglected. I come now to the psychological side, which is what really concerns us in this chapter.

The two questions we have to answer, apart from the problems raised by sentences as opposed to words, are: First, what sort of behaviour is stimulated by hearing a word? And secondly, what sort of occasion stimulates us to the behaviour that consists in pronouncing a word? I put the questions in this order because children learn to react to the words of others before they learn to use words themselves. It might be objected that, in the history of the race, the first spoken word must have preceded the first heard word, at least by a fraction of a second. But this is not very relevant, nor is it certainly true. A noise may have meaning to the hearer, but not to the utterer; in that case it is a heard word but not a spoken word. (I shall explain what I mean by 'meaning' shortly.) Friday's footprint had 'meaning' for Robinson Crusoe but not for Friday. However that may be, we shall do better to avoid the very hypothetical parts of anthropology that would be involved, and take up the learning of language as it can be observed in the human infant of the present day. And in the human infant as we know him, definite reactions to the words of others come much earlier than the power of uttering words himself.

A child learns to understand words exactly as he learns any other process of bodily association. If you always say 'bottle' when you give a child his bottle, he presently reacts to the word 'bottle', within limits, as he formerly reacted to the bottle. This is merely an example of the law of association which we considered in the preceding chapter. When the association has been established, parents say that the child 'understands' the word 'bottle', or knows what the word 'means'. Of course the word does not have *all* the effects that the actual bottle has. It does not exert gravitation, it does not nourish, it cannot bump on to the child's head. The effects which are shared by the word and the thing are those which depend upon the law of association or 'conditioned reflexes' or 'learned reactions'. These may be called 'associative' effects or 'mnemic' effects – the latter name being derived from Semon's book *Mneme*[1], in which he traces all phenomena analogous to memory to a law which is, in effect, not very different from the law of association or 'conditioned reflexes'.

It is possible to be a little more precise as to the class of effects concerned. A physical object is a centre from which a variety of

[1]London: George Allen & Unwin, Ltd.

causal chains emanate. If the object is visible to John Smith, one of the causal chains emanating from it consists first of light-waves (or light-quanta) which travel from the object to John Smith's eye, then of events in his eye and optic nerve, then of events in his brain, and then (perhaps) of a reaction on his part. Now mnemic effects belong only to events in living tissue; therefore only those effects of the bottle which happen either inside John Smith's body, or as a result of his reaction to the bottle, can become associated with his hearing the word 'bottle'. And even then only certain events can be associated: nourishment happens in the body, yet the word 'bottle' cannot nourish. The law of conditioned reflexes is subject to ascertainable limitations, but within its limits it supplies what is wanted to explain the understanding of words. The child becomes excited when he sees the bottle; this is already a conditioned reflex, due to experience that this sight precedes a meal. One further stage in conditioning makes the child grow excited when he hears the word 'bottle'. He is then said to 'understand' the word.

We may say, then, that a person understands a word which he hears if, so far as the law of conditioned reflexes is applicable, the effects of the word are the same as those of what it is said to 'mean'. This of course only applies to words like 'bottle', which denote some concrete object or some class of concrete objects. To understand a word such as 'reciprocity' or 'republicanism' is a more complicated matter, and cannot be considered until we have dealt with sentences. But before considering sentences we have to examine the circumstances which make us use a word, as opposed to the consequences of hearing it used.

Saying a word is more difficult than using it, except in the case of a few simple sounds which infants make before they know that they are words, such as 'ma-ma' and 'da-da'. These two are among the many random sounds that all babies make. When a child says 'ma-ma' in the presence of his mother by chance she thinks he knows what this noise means, and she shows pleasure in ways that are agreeable to the infant. Gradually, in accordance with Thorndike's law of effect, he acquires the habit of making this noise in the presence of his mother, because in these circumstances the consequences are pleasant. But it is only a very small number of words that are acquired in this way. The great majority of words are acquired by imitation, combined with the association between thing and word which the parents deliberately establish in the early stages (after the very first stage). It is obvious that using words oneself involves something over and above the association between the *sound* of the word and its meaning.

Dogs understand many words, and infants understand far more than they can say. The infant has to discover that it is possible and profitable to make noises like those which he hears. (This statement must not be taken quite literally, or it would be too intellectualistic.) He would never discover this if he did not make noises at random, without the intention of talking. He then gradually finds that he can make noises like those which he hears, and in general the consequences of doing so are pleasant. Parents are pleased, desired objects can be obtained, and – perhaps most important of all – there is a sense of power in making intended instead of accidental noises. But in this whole process there is nothing essentially different from the learning of mazes by rats. It resembles this form of learning, rather than that of Köhler's apes, because no amount of intelligence could enable the child to find out the names of things – as in the case of the mazes, experience is the only possible guide.

When a person knows how to speak, the conditioning proceeds in the opposite direction to that which operates in understanding what others say. The reaction of a person who knows how to speak, when he notices a cat, is naturally to utter the word 'cat'; he may not actually do so, but he will have a reaction leading towards this act, even if for some reason the overt act does not take place. It is true that he may utter the word 'cat' because he is 'thinking' about a cat, not actually seeing one. This, however, as we shall see in a moment, is merely one further stage in the process of conditioning. The use of single words, as opposed to sentences, is wholly explicable, so far as I can see, by the principles which apply to animals in mazes.

Certain philosophers who have a prejudice against analysis contend that the sentence comes first and the single word later. In this connection they always allude to the language of the Patagonians, which their opponents, of course, do not know. We are given to understand that a Patagonian can understand you if you say 'I am going to fish in the lake behind the western hill', but that he cannot understand the word 'fish' by itself. (This instance is imaginary, but it represents the sort of thing that is asserted.) Now it may be that Patagonians are peculiar – indeed they must be, or they would not choose to live in Patagonia. But certainly infants in civilised countries do not behave in this way, with the exception of Thomas Carlyle and Lord Macaulay. The former never spoke before the age of three, when, hearing his younger brother cry, he said 'What ails wee Jock?' Lord Macaulay 'learned in suffering what he taught in song', for, having spilt a cup of hot tea over himself at a party, he began his career as a talker by saying to his hostess, after a time, 'Thank you, Madam, the agony is abated'. These, however, are facts about biographers, not about the beginnings of speech in infancy. In all children that have been carefully observed, sentences come much later than single words.

Children, at first, are limited as to their power of producing sounds, and also by the paucity of their learned associations. I am sure the reason why 'ma-ma' and 'da-da' have the meaning they have is that they are sounds which infants make spontaneously at an early age, and are therefore convenient as sounds to which the elders can attach meaning. In the very beginning of speech there is not imitation of grown-ups, but the discovery that sounds made spontaneously have agreeable results. Imitation comes later, after the child has discovered that sounds can have this quality of 'meaning'. The type of skill involved is throughout exactly similar to that involved in learning to play a game or ride a bicycle.

We may sum up this theory of meaning in a simple formula. When through the law of conditioned reflexes, A has come to be a cause of C, we will call A an 'associative' cause of C, and C an 'associative' effect of A. We shall say that, to a given person, the word A, when he hears it, 'means' C, if the associative effects of A are closely similar to those of C; and we shall say that the word A, when he utters it, 'means' C, if the utterance of A is an associative effect of C, or of something previously associated with C. To put the matter more concretely, the word 'Peter' means a certain person if the associative effects of hearing the word 'Peter' are closely similar to those of seeing Peter and the associative causes of uttering the word 'Peter' are occurrences previously associated with Peter. Of course as our experience increases in complexity this simple schema becomes obscured and overlaid, but I think it remains fundamentally true.

There is an interesting and valuable book by Messrs. C. K. Ogden and I. A. Richards, called *The Meaning of Meaning*. This book, owing to the fact that it concentrates on the causes of uttering words, not on the effects of hearing them, gives only half the above theory, and that in a somewhat incomplete form. It says that a word and its meaning have the same *causes*. I should distinguish between *active* meaning, that of the man uttering the word, and *passive* meaning, that of the man hearing the word. In active meaning the word is associatively caused by what it means or something associated with this; in passive meaning, the associative effects of the word are approximately the same as those of what it means.

On behaviourist lines, there is no important difference between proper names and what are called 'abstract' or 'generic' words. A child learns to use the word 'cat', which is general, just as he learns to use the word 'Peter', which is a proper name. But in actual fact 'Peter' really covers a number of different occurrences, and is in a sense general. Peter may be near or far, walking or standing or sitting, laughing or frowning. All these produce different stimuli, but the stimuli have enough in common to produce the reaction consisting of the word 'Peter'. Thus there is no essential difference, from a behaviourist point of view, between 'Peter' and 'man'. There are more resemblances between the various stimuli to the word 'Peter' than between those to the word 'man', but this is only a difference of degree. We have no names for the fleeting particular occurrences which make up the several appearances of Peter, because they are not of much practical importance; their importance, in fact, is purely theoretic and philosophical. As such, we shall have a good deal to say about them at a later stage. For the present, we notice that there are many occurrences of Peter, and many occurrences of the word 'Peter'; each, to the man who sees Peter, is a set of events having certain similarities. More exactly, the occurrences of Peter are *causally* connected, whereas the occurrences of the word 'Peter' are connected by similarity. But this is a distinction which need not concern us yet.

General words such as 'man' or 'cat' or 'triangle' are said to denote 'universals', concerning which, from the time of Plato to the present day, philosophers have never ceased to debate. Whether there are universals, and, if so, in what sense, is a metaphysical question, which need not be raised in connection with the use of language. The only point about universals that needs to be raised at this stage is that the correct use of general words is no evidence that a man can think about universals. It has often been supposed that, because we can use a word like 'man' correctly, we must be capable of a corresponding 'abstract idea' of man, but this is quite a mistake. Some reactions are appropriate to one man, some to another, but all have certain elements in common. If the word 'man' produces in us the reactions which are common but no others, we may be said to understand the word 'man'. In learning geometry, one acquires the habit of avoiding special interpretations of such a word as 'triangle'. We know that, when we have a proposition about triangles in general, we must not think specially of a right-angled triangle or any one kind of triangle. This is essentially the process of learning to associate with the word what is associated with *all* triangles; when we have learnt this, we understand the word 'triangle'. Consequently there is no need to suppose that we ever apprehend universals, although we use general words correctly.

Hitherto we have spoken of single words, and among these we have considered only those that can naturally be employed singly. A child uses single words of a certain kind before constructing sentences; but some words presuppose sentences. No one would use the word 'paternity' until after using such sentences as 'John is the father of James'; no one would use the word 'causality' until after using such sentences as 'the fire makes me warm'. Sentences introduce new considerations, and are not quite so easily explained on behaviourist lines. Philosophy, however, imperatively demands an understanding of sentences, and we must therefore consider them.

As we found earlier, all infants outside Patagonia begin with single words, and only achieve sentences later. But they differ enormously in the speed with which they advance from the one to the other. My own two children adopted entirely different methods. My son first practised single letters, then single words, and only achieved correct sentences of more than three or four words at the age of two years and three months. My daughter, on the contrary, advanced very quickly to sentences, in which there was hardly ever an error. At the age of eighteen months, when supposed to be sleeping, she was overheard saying to herself: 'Last year I used to dive off the diving-board, I *did*.' Of course 'last year' was merely a phrase repeated without understanding. And no doubt the first sentences used by children are always repetitions, unchanged, of sentences they have heard used by others. Such cases raise no new principle not involved in the learning of words. What does raise a new principle is the power of putting together known words into a sentence which has never been heard, but which expresses correctly what the infant wishes to convey. This involves the power to manipulate form and structure. It does not of course involve the apprehension of form or structure in the abstract, any more than the use of the word 'man' involves apprehension of a universal. But it does involve a causal connection between the form of the stimulus and the form of the reaction. An infant very soon learns to be differently affected by the statement 'cats eat mice' from the way he would be affected by the statement 'mice eat cats'; and not much later he learns to make one of these statements rather than the other. In such a case, the cause (in hearing) or the effect (in speaking) is a whole sentence. It may be that one part of the environment is sufficient to cause one word, while another is sufficient to cause another, but it is only the two parts in their relation that can cause the whole sentence. Thus wherever sentences come in we have a causal relation between two complex facts, namely the fact asserted and the sentence asserting it; the facts as wholes enter into the cause-and-effect relation, which cannot be explained wholly as compounded of relations between their parts. Moreover, as soon as the child has learned to use correctly relational words, such as 'eat', he has become capable of being causally affected by a relational feature of the environment, which involves a new degree of complexity not required for the use of ordinary nouns.

Thus the correct use of relational words, i.e. of sentences, involves what may be correctly termed 'perception of form', i.e. it involves a definite reaction to a stimulus which is a form. Suppose, for example, that a child has learnt to say that one thing is 'above' another when this is in fact the case. The stimulus to the use of the word 'above' is a relational feature of the environment, and we may say that this feature is 'perceived' since it produces a definite reaction. It may be said that the relation *above* is not very like the word 'above'. That is true; but the same is true of ordinary physical objects. A stone, according to the physicists, is not at all like what we see when we look at it, and yet we may be correctly said to 'perceive' it. This, however, is to anticipate. The definite point which has emerged is that, when a person can use sentences correctly, that is a proof of sensitiveness to formal or relational stimuli.

The structure of a sentence asserting some relational fact, such as 'this is above that', or 'Brutus killed Caesar', differs in an important respect from the structure of the fact which it asserts. *Above* is a relation which holds between the two terms 'this' and 'that'; but the *word* 'above' is not a relation. In the sentence the relation is the temporal order of the words (or the spatial order, if they are written), but the word for the relation is itself as substantial as the other words. In inflected languages, such as Latin, the order of the words is not necessary to show the 'sense' of the relation; but in uninflected languages this is the only way of distinguishing between 'Brutus killed Caesar' and 'Caesar killed Brutus'. Words are physical phenomena, having spatial and temporal relations; we make use of these relations in our verbal symbolisation of other relations, chiefly to show the 'sense' of the relation, i.e. whether it goes from A to B or from B to A.

A great deal of the confusion about relations which has prevailed in practically all philosophies comes from the fact, which we noticed just now, that relations are indicated, not by other relations, but by words which, in themselves, are just like other words. Consequently, in thinking about relations, we constantly hover between the unsubstantiality of the relation itself and the substantiality of the word. Take, say, the fact that lightning precedes thunder. If we were to express this by a language closely reproducing the structure of the fact, we should have to say simply: 'lightning, thunder', where the fact that the first word precedes the second means that what the first word means precedes what the second word means. But even if we adopted this method for temporal order, we should still need words for all other relations, because we could not without intolerable ambiguity symbolise them also by the order of our words. All this will be important to remember when we come to consider the structure of the world, since nothing but a preliminary study of language will preserve us from being misled by language in our metaphysical speculations.

Throughout this chapter I have said nothing about the narrative and imaginative uses of words; I have dealt with words in connection with an immediate sensible stimulus closely connected with what they mean. The other uses of words are difficult to discuss until we have considered memory and imagination. In the present chapter I have confined myself to a behaviouristic explanation of the effects of words heard as stimuli, and the causes of words spoken when the words apply to something sensibly present. I think we shall find that other uses of words, such as the narrative and imaginative, involve only new applications of the law of association. But we cannot develop this theme until we have discussed several further psychological questions.

Chapter 5

Perception Objectively Regarded

It will be remembered that the task upon which we are at present engaged is the definition of 'knowledge' as a phenomenon discoverable by an outside observer. When we have said what we can from this objective standpoint, we will ask ourselves whether anything further, and if so what, is to be learnt from the subjective standpoint, in which we take account of facts which can only be discovered when the observer and the observed are the same person. But for the present we will resolutely confine ourselves to those facts about a human being which another human being can observe, together with such inferences as can be drawn from these facts.

The word 'knowledge' is very ambiguous. We say that Watson's rats 'know' how to get out of mazes, that a child of three 'knows' how to talk, that a man 'knows' the people with whom he is acquainted, that he 'knows' what he had for breakfast this morning, and that he 'knows' when Columbus first crossed the ocean. French and German are less ambiguous, since each has two words for different kinds of 'knowing', which we tend to confuse in our thoughts because we confuse them in our language. I shall not attempt as yet to deal with knowledge in general, but rather with certain less general concepts which would ordinarily be included under 'knowledge'. And first of all I will deal with perception – not as it appears to the perceiver, but as it can be tested by an outside observer.

Let us try, first, to get a rough preliminary view of the sort of thing we are going to mean by 'perception'. One may say that a man 'perceives' anything that he notices through his senses. This is not a question of the sense-organs alone, though they are a necessary condition. No man can perceive by sight what is not in his field of vision, but he may look straight at a thing without perceiving it. I have frequently had the experience – supposed to be characteristic of philosophers – of looking everywhere for my spectacles although they were before my eyes when my search began. We cannot therefore tell what a man is perceiving by observing his sense-organs alone, though they may enable us to know that he is *not* perceiving something. The observer can only know that a man is perceiving something if the man reacts in some appropriate manner. If I say to a man 'Please pass the mustard' and he thereupon passes it, it is highly probable that he perceived what I said, although it *may* of course be a mere coincidence that he passed it at that moment. But if I say to him 'The telephone number you want is 2467' and he proceeds to call that number, the odds against his doing so by mere chance are very great – roughly 10,000 to 1. And if a man reads aloud out of a book, and I look over his shoulder and perceive the same words, it becomes quite fantastic to suppose that he does not perceive the words he is uttering. We can thus in many cases achieve practical certainty as to some of the things that other people are perceiving.

Perception is a species of a wider genus, namely *sensitivity*. Sensitivity is not confined to living things; in fact it is best exemplified by scientific instruments. A material object is said to be 'sensitive' to such and such a stimulus if, when that stimulus is present, it behaves in a way noticeably different from that in which it behaves in the absence of the stimulus. A photographic plate is sensitive to light, a barometer is sensitive to pressure, a thermometer to temperature, a galvanometer to electric current, and so on. In all these cases, we might say, in a certain metaphorical sense, that an instrument 'perceives' the stimulus to which it is sensitive. We do not in fact say so; we feel that perception involves something more than we find in scientific instruments. What is this something more?

The traditional answer would be: consciousness. But this answer, right or wrong, is not what we are seeking at the moment, because we are considering the percipient as he appears to an outside observer, to whom his 'consciousness' is only an inference. Is there anything in perception as viewed from without that distinguishes it from the sensitivity of a scientific instrument?

There is, of course, the fact that human beings are sensitive to a greater variety of stimuli than any instrument. Each separate sense-organ can be surpassed by something made artificially sensitive to its particular stimulus. Photographic plates can photograph stars that we cannot see; clinical thermometers register differences of temperature that we cannot feel; and so on. But there is no way of combining a microscope, a microphone, a thermometer, a galvanometer, and so on, into a single organism which will react in an integral manner to the combination of all the different stimuli that affect its different 'sense-organs'. This, however, is perhaps only a proof that our mechanical skill is not so great as it may in time become. It is certainly not enough to define the difference between a dead instrument and a living body.

The chief difference – perhaps the only one from our present point of view – is that living bodies are subject to the law of association or of the 'conditioned reflex'. Consider, for instance, an automatic machine. It has a reflex which makes it sensitive to pennies, in response to which it gives up chocolate. But it never learns to give up chocolate on merely seeing a penny, or hearing the word 'penny'. If you kept it in your house, and said 'Abracadabra' to it every time you inserted a penny, it would not in the end be moved to action by the mere word 'Abracadabra'. Its reflexes remain unconditioned, as do some of ours, such as sneezing. But with us sneezing is peculiar in this respect – hence its unimportance. Most of our reflexes can be conditioned, and the conditioned reflex can in turn be conditioned afresh, and so on without limit. This is what makes the reactions of the higher animals, and especially of man, so much more interesting and complicated than the reactions of machines. Let us see whether this one law will suffice to distinguish perception from other forms of sensitivity.

The variability in a human being's responses to a given stimulus has given rise to the traditional distinction between cognition and volition. When one's rich uncle comes for a visit, smiles are the natural response; after he has lost his money, a colder demeanour results from the new conditioning. Thus the reaction to the stimulus has come to be divided into two parts, one purely receptive and sensory, the other active and motor. Perception, as traditionally conceived, is, so to speak, the end term of the receptive-sensory part of the reaction, while volition (in its widest sense) is the first term of the active-motor part of the reaction. It was possible to suppose that the receptive part of the reaction would be always the same for the same stimulus, and that the difference due to experience would only arise in the motor part. The last term of the passive part, as it appears to the person concerned, was called 'sensation'. But in fact the influence of the law of conditioned reflexes goes much deeper than this theory supposed. As we saw, the contraction of the pupil, which is normally due to bright light, can be conditioned so as to result from a loud noise. What we see depends largely upon muscular adjustments of the eyes, which we make quite unconsciously. But apart from the contraction of the pupil only one of them is a true reflex, namely turning the eyes towards a bright light. This is a movement which children can perform on the day of their birth; I know this, not merely from personal observation, but also, what is more, from the text-books. But new-born infants cannot follow a moving light with their eyes, nor can they focus or accommodate. As a consequence, the purely receptive part of their reaction to visual objects, in so far as this reaction is visual, is different from that of adults or older children, whose eye muscles adjust themselves so as to see clearly.

But here again all sorts of factors enter in. Innumerable objects are in our field of vision, but only some (at most) are interesting to us. If someone says 'look, there's a snake', we adjust our eyes afresh and obtain a new 'sensation'. Then, when the purely visual part is finished, there are stimulations, by association, of other centres in the brain. There are pictures, in Köhler's book, of apes watching other apes on the top of insecure piles of boxes, and the spectators have their arms raised in sympathetic balancing movements. Anyone who watches gymnastics or skilful dancing is liable to experience sympathetic muscular contractions. Any visual object that we might be touching will stimulate incipient touch reactions, but the sun, moon, and stars do not.

Conversely, visual reactions may be stimulated through association with other stimuli. When motor-cars were still uncommon, I was walking one day with a friend when a tyre punctured in our neighbourhood with a loud report. He thought it was a revolver, and averred that he had seen the flash. In dreams, this sort of mechanism operates uncontrolled. Some stimulus – say the noise of the maid knocking at the door – becomes interpreted in fantastic ways which are governed by association. I remember once dreaming that I was in an inn in the country in Germany and was wakened by a choir singing outside my window. Finally I really woke, and found that a spring shower was making a very musical noise on the roof. At least, I heard a very musical noise, and now re-interpreted it as a shower on the roof. This hypothesis I confirmed by looking out of the window. In waking life we are critical of the interpretative hypotheses that occur to us, and therefore do not make such wild mistakes as in dreams. But the creative, as opposed to the critical, mechanism is the same in waking life as it is in dreams: there is always far more richness in the experience than the sensory stimulus alone would warrant. All adaptation to environment acquired during the life of the individual might be regarded as learning to dream dreams that succeed rather than dreams that fail. The dreams we have when we are asleep usually end in a surprise: the dreams we have in waking life are less apt to do so. Sometimes they do, as when pride goes before a fall;

but in that case they are regarded as showing maladjustment, unless there is some large external cause, such as an earthquake. One might say that a person properly adapted to his environment is one whose dreams never end in the sort of surprise that would wake him up. In that case, he will think that his dreams are objective reality. But if modern physics is to be believed, the dreams we call waking perceptions have only a very little more resemblance to objective reality than the fantastic dreams of sleep. They have *some* truth, but only just so much as is required to make them useful.

Until we begin to reflect, we unhesitatingly assume that what we see is really 'there' in the outside world, except in such cases as reflections in mirrors. Physics and the theory of the way in which perceptions are caused show that this naïve belief cannot be quite true. Perception may, and I think does, enable us to know something of the outer world, but it is not the direct revelation that we naturally suppose it to be. We cannot go into this question adequately until we have considered what the philosopher has to learn from physics; I am merely giving, by anticipation, the reasons for regarding perception as a form of reaction to the environment, displayed in some bodily movement, rather than as a form of knowledge. When we have considered further what constitutes knowledge, we may find that perception is, after all, a form of knowledge, but only because knowledge is not quite what we naturally suppose it to be. For the present, let us stick to the view of perception that can be obtained by the external observer, i.e. as something displayed in the manner of reacting to the environment.

From the point of view of the external observer, perception is established just like any other causal correlation. We observe that, whenever a certain object stands in a certain spatial relation to a man's body, the man's body makes a certain movement or set of movements; we shall then say that the man 'perceives' the object. So the new-born baby turns its eyes slowly towards a bright light which is not in the centre of the field of vision; this entitles us to say that the baby 'perceives' the light. If he is blind, his eyes do not move in this way. A bird flying about in a wood does not bump into the branches, whereas in a room it will bump into the glass of the window. This entitles us to say that the bird perceives the branches but not the glass. Do we 'perceive' the glass or do we merely know that it is there? This question introduces us to the complications produced by association. We know by experience, from the sense of touch, that there is usually glass in window-frames; this makes us react to the

window-frames as if we could see the glass. But sometimes there is
no glass, and still we shall perhaps behave as if there were. If this
can happen, it shows that we do not perceive the glass, since our
reaction is the same whether there is glass or not. If, however, the
glass is coloured, or slightly distorting, or not perfectly clean, a person
accustomed to glass will be able to distinguish a frame containing glass
from one which has none. In that case it is more difficult to decide
whether we are to say that he 'perceives' the glass or not. It is certain
that perception is affected by experience. A person who can read
perceives print where another would not. A musician perceives
differences between notes which to an untrained ear are indistinguishable. People unaccustomed to the telephone cannot understand what
they hear in it; but this is perhaps not really a case in point.

The difficulty we are considering arises from the fact that a human
body, unlike a scientific instrument, is perpetually changing its reaction
to a given stimulus, under the influence of the law of association.
Moreover, the human body is always doing something. How, then,
are we to know whether what it is doing is the result of a given
stimulus or not? In most cases, however, this difficulty is not very
serious, particularly when we are dealing with people old enough to
speak. When you go to the oculist he asks you to read a number of
letters growing gradually smaller; at some point you fail. Where you
have succeeded, he knows that you have perceived enough to make
out what letter it is. Or you take a pair of compasses and press the
points into a man's back, asking him if he feels two pricks or only
one. He may say one when the two points are near together; if he is
on his guard against this error he may say two when in fact there is
only one. But if the points are sufficiently far apart he will never make
a mistake. That is to say, the bodily movement consisting in
pronouncing the word 'two' will invariably result from a certain
stimulus. (Invariably, I mean, for a given subject on a given day.)
This entitles us to say that the man can perceive that there are
two points provided they are not too near together. Or you say,
'What can you see on the horizon?' One man says, 'I see a
ship'. Another says, 'I see a steamer with two funnels'. A third says,
'I see a Cunarder going from Southampton to New York'. How much
of what these three people say is to count as perception? They may
all three be perfectly right in what they say, and yet we should not
concede that a man can 'perceive' that the ship is going from
Southampton to New York. This, we should say, is inference. But
it is by no means easy to draw the line; some things which are, in an

important sense, inferential, must be admitted to be perceptions. The man who says 'I see a ship' is using inference. Apart from experience, he only sees a queerly shaped dark dot on a blue background. Experience has taught him that that sort of dot 'means' a ship; that is to say, he has a conditioned reflex which causes him to utter, aloud or to himself, the word 'ship' when his eye is stimulated in a certain way. To disentangle what is due to experience, and what not, in the perceptions of an adult, is a hopeless task. Practically, if a word comes without previous verbal intermediaries, the ordinary man would include what the word means in the perception, while he would not do so if the man arrives at the word after verbal preliminaries, overt or internal. But this is itself a question of familiarity. Show a child a pentagon, and he will have to count the sides to know how many there are; but after a little experience of geometrical figures, the word 'pentagon' will arise without any previous words. And in any case such a criterion is theoretically worthless. The whole affair is a matter of degree, and we cannot draw any sharp line between perception and inference. As soon as this is realised, our difficulties are seen to be purely verbal and therefore unimportant.

It will be observed that we are not attempting at present to say what constitutes perception, but only what kind of behaviour on the part of a person whom we are observing will justify us in saying that he has perceived this or that feature of his environment. I suggest that we are justified in saying that a man 'perceives' such a feature if, throughout some such period as a day, there is some bodily act which he performs whenever that feature is present, but not at any other time. This condition is clearly sufficient, but not necessary – that is to say, there may be perception even when it is not fulfilled. A man's reaction may change through conditioning, even in so short a period as a day. Again, there may be a reaction, but one which is too slight to be observable; in this case the criterion of perception is theoretically satisfied, but not practically, since no one can know that it is. We often have evidence later on that something was perceived, although at the moment there was no discoverable reaction. I have frequently known children repeat afterwards some remark which, at the time, they seemed not to have heard. This sort of case affords another kind of evidence of perception, namely, the evidence afforded by a delayed response. Some people will sit silent and impassive in a company of talkers, giving no evidence that they are listening; yet they may go home and write down the conversation verbatim in their journals. These are the typical writers of memoirs. More remarkable still, I know one man – a man of genius, it is true – who talks incessantly, who yet, after meeting a total stranger, knows exactly what the stranger who would have said if he had been given the chance. How this is managed, I do not know; but such a man is rightly called 'perceptive'.

Obviously, in dealing with human beings old enough to talk, words afford the best evidence of perception. A man's verbal responses to perceptive situations do not change much after the first few years of life. If you see a kingfisher, and at the same moment your companion says 'There's a kingfisher', that is pretty conclusive evidence that he saw it. But, as this case illustrates, our evidence that someone else has perceived something always depends upon our own perceptions. And our own perceptions are known to us in a different way from that in which the perceptions of others are known to us. This is one of the weak spots in the attempt at a philosophy from the objective standpoint. Such a philosophy really assumes knowledge as a going concern, and takes for granted the world which a man derives from his own perceptions. We cannot tackle all our philosophical problems by the objective method, but it is worth while to proceed with it as far as it will take us. This whole question of perception will have to be attacked afresh from a different angle, and we shall then find reason to regard the behaviouristic standpoint as inadequate, though valid so far as it goes. We have still, however, a long road to go before we shall be driven to consider the subjective standpoint; more particularly, we have to define 'knowledge' and 'inference' behaviouristically, and then, making a new start, to consider what modern physics makes of 'matter'. But for the moment there are still some things to be said about perception from the objective standpoint.

It will be seen that, according to our criterion of perception, an object perceived need not be in contact with the percipient's body. The sun, moon, and stars are perceived according to the above criterion. In order, however, that an object not in contact with the body should be perceived, there are physical as well as physiological conditions to be fulfilled. There must be some physical process which takes place at the surface of the body when the object in question is suitably situated, but not otherwise; and there must be sense-organs capable of being affected by such a process. There are, as we know from physics, many processes which fulfil the necessary physical conditions, but fail to affect us through the inadequacy of our sense-organs. Waves of a certain sort make sound, but waves of exactly the same sort become inaudible if they are too short. Waves of a certain sort make light, but if they are too long or too short they are invisible. The waves used in wireless are of the same sort as those that make light, but are too long. There is no reason *a priori* why we should not be aware of wireless messages through our senses, without the need of instruments. X-rays are also of the same sort as those that make light, but in this case they are too short to be seen. They might render the objects from which they come visible, if we had a different sort of eye. We are not sensitive to magnetism, unless it is enormously powerful; but if we had more iron in our bodies, we might have no need of the mariner's compass. Our senses are a haphazard selection of those that the nature of physical processes renders possible; one may suppose that they have resulted from chance variation and the struggle for existence.

It is important to observe that our perceptions are very largely concerned with form or shape or structure. This is the point emphasised by what is called *Gestaltpsychologie*, or psychology of form. Reading is a case in point. Whether we read black letters on white paper or white letters on a blackboard is a matter which we hardly notice; it is the forms of the letters that affect us, not their colour or their size (so long as they remain legible). In this matter, the sense of sight is pre-eminent, although blind men (and others to a less degree) can acquire a good knowledge of form by the sense of touch.

Another point of importance about our perceptions is that they give us, within limits, a knowledge of temporal sequence. If you say to a man 'Brutus killed Caesar', and then 'Caesar killed Brutus', the difference between the two statements is likely to be perceived by him if he is listening; in the one case he will say 'Of course', in the other 'Nonsense', which is evidence of his having different perceptions in the two cases, according to our definition. Further, if you ask him what the difference is, he can tell you that it is a difference in the order of the words. Thus time-order within a short period of time is clearly perceptible.

The objective method, which we have been applying in this chapter, is the only possible one in studying the perceptions of animals or of infants before they can talk. Many animals too low in the scale of evolution to have eyes are yet sensitive to light, in the sense that they move towards it or move away from it. Such animals, according to our criterion, perceive light, though there is no reason to suppose that they perceive colour or visual form or anything beyond the bare presence of light. We can perceive the bare presence of light when our eyes are shut; perhaps one may imagine their sensitiveness to be more or less analogous in its limitations.

It is not to be supposed, in any case, that 'perceiving' an object involves knowing what it is like. That is quite another matter. We shall see later that certain inferences, of a highly abstract character, can be drawn from our perceptions to the objects perceived; but these inferences are at once difficult and not quite certain. The idea that perception, in itself, reveals the character of objects, is a fond delusion, and one, moreover, which it is very necessary to overcome if our philosophy is to be anything more than a pleasant fairy-tale.

Chapter 6

Memory Objectively Regarded

We are concerned in these chapters with what we can know about other men by merely observing their behaviour. In this chapter, I propose to consider everything that would commonly be called 'memory', in so far as it can be made a matter of external observation. And perhaps it may be as well, at this point, to state my own view of the question of 'behaviourism'. This philosophy, of which the chief protagonist is Dr. John B. Watson, holds that everything that can be known about man is discoverable by the method of external observation, i.e. that none of our knowledge depends, essentially and necessarily, upon data in which the observer and the observed are the same person. I do not fundamentally agree with this view, but I think it contains much more truth than most people suppose, and I regard it as desirable to develop the behaviourist method to the fullest possible extent. I believe that the knowledge to be obtained by this method, so long as we take physics for granted, is self-contained, and need not, at any point, appeal to data derived from introspection, i.e. from observations which a man can make upon himself but not upon anyone else. Nevertheless, I hold that there are such observations and that there is knowledge which depends upon introspection. What is more, I hold that data of this kind are required for a critical exposition of physics, which behaviourism takes for granted. I shall, therefore, after setting forth the behaviourist view of man, proceed to a scrutiny of our knowledge of physics, returning thence to man, but now as viewed from within. Then, finally, I shall attempt to draw conclusions as to what we know of the universe in general.

The word 'memory' or 'remembering' is commonly used in a number of different senses, which it is important to distinguish. More especially, there is a broad sense, in which the word applies to the power of repeating any habitual act previously learnt, and a narrow sense, in which it applies only to recollection of past events. It is in the broad sense that people speak of a dog remembering his master or his name,

and that Sir Francis Darwin spoke of memory in plants. Samuel
Butler used to attribute the sort of behaviour that would usually be
called instinctive to memory of ancestral experience, and evidently
he was using the word 'memory' in its widest possible sense. Bergson,
on the contrary, dismisses 'habit-memory' as not true memory at all.
True memory, for him, is confined to the recollection of a past
occurrence, which, he maintains, cannot be a habit, since the event
remembered only occurred once. The behaviourist maintains that this
contention is mistaken, and that all memory consists in the retention of
a habit. For him, therefore, memory is not something requiring special
study, but is merged into the study of habit. Dr. Watson says: 'The
behaviourist never uses the term "memory". He believes that it has
no place in an objective psychology.' He proceeds to give instances,
beginning with a white rat in a maze. On the first occasion, he says,
it took this rat forty minutes to get out of the maze, but after thirty-five
trials he learnt to get out in six seconds, without taking any wrong
turnings. He was then kept away from the maze for six months, and
on being put in it again he got out in two minutes, with six mistakes.
He was just as good as he had been before at the twentieth trial. We
have here a measure of the extent to which the habit of the maze had
been retained. A similar experiment with a monkey showed even more
retentiveness. He was put into a problem box which at first took him
twenty minutes to open, but at the twentieth trial he opened it in two
seconds. He was then kept away from it for six months, and on being
put back in it he opened it in four seconds.

With human beings, we know that many of the habits we learn
are retained through long periods of disuse – skating, bicycling,
swimming, golf, etc., are familiar instances. Perhaps Dr. Watson goes
a trifle too far when he says: 'If a poor shot or an inexpert golfer tells
you that he was good five years ago but that lack of practice has made
him poor, don't believe him; he never was good!' At any rate, this
is not the belief of violinists and pianists, who consider it essential to
practise every day. But even if it be somewhat of an exaggeration, it
is certainly true that we retain bodily habits pretty well. Some, such
as swimming, seem to be more completely retained than others. The
power of talking a foreign language, for example, is one which is
greatly impaired by disuse. The whole matter is quantitative, and
easily tested by experiment.

But memory in the sense of recollection of past events, if it can be
explained as a habit, will have, one might suppose, to be a *verbal*
habit. As to this, Dr. Watson says:

'What the man on the street ordinarily means by an exhibition of
memory is what occurs in some such situation as this: An old friend
comes to see him, after many years' absence. The moment he sees this
friend, he says: "Upon my life! Addison Sims of Seattle! I haven't
seen you since the World's Fair in Chicago. Do you remember the
gay parties we used to have in the Wilderness Hotel? Do you
remember the Midway? Do you remember . . . etc.," *ad infinitum*.
The psychology of this process is so simple that it seems almost an
insult to your intelligence to discuss it, and yet a good many of the
behaviourists' kindly critics have said that behaviourism cannot
adequately explain memory. Let us see if this is a fact.'

He goes on to say that during the period, long ago, when the man
on the street was seeing Mr. Sims, they formed verbal and manual
habits towards one another, so that 'finally, just the sight of the man,
even after months of absence, would call out not only the old verbal
habits, but many other types of bodily and visceral responses.'

He sums up: 'By "memory", then, we mean nothing except the fact
that when we meet a stimulus again after an absence, we do the old
habitual thing (say the old words and show the old visceral – emotional
– behaviour) that we learned to do when we were in the presence of
that stimulus in the first place.'

This theory is preferable to ordinary psychological theories in many
ways. In the first place, it is not an attempt to treat memory as some
sort of mystical 'faculty', and does not suppose that we are always
remembering everything that we should remember if a suitable
stimulus were applied. It is concerned with the causation of specific
acts of remembering, these acts being all externally observable. Is
there any good reason to question it? Bergson's contention that the
recollection of a unique occurrence cannot be explained by habit is
clearly fallacious. There are many instances, both with animals and
with human beings, of a habit becoming firmly established through
one experience. It is, therefore, quite possible that a stimulus associated
with a previous occurrence should set going a train of bodily events
which, in turn, produce words describing that occurrence. There is
here, however, a difficulty. The memory of a past occurrence cannot
be a *verbal* habit, except when the occurrence has been frequently
related. When Watson's man on the street says 'Do you remember
the Midway', he is not using words that have become habitual; very
likely he never used these words before. He is using words which a
verbal habit associates with an event that is now happening in him,
and the event is called up by a habit associated with Mr. Sims. So

at least we must suppose, if we accept Watson's view. But this diminishes the plausibility and the verifiability of his view. It is not our actual language that can be regarded as habitual, but only what our words express. In repeating a poem we have learned by heart, the language is habitual, but not so when we recount a past incident in words we never used before. In this case, it is not the actual words that we repeat, but only their meaning. The habitual element, therefore, if it really accounts for the recollection, must not be sought in words.

This is something of a difficulty in the Watsonian theory of language. When a rat learns a maze, it learns certain definite bodily movements; so do we when we learn by heart. But I may say to one person, 'I met Mr. Jones in the train today', and to another 'Joseph was in the 9.35 this morning.' With the exception of the words 'in the', these two sentences have nothing verbally in common, yet they may relate the same fact, and I may use either indifferently when I recall the fact. Thus my recollection is certainly *not* a definite verbal habit. Yet words are the only overt bodily movements by which I make known my recollections to other people. If the behaviourist tells me that my recollection is bodily habit, and begins by telling me that it is a *verbal* habit, he can be driven by such instances to the admission that it must be some other kind of habit. If he says this, he is abandoning the region of observable fact, and taking refuge in hypothetical bodily movements invoked to save a theory. But these are hardly any better than 'thoughts'.

This question is more general than the problem of memory. Many different forms of words may be used to express the same 'meaning', and there seems no reason in mere habit to account for the fact that we sometimes use one form of words and sometimes another when we 'think' of that which all the various forms of words express. The association seems to go, not direct from stimulus to words, but from stimulus to 'meaning' and thence to words expressing the 'meaning'. You may, for instance, be quite unable to recollect whether you were told 'Jacob is older than Joseph', or 'Joseph is younger than Jacob', though you may remember quite definitely that you were told the fact which both these forms of words express. Again, if you are learning, say, a proof of a mathematical theorem, you do not learn by heart what the book says, unless you are a very bad mathematician; you learn, as people say, to 'understand' the proof, and then you can reproduce it in symbols quite different from those in the book. It is such facts, among others, that make it difficult to explain the mechanism of association, whether in memory or in 'thought' in general, if we assume that words, or even sentences, are the terms associated.

Perhaps, however, the theory as to the 'meaning' of words which we developed in an earlier chapter may help us out of the difficulty. We defined the 'meaning' of a word by means of its associations; therefore, if two words are synonyms, they have the same associations; and any stimulus which calls up one may also call up the other. The question which of two synonyms we use will then depend upon some extraneous circumstance.

This is all very well so far as single words are concerned; it would account satisfactorily, for instance, for the fact that I call a man sometimes by his surname and sometimes by his Christian name. But it is hardly so adequate when we come to the question of sentences. To revert to the illustration of a moment ago, in response to the stimulus 'Did anything happen on your journey?' you may say either 'I met Mr. Jones in the train to-day', or 'Joseph was in the 9.35 this morning', or any one of an indefinite number of other sentences expressive of the same occurrence. Are we to suppose that, while you were in the train, you were rehearsing all these different sentences to yourself, so that each of them became firmly associated with the words 'journey to-day'? Clearly such a supposition would be absurd. Yet all the separate words of your sentence have many other associations; it is only the sentence as a whole that is associated with your journey. You have met other people besides Mr. Jones; you have had other contacts with Mr. Jones besides meeting him this morning; 'train' and 'to-day' equally are appropriate to other occurrences that you might relate. Thus it has to be the whole sentence that is the associative unit, and yet the sentence may never have been in your head before. It seems clear that it is possible to state in words something that you remember, although you never put it into words before. Suppose I say 'What did you have for breakfast to-day'? Probably you will be able to tell me, though it is very likely that you have not given names to the things you ate until this moment.

This whole matter is connected with the distinction between sentences and single words, which we found important when we were discussing language. But even when we confine ourselves to single words, there are difficulties in Dr. Watson's view. Cases are alleged in which children, after learning to speak, can recall incidents which occurred before they could speak, and describe them in correct words. This would show that the memory had persisted in a non-verbal form throughout the period before they learned to speak, and had only subsequently found verbal expression. Such extreme incidents are rare and might be questioned, but in a less extreme form it ought not to be difficult to obtain examples of the same sort of thing. Suppose, for example, that a young child hurt his wrist badly before he knew the word 'wrist', and that some time afterwards he learnt it; I should not be surprised if he could relate that he had hurt his wrist. Such instances, however, would not refute the essence of Watson's theory. He would allow 'visceral' memory, for example, and the association with the word 'wrist' might be grafted on to this. The real difficulty in Dr. Watson's view, to my mind, is the fact that our sentence may vary verbally as much as it likes so long as it retains the same 'meaning', and that we clearly do not rehearse to ourselves beforehand all the possible sentences having the 'meaning' in question.

It should be realised that behaviourism loses much of its attractiveness if it is compelled to postulate movements that no one can observe and that there is no other reason to assume. Dr. Broad, in his book on *The Mind and its Place in Nature*, distinguishes between 'molar' and 'molecular' behaviourism: the former assumes only such bodily movements as can be observed, while the latter allows and utilises hypothetical minute movements, more especially in the brain. Now here we must make a distinction. Physics believes in a large number of phenomena which are too minute to be observed even with the strongest microscope, and if physics is at all correct, there must be minute movements in all parts of a human body, of a sort which we can never hope to see. We cannot reasonably demand of the behaviourist that he should abstain from an hypothesis which physics asserts for very good reasons. And in the process which leads from stimulus to reaction there are bound to be small occurrences in the brain which, though they cannot be observed, are essential to the physiological explanation of what occurs. But when the behaviourist assumes small occurrences for which there is no ground in physics, and which are needed solely in order to safeguard his theory, he is in a less strong position. Dr. Watson asserts, for instance, that whenever we 'think' there are small movements in the larynx which are beginnings of the movements we should make as if we spoke words out loud. It may be that this is true; certainly I am not prepared to deny it. But I am not prepared to say that it *must* be true merely because, if it were not, behaviourism would be false. We do not know in advance that behaviourism is true; we have to find out whether it will explain observed facts. Whenever it has to postulate something unobserved merely in order to avoid a refutation, it weakens its case. And if it maintains, as, from Dr. Watson's language, it seems to do, that we only remember an occurrence by forming a verbal habit in connection with it, then it is obliged to postulate much implicit use of words of which we have no evidence.

To sum up this discussion. While it is quite possible, by behaviourist methods, to ascertain whether a person remembers a past occurrence or not, unless he is deliberately obstructing the observer, and while much memory can be quite adequately explained as habit, there do seem to be great difficulties in the view that memory consists *entirely* of habit, at least in the case of the recollection of an event. These difficulties seem insuperable if we suppose memory to be *essentially* a verbal habit. They are not insuperable if we postulate sufficient minute unobservable bodily movements. We have not considered whether they can be overcome by introducing data derived from introspection, since we wish, for the present, to maintain a strictly objective attitude to human behaviour. The introspective discussion of memory will be taken up at a later stage.

Chapter 7

Inference as a Habit

In this chapter, we are concerned with inference as it can be observed when practised by someone else. Inference is supposed to be a mark of intelligence and to show the superiority of men to machines. At the same time, the treatment of inference in traditional logic is so stupid as to throw doubt on this claim, and syllogistic inference, which was taken as the type from Aristotle to Bacon (exclusive), is just the sort of thing that a calculating machine could do better than a professor. In syllogistic inference, you are supposed to know already that all men are mortal and that Socrates is a man; hence you deduce, what you never suspected before, that Socrates is mortal. This form of inference does actually occur, though very rarely. The only instance I have ever heard of was supplied by Dr. F. C. S. Schiller. He once produced a comic number of the philosophical periodical *Mind,* and sent copies to various philosophers, among others to a certain German, who was much puzzled by the advertisements. But at last he argued: 'Everything in this book is a joke, therefore the advertisements are jokes.' I have never come across any other case of new knowledge obtained by means of a syllogism. It must be admitted that, for a method which dominated logic for two thousand years, this contribution to the world's stock of information cannot be considered very weighty.

The inferences that we actually make in daily life differ from those of syllogistic logic in two respects, namely, that they are important and precarious, instead of being trivial and safe. The syllogism may be regarded as a monument to academic timidity: if an inference might be wrong, it was dangerous to draw it. So the mediaeval monks, in their thinking as in their lives, sought safety at the expense of fertility.

With the Renaissance, a more adventurous spirit came into the world, but at first, in philosophy, it only took the form of following Greeks other than Aristotle, and more especially Plato. It is only with Bacon and Galileo that the inductive method arrived at due recognition: with Bacon as a programme which was largely faulty, but with Galileo as something which actually led to brilliant results, namely, the foundation of modern mathematical physics. Unfortunately, when the pedants got hold of induction, they set to work to make it as tame and scholastic as deduction had been. They searched for a way of making it *always* lead to true results, and in so doing robbed it of its adventurous character. Hume turned upon them with sceptical arguments, proving quite conclusively that if an induction is worth making it may be wrong. Thereupon Kant deluged the philosophic world with muddle and mystery, from which it is only now beginning to emerge. Kant has the reputation of being the greatest of modern philosophers, but to my mind he was a mere misfortune.

Induction, as it appears in the text-books, consists, roughly speaking, in the inference that, because A and B have been found often together and never apart, therefore they are probably always together, and either may be taken as a sign of the other. I do not wish, at this stage, to examine the logical justification of this form of argumentation; for the present, I am considering it as a *practice*, which we can observe in the habits of men and animals.

As a practice, induction is nothing but our old friend, the law of conditioned reflexes or of association. A child touches a knob that gives him an electric shock; after that, he avoids touching the knob. If he is old enough to speak, he may state that the knob hurts when it is touched; he has made an induction based on a single instance. But the induction will exist as a bodily habit even if he is too young to speak, and it occurs equally among animals, provided they are not too low in the scale. The theories of induction in logic are what Freudians call a 'rationalisation'; that is to say, they consist of reasons invented afterwards to prove that what we have been doing is sensible. It does not follow that they are bad reasons: in view of the fact that we and our ancestors have managed to exist since the origin of life, our behaviour and theirs must have been fairly sensible, even if we and they were unable to prove that it was. This, however, is not the point that concerns us at present. What concerns us at present is the fact that verbal induction is a late development of induction in behaviour, which is nothing more nor less than the principle of 'learned reactions'.

This principle, as the reader will remember, states that, if a certain event calls out a certain response, and if another event is experienced just before it, or at the same moment, in time that other event will tend to call out the response which, originally, only the first event would call out. This applies both to muscles and to glands; it is because it applies to glands that words are capable of causing emotions.

Moreover, we cannot set limits to the length of the chain of associations that may be established. If you hold an infant's limbs, you call out a rage reaction; this appears to be an 'unlearned reaction'. If you, and no one else, repeatedly hold an infant's limbs, the mere sight of you will call out a rage reaction after a time. When the infant learns to talk your name may have the same effect. If, later, he learns that you are an optician, he may come to hate all opticians; this may lead him to hate Spinoza because he made spectacles, and thence he may come to hate metaphysicians and Jews. For doing so he will no doubt have the most admirable reasons, which will seem to him to be his real ones; he will never suspect the process of conditioning by which he has in fact arrived at his enthusiasm for the Ku Klux Klan. This is an example of conditioning in the emotional sphere; but it is rather in the muscular sphere that we must seek the origin of the practice of induction.

Domestic animals which are habitually fed by a certain person will run towards that person as soon as they see him. We say that they expect food, and in fact their behaviour is very like what it would be if they saw food. But really we have only an example of 'conditioning': they have often seen first the farmer and then the food, so that in time they react to the farmer as they originally reacted to the food. Infants soon learn to react to the sight of the bottle, although at first they only react to the touch of it. When they can speak, the same law makes them say 'dinner' when they hear the dinner-bell. It is quite unnecessary to suppose that they first think 'that bell means dinner', and then say 'dinner'. The sight of dinner (by a previous 'learned reaction') causes the word 'dinner': the bell frequently precedes the sight of dinner; therefore in time the bell produces the word 'dinner'. It is only subsequent reflection, probably at a much later age, that makes the child say 'I knew dinner was ready because I heard the bell'. Long before he can say this, he is acting as if he knew it. And there is no good reason for denying that he knows it, when he acts as if he did. If knowledge is to be displayed by behaviour, there is no reason to confine ourselves to *verbal* behaviour as the sole kind by which knowledge can manifest itself.

The situation, stated abstractly, is as follows. Originally, stimulus A produced reaction C; now stimulus B produces it, as a result of association. Thus B has become a 'sign' of A, in the sense that it causes the behaviour appropriate to A. All sorts of things may be signs of other things, but with human beings words are the supreme example of signs. All signs depend upon some practical induction. Whenever we read or hear a statement, its effect upon us depends upon induction in this sense, since the words are signs of what they mean, in the sense that we react to them, in certain respects, as we should to what they stand for. If someone says to you 'Your house is on fire', the effect upon you is practically the same as if you saw the conflagration. You may, of course, be the victim of a hoax, and in that case your behaviour will not be such as achieves any purpose you have in view. This risk of error exists always, since the fact that two things have occurred together in the past cannot prove conclusively that they will occur together in the future.

Scientific induction is an attempt to regularise the above process, which we may call 'physiological induction'. It is obvious that, as practised by animals, infants, and savages, physiological induction is a frequent source of error. There is Dr. Watson's infant who induced, from two examples, that whenever he saw a certain rat there would be a loud noise. There is Edmund Burke, who induced from one example (Cromwell) that revolutions lead to military tyrannies. There are savages who argue, from one bad season, that the arrival of a white man causes bad crops. The inhabitants of Siena, in 1348, thought that the Black Death was a punishment for their pride in starting to build too large a cathedral. Of such examples there is no end. It is very necessary, therefore, if possible, to find some method by which induction can be practised so as to lead, in general, to correct results. But this is a problem of scientific method, with which we will not yet concern ourselves.

What does concern us at present is the fact that all inference, of the sort that really occurs, is a development of this one principle of conditioning. In practice, inference is of two kinds, one typified by induction, the other by mathematical reasoning. The former is by far the more important, since, as we have seen, it covers all use of signs and all empirical generalisations as well as the habits of which they are the verbal expression. I know that, from the traditional standpoint, it seems absurd to talk of inference in most cases of this sort. For example, you find it stated in the paper that such and such a horse has won the Derby. According to my own use of words, you practise an induction when you arrive thence at the belief that that horse has won. The stimulus consists of certain black marks on white paper – or perhaps on pink paper. This stimulus is only connected with horses and the Derby by association, yet your reaction is one appropriate to the Derby. Traditionally, there was only inference where there was a 'mental process', which, after dwelling upon the 'premisses', was led to assert the 'conclusion' by means of insight into their logical connection. I am not saying that the process which such words as the above are intended to describe never takes place; it certainly does. What I am saying is that, genetically and causally, there is no important difference between the most elaborate induction and the most elementary 'learned reaction'. The one is merely a developed form of the other, not something radically different. And our determination to believe in the results of inductions, even if, as logicians, we see no reason to do so, is really due to the potency of the principle of association; it is an example – perhaps the most important example – of what Dr. Santayana calls 'animal faith'.

The question of mathematical reasoning is more difficult. I think we may lay it down that, in mathematics, the conclusion always asserts merely the whole or part of the premisses, though usually in new language. The difficulty of mathematics consists in seeing that this is so in particular cases. In practice, the mathematician has a set of rules according to which his symbols can be manipulated, and he acquires technical skill in working according to the rules in the same sort of way as a billiard-player does. But there is a difference between mathematics and billiards: the rules of billiards are arbitrary, whereas in mathematics some at least are in some sense 'true'. A man cannot be said to understand mathematics unless he has 'seen' that these rules are right. Now what does this consist of? I think it is only a more complicated example of the process of understanding that 'Napoleon' and 'Bonaparte' refer to the same person. To explain this, however, we must revert to what was said, in the chapter on 'Language', about the understanding of form.

Human beings possess the power of reacting to form. No doubt some of the higher animals also possess it, though to nothing like the same extent as men do; and all animals except a few of the most intelligent species appear to be nearly devoid of it. Among human beings, it differs greatly from one individual to another, and increases, as a rule, up to adolescence. I should take it as what chiefly characterises 'intellect'. But let us see, first, in what the power consists.

When a child is being taught to read, he learns to recognise a given letter, say H, whether it is large or small, black or white or red. However it may vary in these respects his reaction is the same: he says 'H'. That is to say, the essential feature in the stimulus is its *form*. When my boy, at the age of just under three, was about to eat a three-cornered piece of bread and butter, I told him it was a triangle. (His slices were generally rectangular.) Next day, unprompted, he pointed to triangular bits in the pavement of the Albert Memorial, and called them 'triangles'. Thus the form of the bread and butter, as opposed to its edibility, its softness, its colour, etc., was what had impressed him. This sort of thing constitutes the most elementary kind of reaction to form.

Now 'matter' and 'form' can be placed, as in the Aristotelian philosophy, in a hierarchy. From a triangle we can advance to a polygon, thence to a figure, thence to a manifold of points. Then we can go on and turn 'point' into a formal concept, meaning 'something that has relations which resemble spatial relations in certain formal respects'. Each of these is a step away from 'matter' and further into the region of 'form'. At each stage the difficulty increases. The difficulty consists in having a uniform reaction (other than boredom) to a stimulus of this kind. When we 'understand' a mathematical expression, that means that we can react to it in an appropriate manner, in fact, that it has 'meaning' for us. This is also what we mean by 'understanding' the word 'cat'. But it is easier to understand the word 'cat', because the resemblances between different cats are of a sort which causes even animals to have a uniform reaction to all cats. When we come to algebra, and have to operate with x and y, there is a natural desire to know what x and y really are. That, at least, was my feeling: I always thought the teacher knew what they really were, but would not tell me. To 'understand' even the simplest formula in algebra, say $(x+y)^2 = x^2 + 2xy + y^2$, is to be able to react to two sets of symbols in virtue of the form which they express, and to perceive that the form is the same in both cases. This is a very elaborate business, and it is no wonder that boys and girls find algebra a bugbear. But there is no novelty *in principle* after the first elementary perceptions of form. And perception of form consists merely in reacting alike to two stimuli which are alike in form but very different in other respects. For, when we can do that, we can say, on the appropriate occasion, 'that is a triangle'; and this is enough to satisfy the examiner that we know what a triangle is, unless he is so old-fashioned as to expect us to reproduce the verbal definition, which is of course a far easier matter, in which, with patience, we might teach even a parrot to succeeed.

The meanings of complex mathematical symbols are always fixed by rules in relation to the meaning of simpler symbols; thus their meanings are analogous to those of sentences, not to those of single words. What was said earlier about the understanding of sentences applies, therefore, to any group of symbols which, in mathematics, will be declared to have the same meaning as another group, or part of that meaning.

We may sum up this discussion by saying that mathematical inference consists in attaching the same reactions to two different groups of signs, whose meanings are fixed by convention in relation to their constitutent parts, whereas induction consists, first, in taking something as a sign of something else, and later, when we have learned to take A as a sign of B, in taking A as also a sign of C. Thus the usual cases of induction and deduction are distinguished by the fact that, in the former, the inference consists in taking one sign as a sign of two different things, while in the latter the inference consists in taking two different signs as signs of the same thing. This statement is a little too antithetical to be taken as an exact expression of the whole truth in the matter. What is true, however, is that both kinds of inference are concerned with the relation of a sign to what it signifies, and therefore come within the scope of the law of association.

Chapter 8

Knowledge Behaviouristically Considered

The word 'knowledge', like the word 'memory', is avoided by the behaviourist. Nevertheless there is a phenomenon commonly called 'knowledge', which is tested behaviouristically in examinations. I want to consider this phenomenon in this chapter, with a view to deciding whether there is anything in it that the behaviourist cannot deal with adequately.

It will be remembered that, in Chapter 2, we were led to the view that knowledge is a characteristic of the complete process from stimulus to reaction, or even, in the cases of sight and hearing, from an external object to a reaction, the external object being connected with the stimulus by a chain of physical causation in the outer world. Let us, for the moment, leave on one side such cases as sight and hearing, and confine ourselves, for the sake of definiteness, to knowledge derived from touch.

We can observe touch producing reactions in quite humble animals, such as worms and sea anemones. Are we to say that they have 'knowledge' of what they touch? In some sense, yes. Knowledge is a matter of degree. When it is regarded in a purely behaviouristic manner, we shall have to concede that it exists, in some degree, wherever there is a characteristic reaction to a stimulus of a certain kind, and this reaction does not occur in the absence of the right kind of stimulus. In this sense, 'knowledge' is indistinguishable from 'sensitivity', which we considered in connection with perception. We might say that a thermometer 'knows' the temperature, and that a compass 'knows' the direction of the magnetic north. This is the only sense in which, on grounds of observation, we can attribute knowledge to animals that are low in the scale. Many animals, for example, hide themselves when exposed to light, but as a rule not otherwise. In this, however, they do not differ from a radiometer. No doubt the mechanism is different, but the observed molar motion has similar characteristics. Wherever there is a reflex, an animal may be said, in a sense, to 'know' the stimulus. This is, no doubt, not the usual sense of 'knowledge', but it is the germ out of which knowledge in the usual sense has grown, and without which no knowledge would be possible.

Knowledge in any more advanced sense is only possible as a result of learning, in the sense considered in Chapter 3. The rat that has learned the maze 'knows' the way out of it; the boy who has learned certain verbal reactions 'knows' the multiplication table. Between these two cases there is no important difference. In both cases, we say that the subject 'knows' something because he reacts in a manner advantageous to himself, in which he could not react before he had had certain experiences. I do not think, however, that we ought to use such a notion as 'advantageous' in connection with knowledge. What we can observe, for instance, with the rat in the maze, is violent activity until the food is reached, followed by eating when it is reached; also a gradual elimination of acts which do not lead to the food. Where this sort of behaviour is observed, we may say that it is directed towards the food, and that the animal 'knows' the way to the food when he gets to it by the shortest possible route.

But if this view is right, we cannot define any knowledge acquired by learning except with reference to circumstances towards which an animal's activity is directed. We should say, popularly, that the animal 'desires' such circumstances. 'Desire', like 'knowledge', is capable of a behaviouristic definition, and it would seem that the two are correlative. Let us, then, spend a little time on the behaviouristic treatment of 'desire'.

The best example of desire, from this point of view, is hunger. The stimulus to hunger is a certain well-ascertained bodily condition. When in this condition, an animal moves restlessly; if he sees or smells food, he moves in a manner which, in conditions to which he is accustomed, would bring him to the food; if he reaches it, he eats it, and if the quantity is sufficient he then becomes quiescent. This kind of behaviour may be summarised by saying that a hungry animal 'desires' food. It is behaviour which is in various ways different from that of inanimate matter, because restless movements persist until a certain condition is realised. These movements may or may not be the best adapted to realising the condition in question. Everyone knows about the pike that was put on one side of a glass partition, with minnows on the other side. He continually bumped his nose on the glass, and after six weeks gave up the attempt to catch them. When, after this, the partition was removed, he still refrained from pursuing them. I do not know whether the experiment was tried of leaving a possibility of getting to the minnows by a roundabout route. To have learned to take a roundabout route would perhaps have required a degree of intelligence beyond the capacity of fishes; this is a matter, however, which offers little difficulty to dogs or monkeys.

What applies to hunger applies equally to other forms of 'desire'. Every animal has a certain congenital apparatus of 'desires'; that is to say, in certain bodily conditions he is stimulated to restless activities which tend towards the performance of some reflex, and if a given situation is often repeated the animal arrives more and more quickly at the performance of the reflex. This last, however, is only true of the higher animals; in the lower, the whole process from beginning to end is reflex, and can therefore only succeed in normal circumstances. The higher animals, and more especially men, have a larger proportion of learning and a smaller proportion of reflexes in their behaviour, and are therefore better able to adapt themselves to new circumstances. The helplessness of infants is a necessary condition for the adaptability of adults; infants have fewer useful reflexes than the young of animals, but have far more power of forming useful habits, which can be adapted to circumstances and are not fatally fixed from birth. This fact is intimately connected with the superiority of the human intelligence above that of the brutes.

Desire is extremely subject to 'conditioning'. If A is a primitive desire and B has on many occasions been a means to A, B comes to be desired in the same sense in which A was previously desired. It may even happen, as in misers, that the desire for B completely displaces the desire for A, so that B, when attained, is no longer used as a means to A. This, however, is more or less exceptional. In general, the desire for A persists, although the desire for B has a more or less independent life.

The 'conditioning' of primitive desires in human beings is the source of much that distinguishes our life from that of animals. Most animals only seek food when they are hungry; they may, then, die of starvation before they find it. Men, on the contrary, must have early acquired pleasure in hunting as an art, and must have set out on hunting expeditions before they were actually hungry. A further stage in the conditioning of hunger came with domestic animals; a still further stage with agriculture. Nowadays, when a man sets to work to earn his living, his activity is still connected, though not very directly, with hunger and the other primitive desires that can be gratified by means of money. These primitive desires are still, so to speak, the power station, though their energy is widely distributed to all sorts of undertakings that seem, at first sight, to have no connection with them. Consider 'freedom' and the political activities it inspires; this is derivable, by 'conditioning', from the emotion of rage which Dr. Watson observed in infants whose limbs are not 'free'. Again we speak of the 'fall' of empires and of 'fallen' women; this is connected with the fear which infants display when left without support.

After this excursion into the realm of desire, we can now return to 'knowledge', which, as we saw, is a term correlative to 'desire', and applicable to another feature of the same kind of activity. We may say, broadly, that a response to a stimulus of the kind involving desire in the above sense shows 'knowledge' if it leads by the quickest or easiest route to the state of affairs which, in the above sense, is behaviouristically the object of desire. Knowledge is thus a matter of degree: the rat, during its progressive improvements in the maze, is gradually acquiring more and more knowledge. Its 'intelligence quotient', so far as that particular task is concerned, will be the ratio of the time it took on the first trial to the time it takes now to get out of the maze. Another point, if our definition of knowledge is accepted, is, that there is no such thing as purely contemplative knowledge: knowledge exists only in relation to the satisfaction of desire, or, as we say, in the capacity to choose the right means to achieve our ends.

But can such a definition as the above really stand? Does it represent at all the sort of thing that would commonly be called knowledge? I think it does in the main, but there is need of some discussion to make this clear.

In some cases, the definition is obviously applicable. These are the cases that are analogous to the rat in the maze, the consideration of which led us to our definition. Do you 'know' the way from Trafalgar Square to St. Pancras? Yes, if you can walk it without taking any wrong turnings. In practice, you can give verbal proof of such knowledge, without actually having to walk the distance; but that depends upon the correlation of names with streets, and is part of the process of substituting words for things. There may, it is true, come doubtful cases. I was once on a bus in Whitehall, and my neighbour asked 'What street is this?' I answered him, not without surprise at his ignorance. He then said, 'What building is that?' and I replied 'The Foreign Office'. To this he retorted, 'But I thought the Foreign Office was in Downing Street'. This time, it was his knowledge that surprised me. Should we say that he knew where the Foreign Office is? The answer is yes or no according to his purpose. From the point of view of sending a letter to it, he knew; from the point of view of walking to it, he did not know. He had, in fact, been a British Consul in South America, and was in London for the first time.

But now let us come to cases less obviously within the scope of our definition. The reader 'knows' that Columbus crossed the ocean in 1492. What do we mean by saying that he 'knows' this? We mean, no doubt, primarily that writing down this statement is the way to pass examinations, which is just as useful to us as getting out of the maze is to the rat. But we do not mean only this. There is historical evidence of the fact, at least I suppose there is. The historical evidence consists of printed books and manuscripts. Certain rules have been developed by historians as to the conditions in which statements in books or manuscripts may be accepted as true, and the evidence in our case is (I presume) in accordance with these rules. Historical facts often have importance in the present; for example, wills, or laws not yet repealed. The rules for weighing historical evidence are such as will, in general, bring out self-consistent results. Two results are self-consistent when, in relation to a desire to which both are relevant, they enjoin the same action, or actions which can form part of one movement towards the goal. At Coton, near Cambridge, there is (or was in my time) a signpost with two arms pointing in diametrically opposite directions, and each arm said 'To Cambridge'. This was a perfect example of self-contradiction, since the two arms made statements representing exactly opposite actions. And this case illustrates why self-contradiction is to be avoided. But the avoidance of self-contradiction makes great demands upon us; Hegel and Bradley imagined that we could know the nature of the universe by means of this principle alone. In this they were pretty certainly mistaken, but nevertheless a great deal of our 'knowledge' depends upon this principle to a greater or less extent.

Most of our knowledge is like that in a cookery book, maxims to be followed when occasion arises, but not useful at every moment of every day. Since knowledge may be useful at any time, we get gradually, through conditioning, a general desire for knowledge. The learned man who is helpless in practical affairs is analogous to the miser, in that he has become absorbed in a means. It should be observed, also, that knowledge is neutral as among different purposes. If you know that arsenic is a poison, that enables you equally to avoid it if you wish to remain in health, and to take it if you wish to commit suicide. You cannot judge from a man's conduct in relation to arsenic whether he knows that it is a poison or not, unless you know his desires. He may be tired of life, but avoid arsenic because he has been told that it is a good medicine; in this case, his avoidance of it is evidence of *lack* of knowledge.

But to return to Columbus: surely, the reader will say, Columbus really did cross the Atlantic in 1492, and that is why we call this statement 'knowledge'. This is the definition of 'truth' as 'correspondence with fact'. I think there is an important element of correctness in this definition, but it is an element to be elicited at a later stage, after we have discussed the physical world. And it has the defect – as pragmatists have urged – that there seems no way of getting at 'facts' and comparing them with our beliefs: all that we ever reach consists of other beliefs. I do not offer our present behaviouristic and pragmatic definition of 'knowledge' as the only possible one, but I offer it as the one to which we are led if we wish to regard knowledge as something causally important, to be exemplified in our reactions to stimuli. This is the appropriate point of view when we are studying man from without, as we have been doing hitherto.

There is, however, within the behaviourist philosophy, one important addition to be made to our definition. We began this chapter with sensitivity, but we went on to the consideration of learned reactions, where the learning depended upon association. But there is another sort of learning – at least it is *prima facie* another sort – which consists of increase of sensitivity. All sensitivity in animals and human beings must count as a sort of knowledge; that it so say, if an animal behaves, in the presence of a stimulus of a certain kind, as it would not behave in the absence of that stimulus, then, in an important sense, it has 'knowledge' as regards the stimulus. Now it appears that practice – e.g. in music – very greatly increases sensitivity. We learn to react differently to stimuli which only differ slightly; what is more, we learn to react to differences. A violin-player can react with great precision to an interval of a fifth; if the interval is very slightly greater or less, his behaviour in tuning is influenced by the difference from a fifth. And as we have already had occasion to notice, we become, through practice, increasingly sensitive to form. All this increased sensitivity must count as increase of knowledge.

But in saying this we are not saying anything inconsistent with our earlier definition of knowledge. Sensitivity is essential to choosing the right reaction in many cases. To take the cookery-book again: when it says 'take a pinch of salt', a good cook knows how much to take, which is an instance of sensitivity. Accurate scientific observation, which is of great practical importance, depends upon sensitivity. And so do many of our practical dealings with other people: if we cannot 'feel' their moods, we shall be always getting at cross purposes.

The extent to which sensitivity is improved by practice is astonishing. Town-bred people do not know whether the weather is warm or cold until they read the weather reports in the paper. An entomologist perceives vastly more beetles in the course of a country walk than other people do. The subtlety with which connoisseurs can distinguish among wines and cigars is the despair of youths who wish to become men of the world. Whether this increase of sensitivity can be accounted for by the law of association, I do not know. In many cases, probably, it can, but I think sensitiveness to form, which is the essential element in the more difficult forms of abstract thought as well as in many other matters, cannot be regarded as derivative from the law of association, but is more analogous to the development of a new sense. I should therefore include improvement in sensitivity as an independent element in the advancement of knowledge. But I do so with some hesitation.

The above discussion does not pretend to cover the whole of the ground that has to be covered in discussing the definition of 'knowledge'. There are other points of view, which are also necessary to a complete consideration of the question. But these must wait until, after considering the physical world, we come to the discussion of man as viewed from within.

Chapter 9

The Structure of the Atom

In all that we have said hitherto on the subject of man from without, we have taken a common-sense view of the material world. We have not asked ourselves: What *is* matter? Is there such a thing, or is the outside world composed of stuff of a different kind? And what light does a correct theory of the physical world throw upon the process of perception? These are questions which we must attempt to answer in the following chapters. And in doing so the science upon which we must depend is physics. Modern physics, however, is very abstract, and by no means easy to explain in simple language. I shall do my best, but the reader must not blame me too severely if, here and there, he finds some slight difficulty or obscurity. The physical world, both through the theory of relativity and through the most recent doctrines as to the structure of the atom, has become very different from the world of everyday life, and also from that of scientific materialism of the eighteenth-century variety. No philosophy can ignore the revolutionary changes in our physical ideas that the men of science have found necessary; indeed it may be said that all traditional philosophies have to be discarded, and we have to start afresh with as little respect as possible for the systems of the past. Our age has penetrated more deeply into the nature of things than any earlier age, and it would be a false modesty to over-estimate what can still be learned from the metaphysicians of the seventeenth, eighteenth and nineteenth centuries.

What physics has to say about matter, and the physical world generally, from the standpoint of the philosopher, comes under two main heads: first, the structure of the atom; secondly, the theory of relativity. The former was, until recently, the less revolutionary philosophically, though the more revolutionary in physics. Until 1925, theories of the structure of the atom were based upon the old conception of matter as indestructible substance, although this was already regarded as no more than a convenience. Now, owing chiefly to two German physicists, Heisenberg and Schrödinger, the last vestiges of the old solid atom have melted away, and matter has become as ghostly as anything in a spiritualist séance. But before tackling these newer views, it is necessary to understand the much simpler theory which they have displaced. This theory does not, except here and there, take account of the new doctrines on fundamentals that have been introduced by Einstein, and it is much easier to understand than relativity. It explains so much of the facts that, whatever may happen, it must remain a stepping-stone to a complete theory of the structure of the atom; indeed, the newer theories have grown directly out of it, and could hardly have arisen in any other way. We must therefore spend a little time in giving a bare outline, which is the less to be regretted as the theory is in itself fascinating.

The theory that matter consists of 'atoms', i.e. of little bits that cannot be divided, is due to the Greeks, but with them it was only a speculation. The evidence for what is called the atomic theory was derived from chemistry, and the theory itself, in its nineteenth-century form, was mainly due to Dalton. It was found that there were a number of 'elements', and that other substances were compounds of these elements. Compound substances were found to be composed of 'molecules', each molecule being composed of 'atoms' of one substance combined with 'atoms' of another or of the same. A molecule of water consists of two atoms of hydrogen and one atom of oxygen; they can be separated by electrolysis. It was supposed, until radio-activity was discovered, that atoms were indestructible and unchangeable. Substances which were not compounds were called 'elements'. The Russian chemist Mendeléev discovered that the elements can be arranged in a series by means of progressive changes in their properties; in his time, there were gaps in this series, but most of them have since been filled by the discovery of new elements. If all the gaps were filled, there would be 92 elements; actually, the number known is 87, or, including three about which there is still some doubt, 90. The place of an element in this series is called its 'atomic number'. Hydrogen is the first, and has the atomic number 1; helium is the second, and has the atomic number 2; uranium is the last, and has the atomic number 92. Perhaps in the stars there are elements with higher atomic numbers, but so far none have been actually observed.

The discovery of radio-activity necessitated new views as to 'atoms'. It was found that an atom of one radio-active element can break up into an atom of another element and an atom of helium, and that there is also another way in which it can change. It was found also that there can be different elements having the same place in the series; these are called 'isotopes'. For example, when radium disintegrates it gives rise, in the end, to a kind of lead, but this is somewhat different from the lead found in lead-mines. A great many 'elements' have been shown by Dr. F. W. Aston to be really mixtures of isotopes, which can be sorted out by ingenious methods. All this, but more especially the transmutation of elements in radio-activity, led to the conclusion that what had been called 'atoms' were really complex structures, which could change into atoms of a different sort by losing a part. After various attempts to imagine the structure of an atom, physicists were led to accept the view of Sir Ernest Rutherford, which was further developed by Niels Bohr.

In this theory, which, in spite of recent developments, remains substantially correct, all matter is composed of two sorts of units, electrons and protons. All electrons are exactly alike, and all protons are exactly alike. All protons carry a certain amount of positive electricity, and all electrons carry an equal amount of negative electricity. But the mass of a proton is about 1835 times that of an electron: it takes 1835 electrons to weigh as much as one proton. Protons repel each other, and electrons repel each other, but an electron and a proton attract each other. Every atom is a structure consisting of electrons and protons. The hydrogen atom, which is the simplest, consists of one proton with one electron going round it as a planet goes round the sun. The electron may be lost, and the proton left alone; the atom is then positively electrified. But when it has its electron, it is as a whole, electrically neutral, since the positive electricity of the proton is exactly balanced by the negative electricity of the electron.

The second element, helium, has already a much more complicated structure. It has a nucleus, consisting of four protons and two electrons very close together, and in its normal state it has two planetary electrons going round the nucleus. But it may lose either or both of these, and it is then positively electrified.

All the later elements consist, like helium, of a nucleus composed of protons and electrons, and a number of planetary electrons going round the nucleus. There are more protons than electrons in the nucleus, but the excess is balanced by the planetary electrons when the atom is unelectrified. The number of protons in the nucleus gives the 'atomic weight' of the element: the excess of protons over electrons in the nucleus gives the 'atomic number', which is also the number of planetary electrons when the atom is unelectrified. Uranium, the last element, has 238 protons and 146 electrons in the nucleus, and when unelectrified it has 92 planetary electrons. The arrangement of the planetary electrons in atoms other than hydrogen is not accurately known, but it is clear that, in some sense, they form different rings, those in the outer rings being more easily lost than those nearer the nucleus.

I come now to what Bohr added to the theory of atoms as developed by Rutherford. This was a most curious discovery, introducing, in a new field, a certain type of discontinuity which was already known to be exhibited by some other natural processes. No adage had seemed more respectable in philosophy than *natura non facit saltum*, Nature makes no jumps. But if there is one thing more than another that the experience of a long life has taught me, it is that Latin tags always express falsehoods; and so it has proved in this case. Apparently Nature does make jumps, not only now and then, but whenever a body emits light, as well as on certain other occasions. The German physicist Planck was the first to demonstrate the necessity of jumps. He was considering how bodies radiate heat when they are warmer than their surroundings. Heat, as has long been known, consists of vibrations, which are distinguished by their 'frequency', i.e. by the number of vibrations per second. Planck showed that, for vibrations having a given frequency, not all amounts of energy are possible, but only those having to the frequency a ratio which is a certain quantity h multiplied by 1 or 2 or 3 or some other whole number, in practice always a small whole number. The quantity h is known as 'Planck's constant'; it has turned out to be involved practically everywhere where measurement is delicate enough to know whether it is involved or not. It is such a small quantity that, except where measurement can reach a very high degree of accuracy, the departure from continuity is not appreciable[1].

Bohr's great discovery was that this same quantity h is involved in the orbits of the planetary electrons in atoms, and that it limits the possible orbits in ways for which nothing in Newtonian dynamics had prepared us, and for which, so far, there is nothing in relativity—

[1]The dimensions of h are those of 'action', i.e. energy multiplied by time, or moment of momentum, or mass multiplied by length multiplied by velocity. Its magnitude is about 6.55×10^{-27} erg secs.

dynamics to account. According to Newtonian principles, an electron ought to be able to go round the nucleus in any circle with the nucleus in the centre, or in any ellipse with the nucleus in a focus; among possible orbits, it would select one or another according to its direction and velocity. But in fact only certain out of all these orbits occur. Those that occur are among those that are possible on Newtonian principles, but are only an infinitesimal selection from among these. It will simplify the explanation if we confine ourselves, as Bohr did at first, to circular orbits; moreover we will consider only the hydrogen atom, which has one planetary electron and a nucleus consisting of one proton. To define the circular orbits that are found to be possible, we proceed as follows: multiply the mass of the electron by the circumference of its orbit, and this again by the velocity of the electron; the result will always be h or $2h$, or $3h$, or some other small exact multiple of h, where h, as before, is 'Planck's constant'. There is thus a smallest possible orbit, in which the above product is h; the radius of the next orbit, in which the above product is $2h$, will have a length four times this minimum; the next, nine times; the next, sixteen times; and so on through the 'square numbers' (i.e. those got by multiplying a number by itself). Apparently no other circular orbits than these are possible in the hydrogen atom. Elliptic orbits are possible, and these again introduce exact multiples of h; but we need not, for our purposes, concern ourselves with them.

When a hydrogen atom is left to itself, if the electron is in the minimum orbit it will continue to rotate in that orbit so long as nothing from outside disturbs it; but if the electron is in any of the larger possible orbits, it may sooner or later jump suddenly to a smaller orbit, either the minimum or one of the intermediate possible orbits. So long as the electron does not change its orbit, the atom does not radiate energy, but when the electron jumps to a smaller orbit, the atom loses energy, which is radiated out in the form of a light-wave. This light-wave is always such that its energy divided by its frequency is exactly h. The atom may absorb energy from without, and it does so by the electron jumping to a larger orbit. It may then afterwards, when the external source of energy is removed, jump back to the smaller orbit; this is the cause of fluorescence, since, in doing so, the atom gives out energy in the form of light.

The same principles, with greater mathematical complications, apply to the other elements. There is, however, with some of the latest elements, a phenomenon which cannot have any analogue in hydrogen, and that is radio-activity. When an atom is radio-active, it emits rays of three kinds, called respectively α-rays, β-rays, and γ-rays. Of these, the γ-rays are analogous to light, but of much higher frequencies, or shorter wave-lengths; we need not further concern ourselves with them. The α-rays and β-rays, on the contrary, are important as our chief source of knowledge concerning the nuclei of atoms. It is found that the α-rays consist of helium nuclei, while the β-rays consist of electrons. Both come out of the nucleus, since the atom after radio-activity disruption is a different element from what it was before. But no one knows just why the nucleus disintegrates when it does, nor why, in a piece of radium, for example, some atoms break down while others do not.

The three principal sources of our knowledge concerning atoms have been the light they emit, X-rays, and radio-activity. As everyone knows, when the light emitted by a glowing gas is passed through a prism, it is found to consist of well-defined lines of different colours, which are characteristic for each element, and constitute what is called its 'spectrum'. The spectrum extends beyond the range of visible light, both into the infra-red and into the ultra-violet. In the latter direction, it extends right into the region of X-rays, which are only ultra-ultra-violet light. By means of crystals, it has been found possible to study X-ray spectra as exactly as those of ordinary light. The great merit of Bohr's theory was that it explained why elements have the spectra they do have, which had, before, been a complete mystery. In the cases of hydrogen and positively electrified helium, the explanation, particularly as extended by the German physicist Sommerfeld, gave the most minute numerical agreement between theory and observation; in other cases, mathematical difficulties made this completeness impossible, but there was every reason to think that the same principles were adequate. This was the main reason for accepting Bohr's theory; and certainly it was a very strong one. It was found that visible light enabled us to study the outer rings of planetary electrons, X-rays enabled us to study the inner rings, and radio-activity enabled us to study the nucleus. For the latter purpose, there are also other methods, more particularly Rutherford's 'bombardment', which aims at breaking up nuclei by firing projectiles at them, and sometimes succeeds in making a hit in spite of the smallness of the target.

The theory of atomic structure that has just been outlined, like everything in theoretical physics, is capable of expression in mathematical formulæ; but like many things in theoretical physics, it is also capable of expression in the form of an imaginative picture. But here, as always, it is necessary to distinguish sharply between the mathematical symbols and the pictorial words. The symbols are pretty sure to be right, or nearly so; the imaginative picture, on the other hand, should not be taken too seriously. When we consider the nature of the evidence upon which the above theory of the atom is based, we can see that the attempt to make a picture of what goes on has led us to be far more concrete than we have any right to be. If we want to assert only what we have good reason to believe, we shall have to abandon the attempt to be concrete about what goes on in the atom, and say merely something like this. An atom with its electrons is a system characterised by certain integers, all small, and all capable of changing independently. These integers are the multiples of *h* involved. When any of them changes to a smaller integer, energy of a definite amount is emitted, and its frequency will be obtained by dividing the energy by *h*. When any of the integers concerned changes to a larger integer, energy is absorbed, and again the amount absorbed is definite. But we cannot know what goes on when the atom is neither absorbing nor radiating energy, since then it has no effects in surrounding regions; consequently all evidence as to atoms is as to their changes, not as to their steady states.

The point is not that the facts do not fit with the hypothesis of the atom as a planetary system. There are, it is true, certain difficulties which afford empirical grounds for the newer theory which has superseded Bohr's, and which we shall shortly consider. But even if no such grounds existed, it would be obvious that Bohr's theory states more than we have a right to infer from what we can observe. Of theories that state so much, there must be an infinite number that are compatible with what is known, and it is only what all of these have in common that we are really entitled to assert. Suppose your knowledge of Great Britain were entirely confined to observing the people and goods that enter and leave the ports; you could, in that case, invent many theories as to the interior of Great Britain, all of which would agree with all known facts. This is an exact analogy. If you delimit in the physical universe any region, large or small, not containing a scientific observer, all scientific observers will have exactly the same experiences whatever happens inside this region, provided it does not affect the flow of energy across the boundary of the region. And so, if the region contains one atom, any two theories which give the same results as to the energy that the atom radiates or absorbs are empirically indistinguishable, and there can be no reason except simplicity for preferring one of them to the other. On this ground, even if on no other, prudence compels us to seek a more abstract theory of the atom than that which we owe to Rutherford and Bohr.

The newer theory has been put forward mainly by two physicists already mentioned, Heisenberg and Schrödinger, in forms which look different, but are in fact mathematically equivalent. It is as yet an impossible task to describe this theory in simple language, but something can be said to show its philosophical bearing. Broadly speaking, it describes the atom by means of the radiations that come out of it. In Bohr's theory, the planetary electrons are supposed to describe orbits over and over again while the atom is not radiating; in the newer theory, we say nothing at all as to what happens at these times. The aim is to confine the theory to what is empirically verifiable, namely radiations; as to what there is where the radiations come from, we cannot tell, and it is scientifically unnecessary to speculate. The theory requires modifications in our conception of space, of a sort not yet quite clear. It also has the consequence that we cannot identify an electron at one time with an electron at another, if, in the interval, the atom has radiated energy. The electron ceases altogether to have the properties of a 'thing' as conceived by common sense; it is merely a region from which energy may radiate.

On the subject of discontinuity, there is disagreement between Schrödinger and other physicists. Most of them maintain that quantum changes – i.e. the changes that occur in an atom when it radiates or absorbs energy – must be discontinuous. Schrödinger thinks otherwise. This is a matter in debate among experts, as to which it would be rash to venture an opinion. Probably it will be decided one way or other before very long.

The main point for the philosopher in the modern theory is the disappearance of matter as a 'thing'. It has been replaced by emanations from a locality – the sort of influences that characterise haunted rooms in ghost stories. As we shall see in the next chapter, the theory of relativity leads to a similar destruction of the solidity of matter, by a different line of argument. All sorts of events happen in the physical world, but tables and chairs, the sun and moon, and even our daily bread, have become pale abstractions, mere laws exhibited in the successions of events which radiate from certain regions.

Chapter 10

Relativity

We have seen that the world of the atom is a world of revolution rather than evolution: the electron which has been moving in one orbit hops quite suddenly into another, so that the motion is what is called 'discontinuous', that is to say, the electron is first in one place and then in another, without having passed over any intermediate places. This sounds like magic, and there may be some way of avoiding such a disconcerting hypothesis. At any rate, nothing of the sort seems to happen in the regions where there are no electrons and protons. In these regions, so far as we can discover, there is continuity, that is to say, everything goes by gradual transitions, not by jumps. The regions in which there are no electrons and protons may be called 'æther' or 'empty space' as you prefer: the difference is only verbal. The theory of relativity is especially concerned with what goes on in these regions, as opposed to what goes on where there are electrons and protons. Apart from the theory of relativity, what we know about these regions is that waves travel across them, and that these waves, when they are waves of light or electromagnetism (which are identical), behave in a certain fashion set forth by Maxwell in certain formulæ called 'Maxwell's equations'. When I say we 'know' this, I am saying more than is strictly correct, because all we know is what happens when the waves reach our bodies. It is as if we could not see the sea, but could only see the people disembarking at Dover, and inferred the waves from the fact that the people looked green. It is obvious, in any case, that we can only know so much about the waves as is involved in their having such and such causes at one end and such-and-such effects at the other. What can be inferred in this way will be, at best, something wholly expressible in terms of mathematical structure. We must not think of the waves as being necessarily 'in' the æther or 'in' anything else; they are to be thought of merely as progressive periodic processes, whose laws are more or less known, but whose intrinsic character is not known and never can be.

The theory of relativity has arisen from the study of what goes on in the regions where there are no electrons and protons. While the study of the atom has led us to discontinuities, relativity has produced a completely continuous theory of the intervening medium – far more continuous than any theory formerly imagined. At the moment, these two points of view stand more or less opposed to each other, but no doubt before long they will be reconciled. There is not, even now, any logical contradiction between them; there is only a fairly complete lack of connection.

For philosophy, far the most important thing about the theory of relativity is the abolition of the one cosmic time and the one persistent space, and the substitution of space-time in place of both. This is a change of quite enormous importance, because it alters fundamentally our notion of the structure of the physical world, and has, I think, repercussions in psychology. It would be useless, in our day, to talk about philosophy without explaining this matter. Therefore I shall make the attempt, in spite of some difficulty.

Common-sense and pre-relativity physicists believed that, if two events happen in different places, there must always be a definite answer, in theory, to the question whether they were simultaneous. This is found to be a mistake. Let us suppose two persons A and B a long way apart, each provided with a mirror and a means of sending out light-signals. The events that happen to A still have a perfectly definite time-order, and so have those that happen to B; the difficulty comes in connecting A's time with B's. Suppose A sends a flash to B, B's mirror reflects it, and it returns to A after a certain time. If A is on the earth and B on the sun, the time will be about sixteen minutes. We shall naturally say that the time when B received the light-signal is half-way between the times when A sent it out and received it back. But this definition turns out to be not unambiguous; it will depend upon how A and B are moving relatively to each other. The more this difficulty is examined, the more insuperable it is seen to be. Anything that happens to A after he sends out the flash and before he gets it back is neither definitely before nor definitely after nor definitely simultaneous with the arrival of the flash at B. To this extent, there is no unambiguous way of correlating times in different places.

The notion of a 'place' is also quite vague. Is London a 'place'? But the earth is rotating. Is the earth a 'place'? But it is going round the sun. Is the sun a 'place'? But it is moving relatively to the stars. At best you could talk of a place at a given time; but then it is ambiguous what is a given time, unless you confine yourself to one place. So the notion of 'place' evaporates.

We naturally think of the universe as being in one state at one time and in another at another. This is a mistake. There is no cosmic time, and so we cannot speak of the state of the universe at a given time. And similarly we cannot speak unambiguously of the distance between two bodies at a given time. If we take the time appropriate to one of the two bodies, we shall get one estimate; if the time of the other, another. This makes the Newtonian law of gravitation ambiguous, and shows that it needs restatement, independently of empirical evidence.

Geometry also goes wrong. A straight line, for example, is supposed to be a certain track in space whose parts all exist simultaneously. We shall now find that what is a straight line for one observer is not a straight line for another. Therefore geometry ceases to be separable from physics.

The 'observer' need not be a mind, but may be a photographic plate. The peculiarities of the 'observer' in this region belong to physics, not to psychology.

So long as we continue to think in terms of bodies moving, and try to adjust this way of thinking to the new ideas by successive corrections, we shall only get more and more confused. The only way to get clear is to make a fresh start, with *events* instead of bodies. In physics, an 'event' is anything which, according to the old notions, would be said to have both a date and a place. An explosion, a flash of lightning, the starting of a light-wave from an atom, the arrival of the light-wave at some other body, any of these would be an 'event'. Some strings of events make up what we regard as the history of one body; some make up the course of one light-wave; and so on. The unity of a body is a unity of history – it is like the unity of a tune, which takes time to play, and does not exist whole in any one moment. What exists at any one moment is only what we call an 'event'. It may be that the word 'event', as used in physics, cannot be quite identified with the same word as used in psychology; for the present we are concerned with 'events' as the constituents of physical processes, and need not trouble ourselves about 'events' in psychology.

The events in the physical world have relations to each other which are of the sort that have led to the notions of space and time. They have relations of order, so that we can say that one event is nearer to a second than to a third. In this way we can arrive at the notion of the 'neighbourhood' of an event: it will consist roughly speaking of all the events that are very near the given event. When we say that neighbouring events have a certain relation, we shall mean that the nearer two events are to each other, the more nearly they have this relation, and that they approximate to having it without limit as they are taken nearer and nearer together.

Two neighbouring events have a measurable quantitative relation called 'interval', which is sometimes analogous to distance in space, sometimes to lapse of time. In the former case it is called space-like, in the latter time-like. The interval between two events is time-like when one body might be present at both – for example, when both are parts of the history of your body. The interval is space-like in the contrary case. In the marginal case between the two, the interval is zero; this happens when both are parts of one light-ray.

The interval between two neighbouring events is something objective, in the sense that any two careful observers will arrive at the same estimate of it. They will not arrive at the same estimate for the distance in space or the lapse of time between the two events, but the interval is a genuine physical fact, the same for all. If a body can travel freely from one event to the other, the interval between the two events will be the same as the time between them as measured by a clock travelling with the body. If such a journey is physically impossible, the interval will be the same as the distance as estimated by an observer to whom the two events are simultaneous. But the interval is only definite when the two events are very near together; otherwise the interval depends upon the route chosen for travelling from the one event to the other.

Four numbers are needed to fix the position of an event in the world; these correspond to the time and the three dimensions of space in the old reckoning. These four numbers are called the co-ordinates of the event. They may be assigned on any principle which gives neighbouring co-ordinates to neighbouring events; subject to this condition, they are merely conventional. For example, suppose an aeroplane has had an accident. You can fix the position of the accident by four numbers: latitude, longitude, altitude above sea-level, and Greenwich Mean Time. But you cannot fix the position of the explosion in space–time by means of less than four numbers.

Everything in relativity-theory goes (in a sense) from next to next; there are no direct relations between distant events, such as distance in time or space. And of course there are no forces acting at a distance; in fact, except as a convenient fiction, there are no 'forces' at all. Bodies take the course which is easiest at each moment, according to the character of space–time in the particular region where they are; this course is called a *geodesic*.

Now it will be observed that I have been speaking freely of bodies and motion, although I said that bodies were merely certain strings of events. That being so, it is of course necessary to say what strings of events constitute bodies, since not all continuous strings of events do so, nor even all geodesics. Until we have defined the sort of thing that makes a body, we cannot legitimately speak of motion, since this involves the presence of one body on different occasions. We must therefore set to work to define what we mean by the persistence of a body, and how a string of events constituting a body differs from one which does not. This topic will occupy the next chapter.

But it may be useful, as a preliminary, to teach our imagination to work in accordance with the new ideas. We must give up what Whitehead admirably calls the 'pushiness' of matter. We naturally think of an atom as being like a billiard-ball; we should do better to think of it as like a ghost, which has no 'pushiness' and yet can make you fly. We have to change our notions both of substance and of cause. To say that an atom persists is like saying that a tune persists. If a tune takes five minutes to play, we do not conceive of it as a single thing which exists throughout that time, but as a series of notes, so related as to form a unity. In the case of the tune, the unity is aesthetic; in the case of the atom, it is causal. But when I say 'causal' I do not mean exactly what the word naturally conveys. There must be no idea of compulsion or 'force', neither the force of contact which we imagine we see between billiard balls nor the action at a distance which was formerly supposed to constitute gravitation. There is merely an observed law of succession from next to next. An event at one moment is succeeded by an event at a neighbouring moment, which, to the first order of small quantities, can be calculated from the earlier event. This enables us to construct a string of events, each, approximately, growing out of a slightly earlier event according to an intrinsic law. Outside influences only affect the second order of small quantities. A string of events connected, in this way, by an approximate intrinsic law of development is called one piece of matter. This is what I mean by saying that the unity of a piece of matter is causal. I shall explain this notion more fully in later chapters.

Chapter 11

Causal Laws in Physics

In the last chapter we spoke about the substitution of space–time for space and time, and the effect which this has had in substituting strings of events for 'things' conceived as substances. In this chapter we will deal with cause and effect as they appear in the light of modern science. It is at least as difficult to purge our imagination of irrelevances in this matter as in regard to substance. The old-fashioned notion of cause appeared in dynamics as 'force'. We still speak of forces just as we still speak of the sunrise, but we recognise that this is nothing but a convenient way of speaking, in the one case as in the other.

Causation is deeply embedded in language and common sense. We say that people build houses or make roads: to 'build' and to 'make' are both notions involving causality. We say that a man is 'powerful', meaning that his volitions are causes over a wide range. Some examples of causation seem to us quite natural, others less so. It seems natural that our muscles should obey our will, and only reflection makes us perceive the necessity of finding an explanation of this phenomenon. It seems natural that when you hit a billiard-ball with a cue it moves. When we see a horse pulling a cart, or a heavy object being dragged by a rope, we *feel* as if we understood all about it. It is events of this sort that have given rise to the common-sense belief in causes and forces.

But as a matter of fact the world is incredibly more complicated than it seems to commonsense. When we think we understand a process – I mean by 'we' the non-reflective part in each of us – what really happens is that there is some sequence of events so familiar through past experience that at each stage we expect the next stage. The whole process seems to us peculiarly intelligible when human desires enter in, for example, in watching a game: what the ball does and what the players do seems 'natural', and we feel as if we quite understood how the stages succeed each other. We thus arrive at the notion of what is called 'necessary' sequence. The text-books say that A is the cause of B if A is 'necessarily' followed by B. This notion of 'necessity' seems to be purely anthropomorphic, and not based upon anything that is a discoverable feature of the world. Things happen according to certain rules; the rules can be generalised, but in the end remain brute facts. Unless the rules are concealed conventions or definitions, no reason can be given why they should not be completely different.

To say that A is 'necessarily' followed by B is thus to say no more than that there is some general rule, exemplified in a very large number of observed instances, and falsified in none, according to which events such as A are followed by events such as B. We must not have any notion of 'compulsion', as if the cause *forced* the effect to happen. A good test for the imagination in this respect is the reversibility of causal laws. We can just as often infer backwards as forwards. When you get a letter, you are justified in inferring that sombody wrote it, but you do not feel that your receiving it *compelled* the sender to write it. The notion of compulsion is just as little applicable to effects as to causes. To say that causes compel effects is as misleading as to say that effects compel causes. Compulsion is anthropomorphic: a man is compelled to do something when he wishes to do the opposite, but except where human or animal wishes come in the notion of compulsion is inapplicable. Science is concerned merely with what happens, not with what *must* happen.

When we look for invariable rules of sequence in nature, we find that they are not such as common sense sets up. Common sense says: thunder follows lightning, waves at sea follow wind, and so on. Rules of this sort are indispensable in practical life, but in science they are all only approximate. If there is any finite interval of time, however short, between the cause and the effect, something may happen to prevent the effect from occurring. Scientific laws can only be expressed in differential equations. This means that, although you cannot tell what may happen after a finite time, you can say that, if you make the time shorter and shorter, what will happen will be more and more nearly according to such-and-such a rule. To take a very simple case: I am now in this room; you cannot tell where I shall be in another second, because a bomb may explode and blow me sky-high, but if you take any two small fragments of my body which are now very close together, you can be sure that, after *some* very short finite time, they will still be very close together. If a second is not short enough, you must take a shorter time; you cannot tell in advance how short a time you may have to take, but you may feel fairly certain that there is a short enough time.

The laws of sequence in physics, apart from quantum phenomena, are of two sorts, which appeared in traditional dynamics as laws of velocity and laws of acceleration. In a very short time, the velocity of a body alters very little, and if the time is taken short enough, the change of velocity diminishes without limit. This is what, in the last chapter, we called an 'intrinsic' causal law. Then there is the effect of the outer world, as it appeared in traditional dynamics, which is shown in acceleration. The small change which does occur in the velocity in a short time is attributed to surrounding bodies, because it is found to vary as they vary, and to vary according to ascertained laws. Thus we think of surrounding bodies as exerting an influence, which we call 'force', though this remains as mysterious as the influence of the stars in astrology.

Einstein's theory of gravitation has done away with this conception in so far as gravitational forces are concerned. In this theory, a planet moving round the sun is moving in the nearest approach to a straight line that the neighbourhood permits. The neighbourhood is supposed to be non-Euclidean, that is to say, to contain no straight lines such as Euclid imagined. If a body is moving freely, as the planets do, it observes a certain rule. Perhaps the simplest way to state this rule is as follows: Suppose you take any two events which happen on the earth, and you measure the time between them by ideally accurate clocks which move with the earth. Suppose some traveller on a magic carpet had meanwhile cruised about the universe, leaving the earth at the time of the first event and returning at the time of the second. By his clocks the period elapsed will be less than by the terrestial clocks. This is what is meant by saying that the earth moves in a 'geodesic', which is the nearest approach to a straight line to be found in the region in which we live. All this is, so to speak, geometrical, and involves no 'forces'. It is not the sun that makes the earth go round, but the nature of space-time where the earth is.

Even this is not quite correct. Space-time does not make the earth go round the sun; it makes us *say* the earth goes round the sun. That is to say, it makes this the shortest way of describing what occurs. We could describe it in other language, which would be equally correct, but less convenient.

The abolition of 'force' in astronomy is perhaps connected with the fact that astronomy depends only upon the sense of sight. On the earth, we push and pull, we touch things, and we experience muscular strains. This all gives us a notion of 'force', but this notion is anthropomorphic. To imagine the laws of motion of heavenly bodies, think of the motions of objects in a mirror; they may move very fast, although in the mirror world there are no forces.

What we really have to substitute for force is laws of correlation. Events can be collected in groups by their correlations. This is all that is true in the old notion of causality. And this is not a 'postulate' or 'category', but an observed fact – lucky, not necessary.

As we suggested before, it is these correlations of events that lead to the definition of permanent 'things'. There is no essential difference, as regards substantiality, between an electron and a light-ray. Each is really a string of events or of sets of events. In the case of the light-ray, we have no temptation to think otherwise. But in the case of the electron, we think of it as a single persistent entity. There *may* be such an entity, but we can have no evidence that there is. What we can discover is (*a*) a group of events spreading outwards from a centre – say, for definiteness, the events constituting a wave of light – and attributed, hypothetically, to a 'cause' in that centre; (*b*) more or less similar groups of events at other times, connected with the first group according to the laws of physics, and therefore attributed to the same hypothetical cause at other times. But all that we ought to assume is series of groups of events, connected by discoverable laws. These series we may *define* as 'matter'. Whether there is matter in any other sense, no one can tell.

What is true in the old notion of causality is the fact that events at different times are connected by laws (differential equations). When there is a law connecting an event A with an event B, the two have a definite unambiguous time-order. But if the events are such that a ray of light starting from A would arrive at any body which was present at B after B had occurred, and vice versa, then there is no definite time order, and no possible causal law connecting A and B. A and B must then be regarded as separate facts of geography.

Perhaps the scope and purpose of this and the foregoing chapters may be made clearer by showing their bearing upon certain popular beliefs which may seem self-evident but are really, in my opinion, either false or likely to lead to falsehood. I shall confine myself to objections which have actually been made to me when trying to explain the philosophical outcome of modern physics[1].

'We cannot conceive of movement apart from some *thing* as moving.' This is, in a sense, a truism; but in the sense in which it is

---

[1] These objections are quoted (with kind permission) from a letter written to me by a well-known engineer, Mr. Percy Griffith, who is also a writer on philosophical subjects.

usually meant, it is a falsehood. We speak of the 'movement' of a drama or piece of music, although we do not conceive either as a 'thing' which exists complete at every moment of the performance. This is the sort of picture we must have in our minds when we try to conceive the physical world. We must think of a string of events, connected together by certain causal connections, and having enough unity to deserve a single name. We then begin to imagine that the single name denotes a single 'thing', and if the events concerned are not all in the same place, we say the 'thing' has 'moved'. But this is only a convenient shorthand. In the cinema, we seem to see a man falling off a skyscraper, catching hold of the telegraph wires, and reaching the ground none the worse. We know that, in fact, there are a number of different photographs, and the appearance of a single 'thing' moving is deceptive. In this respect, the real world resembles the cinema.

In connection with motion one needs to emphasise the very difficult distinction between *experience* and *prejudice*. Experience, roughly, is what you see, and prejudice is what you only think you see. Prejudice tells you that you see the *same* table on two different occasions; you *think* that experience tells you this. If it really were experience, you could not be mistaken; yet a similar table may be substituted without altering the experience. If you look at a table on two different occasions, you have very similar sensations, and memory tells you that they are similar; but there is nothing to show that one identical entity causes the two sensations. If the table is in a cinema, you know that there is not such an entity, even though you can watch it changing with apparent continuity. The experience is just like that with a 'real' table; so in the case of a 'real' table also, there is nothing in the actual experience to show whether there is a persistent entity or not. I say, therefore: I do not know whether there is a persistent entity, but I do know that my experiences can be explained without assuming that there is. Therefore it can be no part of legitimate science to assert or deny the persistent entity; if it does either, it goes beyond the warrant of experience.

The following is a verbally cited passage in the letter referred to objecting to what was said above about 'force':

'The concept of Force is not of physical but of psychological origin. Rightly or wrongly it arises in the most impersonal contemplation of the Stellar Universe, where we observe an infinite number of spherical bodies revolving on their own axes and gyrating in orbits round each other. Rightly or wrongly, we naturally conceive of these as having been so constituted and so maintained by some Force or Forces.'

We do not, in fact, 'observe' what it is here said that we observe; all this is *inferred*. What we observe, in astronomy, is a two-dimensional pattern of points of light, with a few bright surfaces of measurable size when seen through the telescope (the planets), and of course the larger bright surfaces that we call the sun and moon. Most of this pattern (the fixed stars) rotates round the earth once in every twenty-three hours and fifty-six minutes. The sun rotates in varying periods, which average twenty-four hours and never depart very far from the average. The moon and planets have apparent motions which are more irregular. These are the *observed* facts. There is no logical impossibility about the mediaeval doctrine of spheres rotating round the earth, one for each planet and one for the stars. The modern doctrines are simpler, but not one whit more in accordance with observed facts; it is our passion for *simple* laws that has made us adopt them.

The last sentence of the above quotation raises some further points of interest. 'Rightly or wrongly', the writer says, 'we naturally conceive of these as having been so constituted and so maintained by some Force or Forces.' I do not deny this. It is 'natural', and it is 'right or wrong' – more specifically, it is wrong. 'Force' is part of our love of explanations. Everyone knows about the Hindu who thought that the world does not fall because it is supported by an elephant, and the elephant does not fall because it is supported by a tortoise. When his European interlocutor said 'But how about the tortoise?' he replied that he was tired of metaphysics and wanted to change the subject. 'Force', as an explanation, is no better than the elephant and the tortoise. It is an attempt to get at the 'why' of natural processes, not only at the 'how'. What we observe, to a limited extent, is what happens, and we can arrive at laws according to which observable things happen, but we cannot arrive at a reason for the laws. If we invent a reason, it needs a reason in its turn, and so on. 'Force' is a rationalising of natural processes, but a fruitless one since 'force' would have to be rationalised also.

When it is said, as it often is, that 'force' belongs to the world of experience, we must be careful to understand what can be meant. In the first place, it may be meant that calculations which employ the notion of force work out right in practice. This, broadly speaking, is admitted: no one would suggest that the engineer should alter his methods, or should give up working out stresses and strains. But that does not prove that there are stresses and strains. A medical man works his accounts in guineas, although there are none; he obtains a real payment, though he employs a fictitious coin. Similarly, the engineer is concerned with the question whether his bridge will stand: the fact of experience is that it stands (or does not stand), and the stresses and strains are only a way of explaining what sort of bridge will stand. They are as useful as guineas, but equally imaginary.

But when it is said that force is a fact of experience, there is something quite different that may be meant. It may be meant that we experience force when we experience such things as pressure or muscular exertion. We cannot discuss this contention adequately without going into the relation of physics to psychology, which is a topic we shall consider at length at a later stage. But we may say this much: if you press your finger-tip upon a hard object, you have an experience which you attribute to your finger-tip, but there is a long chain of intermediate causes in nerves and brain. If your finger were amputated you could still have the same experience by a suitable operation on the nerves that formerly connected the finger with the brain, so that the force between the finger-tip and the hard object, as a fact of experience, may exist when there is no finger-tip. This shows that force, in this sense, cannot be what concerns physics.

As the above example illustrates, we do not, in fact, experience many things that we think we experience. This makes it necessary to ask, without too much assurance, in what sense physics can be based upon experience, and what must be the nature of its entities and its inferences if it is to make good its claim to be empirically grounded. We shall begin this inquiry in the next chapter.

Chapter 12

Physics and Perception

It will be remembered that we regarded perception, in Chapter 5, as a species of 'sensitivity'. Sensitivity to a given feature of the environment we defined as consisting in some characteristic reaction which is exhibited whenever that feature is present, but not otherwise; this property is possessed more perfectly, in given directions, by scientific instruments than by living bodies, though scientific instruments are more selective as to the stimuli to which they will respond. We decided that what, from the standpoint of an external observer, distinguishes perception from other forms of sensitivity is the law of association or conditioned reflexes. But we also found that this purely external treatment of perception presupposes our knowledge of the physical world as a going concern. We have now to investigate this presupposition, and to consider how we come to know about physics, and how much we really do know.

According to the theory of Chapter 5, it is possible to perceive things that are not in spatial contact with the body. There must be a reaction to a feature of the environment, but that feature may be at a greater or less distance from the body of the percipient; we can even perceive the sun and stars, within the limits of the definition. All that is necessary is that our reaction should depend upon the spatial relation between our body and the feature of the environment. When our back is towards the sun, we do not see it; when our face is towards it, we do.

When we consider perception – visual or auditory – of an external event, there are three different matters to be examined. There is first the process in the outside world, from the event to the percipient's body; there is next the process in his body, in so far as this can be known by an outside observer; lastly, there is the question, which must be faced sooner of later, whether the percipient can perceive something of the process in his body which no other observer could perceive. We will take these points in order.

If it is to be possible to 'perceive' an event not in the percipient's body, there must be a physical process in the outer world such that, when a certain event occurs, it produces a stimulus of a certain kind at the surface of the percipient's body. Suppose, for example, that pictures of different animals are exhibited on a magic lantern to a class of children, and all the children are asked to say the name of each animal in turn. We may assume that the children are sufficiently familiar with animals to say 'cat', 'dog', 'giraffe', 'hippopotamus', etc., at the right moments. We must then suppose – taking the physical world for granted – that some process travels from each picture to the eyes of the various children, retaining throughout these journeys such peculiarities that, when the process reaches their eyes, it can in one case stimulate the word 'cat' and in another the word 'dog'. All this the physical theory of light provides for. But there is one interesting point about language that should be noticed in this connection. If the usual physical theory of light is correct, the various children will receive stimuli which differ greatly according to their distance and direction from the picture, and according to the way the light falls. There are also differences in their reactions, for, though they all utter the word 'cat', some say it loud, others soft, some in a soprano voice, some in a contralto. But the differences in their reactions are much less than the differences in the stimuli. This is still more the case if we consider various different pictures of cats, to all of which they respond with the word 'cat'. Thus language is a means of producing responses which differ less than the stimuli do, in cases where the resemblances between the stimuli are more important to us than the differences. This fact makes us apt to overlook the differences between stimuli which produce nearly identical responses.

As appears from the above, when a number of people simultaneously perceive a picture of a cat, there are differences between the stimuli to their various perceptions, and these differences must obviously involve differences in their reactions. The *verbal* responses may differ very little, but even the verbal responses could be made to differ by putting more complicated questions than merely 'What animal is that?' One could ask: 'Can the picture be covered by your thumb-nail held at arm's length?' Then the answer would be different according as the percipient was near the picture or far off. But the normal percipient, if left to himself, will not notice such differences, that is to say, his verbal response will be the same in spite of the differences in the stimuli.

The fact that it is possible for a number of people to perceive the same noise or the same coloured pattern obviously depends upon the fact that a physical process can travel outward from a centre and retain certain of its characteristics unchanged, or very little changed. The most notable of such characteristics is frequency in a wave-motion. That, no doubt, affords a biological reason for the fact that our most delicate senses, sight and hearing, are sensitive to frequencies, which determine colour in what we see and pitch in what we hear. If there were not, in the physical world, processes spreading out from centres and retaining certain characters practically unchanged, it would be impossible for different percipients to perceive the same object from different points of view, and we should not have been able to discover that we all live in a common world.

We come now to the process in the percipient's body, in so far as this can be perceived by an outside observer. This raises no new philosophical problems, because we are still concerned, as before, with the perception of events outside the observer's body. The observer, now, is supposed to be a physiologist, observing, say, what goes on in the eye when light falls upon it. His means of knowing are, in principle, exactly the same as in the observation of dead matter. An event in an eye upon which light is falling causes lightwaves to travel in a certain manner until they reach the eye of the physiologist. They there cause a process in the physiologist's eye and optic nerve and brain, which ends in what he calls 'seeing what happens in the eye he is observing'. But this event, which happens in the physiologist, is not what happened in the eye he was observing; it is only connected with this by a complicated causal chain. Thus our knowledge of physiology is no more direct or intimate than our knowledge of processes in dead matter; we do not know any more about our eyes than about the trees and fields and clouds that we see by means of them. The event which happens when a physiologist observes an eye is an event in him, not in the eye that he is observing.

We come now at last to the question of self-observation, which we have hitherto avoided. I say 'self-observation' rather than 'introspection', because the latter word has controversial associations that I wish to avoid. I mean by 'self-observation' anything that a man can perceive about himself but that others, however situated, cannot perceive about him. What follows is only preliminary, since the subject will be discussed at length in Chapter 16.

No one can deny that we know things about ourselves which others cannot know unless we tell them. We know when we have toothache, when we feel thirsty, what we were dreaming when we woke up, and so on. Dr. Watson might say that the dentist can know we have toothache by observing a cavity in a tooth. I will not reply that the dentist is often mistaken; this may be merely because the art of dentistry has not been sufficiently perfected. I will concede as possible, in the future, a state of odontology in which the dentist could always know whether I am feeling toothache. But even then his knowledge has a different character from mine. His knowledge is an inference, based upon the inductive law that people with such-and-such cavities suffer pain of a certain kind. But this law cannot be established by observation of cavities alone; it requires that, where these are observed, the people who have them should tell us that they feel toothache. And, more than that, they must be speaking the truth. Purely external observation can discover that people with cavities *say* they have toothache, but not that they have it. Saying one has toothache is a different thing from having it; if not, we could cure toothache by not talking about it, and so save our dentist's bills. I am sure the expert opinion of dentists will agree with me that this is impossible.

To this argument, however, it might be replied that having toothache is a state of the body, and that knowing I have toothache is a response to this bodily stimulus. It will be said that, theoretically, the state of my body when I have toothache can be observed by an outsider, who can then also know that I have toothache. This answer, however, does not really meet the point. When the outside observer knows that I have toothache, not only is his knowledge based upon an inductive inference, as we have already seen, but his knowledge of the inferred term, 'toothache', must be based upon personal experience. No knowledge of dentistry could enable a man to know what toothache is if he had never felt it. If, then, toothache is really a state of the body – which, at the moment, I neither affirm nor deny – it is a state of the body which only the man himself can perceive. In a word, whoever has experienced toothache and can remember it has knowledge that cannot be possessed by a man who has never experienced toothache.

Take next our knowledge of our own dreams. Dr. Watson has not, so far as I know, ever discussed dreams, but I imagine he would say something like this: In dreams, there are probably small laryngeal movements such as, if they were greater, would lead to speech; indeed, people do sometimes cry out in dreams. There may also be stimulations of the sense-organs, which produce unusual reactions owing to the peculiar physiological condition of the brain during sleep: but all these reactions must consist of small movements, which could theoretically be seen from outside, say by some elaboration of X-ray apparatus. This is all very well, but meantime it is hypothetical, and the dreamer himself knows his dreams without all this elaborate inference. Can we say that he really knows these hypothetical small bodily movements, although he thinks he knows something else? That would presumably be Dr. Watson's position, and it must be admitted that, with a definition of 'knowledge' such as we considered in Chapter 8, such a view is not to be dismissed offhand as obviously impossible. Moreover, if we are to say that perception gives knowledge of the physical world, we shall have to admit that what we are perceiving may be quite different from what it seems to be. A table does not look like a vast number of electrons and protons, nor like trains of waves meeting and clashing. Yet that is the sort of thing a table is said to be by modern physicists. If, then, what seems to us to be just a table such as may be seen any day is really this odd sort of thing, it is possible that what seems to us to be a dream is really a number of movements in the brain.

This again is all very well, but there is one point which it fails to explain, namely, what is meant by 'seeming'. If a dream or a table 'seems' to be one sort of thing while it is 'really' another, we shall have to admit that it *really* seems, and that what it seems to be has a reality of its own. Nay more, we only arrive at what it 'really' is by an inference, valid or invalid, from what it seems to be. If we are wrong about the seeming, we must be doubly wrong about the reality, since the sole ground for asserting the table composed of electrons and protons is the table that we see, i.e. the 'seeming' table. We must therefore treat 'seeming' with respect.

Let us consider Dr. Watson watching a rat in a maze. He means to be quite objective, and report only what really goes on. Can he succeed? In one sense he can. He can use words about what he sees which are the same as any other scientifically trained observer will use if he watches the same rat at the same time. But Dr. Watson's objectivity emphatically does not consist in using the same words as other people use; his vocabulary is very different from that of most psychologists. He cannot take as the sole test of truth the consensus of mankind. *Securus judicat orbis terrarum* is another example of a Latin tag which is false, and which certainly Dr. Watson would not consider true. It has happened again and again in human history that a man who said something that had never been said before turned out to be right, while the people who repeated the wise saws of their forefathers were talking nonsense. Therefore, when Dr. Watson endeavours to eliminate subjectivity in observing rats, he does not mean that he says what everybody else says. He means that he refrains from inferring anything about the rat beyond its bodily movements. This is all to the good, but I think he fails to realise that almost as long and difficult an inference is required to give us knowledge of the rat's bodily movements as to give us knowledge of its 'mind'. And what is more, the data from which we must start in order to get to know the rat's bodily movements are data of just the sort that Dr. Watson wishes to avoid, namely private data patent to self-observation but not patent to any one except the observer. This is the point at which, in my opinion, behaviourism *as a final philosophy* breaks down.

When several people simultaneously watch a rat in a maze, or any other example of what we should naturally regard as matter in motion, there is by no means complete identity between the physical events which happen at the surface of their eyes and constitute the stimuli to their perceptions. There are differences of perspective, of light and shade, of apparent size, and so on, all of which will be reproduced in photographs taken from the places where the eyes of the several observers are. These differences produce differences in the reactions of the observers – differences which a quite unthinking person may overlook, but which are familiar to every artist. Now it is contrary to all scientific canons to suppose that the object perceived, in addition to affecting us in the way of stimulus and reaction, also affects us directly by some mystical epiphany; certainly it is not what any behaviourist would care to assert. Our knowledge of the physical world, therefore, must be contained in our reaction to the stimulus which reaches us across the intervening medium; and it seems hardly possible that our reaction should have a more intimate relation to the object than the stimulus has. Since the stimulus differs for different observers, the reaction also differs; consequently, in all our perceptions of physical processes there is an element of subjectivity. If, therefore, physics is true in its broad outlines (as the above argument supposes), what we call 'perceiving' a physical process is something private and subjective, at least in part, and is yet the only possible starting-point for our knowledge of the physical world.

There is an objection to the above argument which might naturally be made, but it would be in fact invalid. It may be said that we do not in fact proceed to *infer* the physical world from our perceptions, but that we begin at once with a rough-and-ready knowledge of the physical world, and only at a late stage of sophistication compel ourselves to regard our knowledge of the physical world as an inference. What is valid in this statement is the fact that our knowledge of the physical world is not at first inferential, but that is only because we take our percepts to *be* the physical world. Sophistication and philosophy come in at the stage at which we realise that the physical world cannot be identified with our percepts. When my boy was three years old, I showed him Jupiter, and told him that Jupiter was larger than the earth. He insisted that I must be speaking of some other Jupiter, because, as he patiently explained, the one he was seeing was obviously quite small. After some efforts, I had to give it up and leave him unconvinced. In the case of the heavenly bodies, adults have got used to the idea that what is really there can only be *inferred* from what they see; but where rats in mazes are concerned, they still tend to think that they are seeing what is happening in the physical world. The difference, however, is only one of degree, and naïve realism is as untenable in the one case as in the other. There are differences in the perceptions of two persons observing the same process; there are sometimes no discoverable differences between two perceptions of the same person observing different processes, e.g. pure water and water full of bacilli. The subjectivity of our perceptions is thus of practical as well as theoretical importance.

I am not maintaining that what we primarily know is our own perceptions. This is largely a verbal question; but with the definition of knowledge given in Chapter 8, it will be correct to say that from the first we know external objects. The question is not as to what are the objects we know, but rather as to how accurately we know them. Our non-inferential knowledge of an object cannot be more accurate than our reaction to it, since it is part of that reaction. And our reaction cannot be more accurate than the stimulus. But what on earth can you mean by the 'accuracy' of a stimulus? I may be asked. I mean just the same as by the accuracy of a map or a set of statistics. I mean a certain kind of correspondence. One pattern is an accurate representation of another if every element of the one can be taken as the representative of just one element of the other, and the relations that make the one set into a pattern correspond with relations making the other set into a pattern. In this sense, writing can represent speech with a certain degree of accuracy; to every spoken word a written word corresponds, and to the time-order of the spoken words the space-order of the written words corresponds. But there are inflexions and tones of voice that cannot be represented in writing, except, to some extent, by musical notation. A gramophone record is a much more accurate representation of vocal sounds than any writing can be; but even the best gramophone record fails to be completely accurate. The impression made upon an observer is very analogous to a gramophone record or a photograph, but usually less accurate owing to the influence of the law of association, and the lack of delicacy in our senses. And whatever limitations there are to the accuracy of our impressions are limitations to the accuracy of our non-inferential knowledge of the external world.

Another point: If we accept the definition of knowledge given in Chapter 8, which was framed so as to be as favourable as possible to behaviourism, a given reaction may be regarded as knowledge of various different occurrences. When we see Jupiter, we have, according to the definition, knowledge of Jupiter, but we also have knowledge of the stimulus at the surface of the eye, and even of the process in the optic nerve. For it is arbitrary at what point we start in the process leading to a certain event in the brain: this event, and the consequent bodily action, may be regarded as a reaction to a process starting at any earlier point. And the nearer our starting-point is to the brain, the more accurate becomes the knowledge displayed in our reaction. A lamp at the top of a tall building might produce the same visual stimulus as Jupiter, or at any rate one practically indistinguishable from that produced by Jupiter. A blow on the nose might make us 'see stars'. Theoretically, it should be possible to apply a stimulus direct to the optic nerve, which should give us a visual sensation. Thus when we think we see Jupiter, we may be mistaken. We are less likely to be mistaken if we say that the surface of the eye is being stimulated in a certain way, and still less likely to be mistaken if we say that the optic nerve is being stimulated in a certain way. We do not eliminate the risk or error completely unless we confine ourselves to saying that an event of a certain sort is happening in the brain; this statement may still be true if we see Jupiter in a dream.

But, I shall be asked, what do you know about what is happening in the brain? Surely nothing. Not so, I reply. I know about what is happening in the brain exactly what naïve realism thinks it knows about what is happening in the outside world. But this needs explaining, and there are other matters that must be explained first.

When the light from a fixed star reaches me, I see the star if it is night and I am looking in the right direction. The light started years ago, probably many years ago, but my reaction is primarily to something that is happening *now*. When my eyes are open, I see the star; when they are shut, I do not. Children discover at a fairly early age that they see nothing when their eyes are shut. They are aware of the difference between seeing and not seeing, and also of the difference between eyes open and eyes shut; gradually they discover that these two differences are correlated – I mean that they have expectations of which this is the intellectualist transcription. Again, children learn to name the colours, and to state correctly whether a thing is blue or red or yellow or what-not. They ought not to be sure that light of the appropriate wave-length started from the object. The sun looks red in a London fog, grass looks blue through blue spectacles, everything looks yellow to a person suffering from jaundice. But suppose you ask: What colour are you seeing? The person who answers, in these cases, red for the sun, blue for the grass, and yellow for the sick-room of the jaundiced patient, is answering quite truly. And in each of these cases he is stating something that he *knows*. What he knows in such cases is what I call a 'percept'. I shall contend later that, from the standpoint of physics, a percept is in the brain; for the present I am only concerned to say that a percept is what is most indubitable in our knowledge of the world.

To behaviourism as a metaphysic one may put the following dilemma. Either physics is valid in its main lines, or it is not. If it is not, we know nothing about the movements of matter; for physics is the result of the most serious and careful study of which the human intelligence has hitherto been capable. If, on the other hand, physics is valid in its main lines, any physical process starting either inside or outside the body will, if it reaches the brain, be different if the intervening medium is different; moreover two processes, initially very different, may become indistinguishable as they spread and grow fainter. On both grounds, what happens in the brain is not connected quite accurately with what happens elsewhere, and our perceptions are therefore infected with subjectivity on purely physical grounds. Even, therefore, when we assume the truth of physics, what we know most indubitably through perception is not the movements of matter, but certain events in ourselves which are connected, in a manner not quite invariable, with the movements of matter. To be specific, when Dr. Watson watches rats in mazes, what he knows, apart from difficult inferences, are certain events in himself. The behaviour of the rats can only be inferred by the help of physics, and is by no means to be accepted as something accurately knowable by direct observation.

I do not in fact entertain any doubts that physics is true in its main lines. The interpretation of physical formulae is a matter as to which a considerable degree of uncertainty is possible; but we cannot well doubt that there is an interpretation which is true roughly and in the main. I shall come to the question of interpretation later; for the present, I shall assume that we may accept physics in its broad outlines, without troubling to consider how it is to be interpreted. On this basis, the above remarks on perception seem undeniable. We are often misled as to what is happening, either by peculiarities of the medium between the object and our bodies, or by unusual states of our bodies, or by a temporary or permanent abnormality in the brain. But in all these cases *something* is really happening, as to which, if we turn our attention to it, we can obtain knowledge that is not misleading. At one time when, owing to illness, I had been taking a great deal of quinine, I became hypersensitive to noise, so that when the nurse rustled the newspaper I thought she was spilling a scuttle of coals on the floor. The interpretation was mistaken, but it was quite true that I heard a loud noise. It is a commonplace that a man whose leg has been amputated can still feel pains in it; here again, he does really feel the pains, and is only mistaken in his belief that they come from his leg. A percept is an observable event, but its interpretation as knowledge of this or that event in the physical world is liable to be mistaken, for reasons which physics and physiology can make fairly clear.

The subjectivity of percepts is a matter of degree. They are more subjective when people are drunk or asleep than when they are sober and awake. They are more subjective in regard to distant objects than in regard to such as are near. They may acquire various peculiar kinds of subjectivity through injuries to the brain or to the nerves. When I speak of a percept as 'subjective' I mean that the physiological inferences to which it gives rise are mistaken or vague. This is always the case to some extent, but much more so in some circumstances than in others. And the sort of defect that leads to mistakes must be distinguished from the sort that leads to vagueness. If you see a man a quarter of a mile away, you can see that it is a man if you have normal eyesight, but you probably cannot tell who it is, even if in fact it is some one you know well. This is vagueness in the percept: the inferences you draw are correct so far as they go, but they do not go very far. On the other hand, if you are seeing double and think there are two men, you have a case of mistake. Vagueness, to a greater or less extent, is universal and inevitable; mistakes, on the other hand, can usually be avoided by taking trouble and by not always trusting to physiological inference. Anybody can see double on purpose, by focussing on a distant object and noticing a near one; but this will not cause mistakes, since the man is aware of the subjective element in his double vision. Similarly we are not deceived by after-images, and only dogs are deceived by gramophones.

From what has been said in this chapter, it is clear that our knowledge of the physical world, if it is to be made as reliable as possible, must start from percepts, and must scrutinise the physiological inferences by which percepts are accompanied. Physiological inference is inference in the sense that it sometimes leads to error; and physics gives reason to expect that percepts will, in certain circumstances, be more or less deceptive if taken as signs of something outside the brain. It is these facts that give a subjective cast to the philosophy of physics, at any rate in its beginnings. We cannot start cheerfully with a world of matter in motion, as to which any two sane and sober observers must agree. To some extent, each man dreams his own dream, and the disentangling of the dream element in our percepts is no easy matter. This is, indeed, the work that scientific physics undertakes to do.

Chapter 13

Physical and Perceptual Space

Perhaps there is nothing so difficult for the imagination as to teach it to feel about space as modern science compels us to think. This is the task which must be attempted in the present chapter.

We said in Chapter 12 that we know about what is happening in the brain exactly what naïve realism thinks it knows about what is happening in the world. This remark may have seemed cryptic; it must now be expanded and expounded.

The gist of the matter is that percepts, which we spoke about at the end of last chapter, are in our heads; that percepts are what we can know with most certainty; and that percepts contain what naïve realism thinks it knows about the world.

But when I say that my percepts are in my head, I am saying something which is ambiguous until the different kinds of space have been explained, for the statement is only true in connection with *physical* space. There is also a space in our percepts, and of this space the statement would not be true. When I say that there is space in our percepts, I mean nothing at all difficult to understand. I mean – to take the sense of sight, which is the most important in this connection – that in what we see at one time there is up and down, right and left, inside and outside. If we see, say, a circle on a blackboard, all these relations exist within what we see. The circle has a top half and bottom half, a right-hand half and a left-hand half, an inside and an outside. These relations alone are enough to make up a space of sorts. But the space of every-day life is filled out with what we derive from touch and movement – how a thing feels when we touch it, and what movements are necessary in order to grasp it. Other elements also come into the genesis of the space in which everybody believes who has not been troubled by philosophy; but it is unnecessary for our purposes to go into this question any more deeply. The point that concerns us is that a man's percepts are private to himself: what I see, no one else sees; what I hear, no one else hears; what I touch, no one else touches; and so on. True, others hear and see something very like what I hear and see, if they are suitably placed; but there are always differences. Sounds are less loud at a distance; objects change their visual appearance according to the laws of perspective. Therefore it is impossible for two persons at the same time to have exactly identical percepts. It follows that the space of percepts, like the percepts, must be private; there are as many perceptual spaces as there are percipients. My percept of a table is outside my percept of my head, in my perceptual space; but it does not follow that it is outside my head as a physical object in physical space. Physical space is neutral and public: in this space, all my percepts are in my head, even the most distant star *as I see it*. Physical and perceptual space have relations, but they are not identical, and failure to grasp the difference between them is a potent source of confusion.

To say that you see a star when you see the light that has come from it is no more correct than to say that you see New Zealand when you see a New Zealander in London. Your perception when (as we say) you see a star is causally connected, in the first instance, with what happens in the brain, the optic nerve, and the eye, then with a light-wave which, according to physics, can be traced back to the star as its source. Your sensations will be closely similar if the light comes from a lamp at the top of a mast. The physical space in which you believe the 'real' star to be is an elaborate inference; what is given is the private space in which the speck of light you see is situated. It is still an open question whether the space of sight has depth, or is merely a surface, as Berkeley contended. This does not matter for our purposes. Even if we admit that sight alone shows a difference between an object a few inches from the eyes and an object several feet distant, yet you certainly cannot, by sight alone, see that a cloud is less distant than a fixed star, though you may *infer* that it is, because it can hide the star. The world of astronomy, from the point of view of sight, is a surface. If you were put in a dark room with little holes cut in the ceiling in the pattern of the stars letting light come through, there would be nothing in your immediate visual data to show that you were not 'seeing the stars'. This illustrates what I mean by saying that what you see is *not* 'out there' in the sense of physics.

We learn in infancy that we can sometimes touch objects we see, and sometimes not. When we cannot touch them at once, we can sometimes do so by walking to them. That is to say, we learn to correlate sensations of sight with sensations of touch, and sometimes with sensations of movement followed by sensations of touch. In this way we locate our sensations in a three-dimensional world. Those which involve sight alone we think of as 'external', but there is no justification for this view. What you see when you see a star is just as internal as what you feel when you feel a headache. That is to say, it is internal from the standpoint of *physical* space. It is distant in your private space, because it is not associated with sensations of touch, and cannot be associated with them by means of any journey you can perform.

Your own body, as known to you through direct experience, is quite different from your own body as considered in physics. You know more about your own body than about any other through direct experience, because your own body can give you a number of sensations that no other body can, for instance all kinds of bodily pains. But you still know it only through sensations; apart from inference, it *is* a bundle of sensations, and therefore quite different, *prima facie,* from what physics calls a body.

Most of the things you see are outside what you see when (as one says) you see your own body. That is to say: you see certain other patches of colour, differently situated in visual space, and say you are seeing things outside your body. But from the point of view of physics, all that you see must count as inside your body; what goes on elsewhere can only be inferred. Thus the whole space of your sensible world with all its percepts counts as one tiny region from the point of view of physics.

There is no direct spatial relation between what one person sees and what another sees, because no two ever see exactly the same object. Each person carries about a private space of his own, which can be located in physical space by indirect methods, but which contains no place in common with another person's private space. This shows how entirely physical space is a matter of inference and construction.

To make the matter definite, let us suppose that a physiologist is observing a living brain – no longer an impossible supposition, as it would have been formerly. It is natural to suppose that what the physiologist sees is in the brain he is observing. But if we are speaking of physical space, what the physiologist sees is in his own brain. it is in no sense in the brain that he is observing, though it is in the percept of that brain, which occupies part of the physiologist's perceptual space. Causal continuity makes the matter perfectly evident: light-waves travel from the brain that is being observed to the eye of the physiologist, at which they only arrive after an interval of time, which is finite though short. The physiologist sees what he is observing only after the light-waves have reached his eye; therefore the event which constitutes his seeing comes at the end of a series of events which travel from the observed brain into the brain of the physiologist. We cannot, without a preposterous kind of discontinuity, suppose that the physiologist's percept, which comes at the end of this series, is anywhere else but in the physiologist's head.

This question is very important, and must be understood if metaphysics is ever to be got straight. The traditional dualism of mind and matter, which I regard as mistaken, is intimately connected with confusions on this point. So long as we adhere to the conventional notions of mind and matter, we are condemned to a view of perception which is miraculous. We suppose that a physical process starts from a visible object, travels to the eye, there changes into another physical process, causes yet another physical process in the optic nerve, finally produces some effect in the brain, simultaneously with which we see the object from which the process started, the seeing being something 'mental', totally different in character from the physical processes which precede and accompany it. This view is so queer that metaphysicians have invented all sorts of theories designed to substitute something less incredible. But nobody noticed an elementary confusion.

To return to the physiologist observing another man's brain: what the physiologist sees is by no means identical with what happens in the brain he is observing, but is a somewhat remote effect. From what he sees, therefore, he cannot judge whether what is happening in the brain he is observing is, or is not, the sort of event that he would call 'mental'. When he says that certain physical events in the brain are accompanied by mental events, he is thinking of physical events as if they were what he sees. He does not see a mental event in the brain he is observing, and therefore supposes there is in that brain a physical process which he can observe and a mental process which he cannot. This is a complete mistake. In the strict sense, he cannot observe anything in the other brain, but only the percepts which he himself has when he is suitably related to that brain (eye to microscope, etc.). We first identify physical processes with our percepts, and then, since our percepts are not other people's thoughts, we argue that the physical processes in their brains are something quite different from their thoughts. In fact, everything that we can directly observe of the physical world happens inside our heads, and consists of 'mental' events in at least one sense of the word 'mental'. It also consists of events which form part of the physical world. The development of this point of view will lead us to the conclusion that the distinction between mind and matter is illusory. The stuff of the world may be called physical or mental or both or neither, as we please; in fact, the words serve no purpose. There is only one definition of the words that is unobjectionable: 'physical' is what is dealt with by physics, and 'mental' is what is dealt with by psychology. When, accordingly, I speak of 'physical' space, I mean the space that occurs in physics.

It is extraordinarily difficult to divest ourselves of the belief that the physical world is the world we perceive by sight and touch; even if, in our philosophic moments, we are aware that this is an error, we nevertheless fall into it again as soon as we are off our guard. The notion that what we see is 'out there' in physical space is one which cannot survive while we are grasping the difference between what physics supposes to be really happening, and what our senses show us as happening; but it is sure to return and plague us when we begin to forget the argument. Only long reflection can make a radically new point of view familiar and easy.

Our illustrations hitherto have been taken from the sense of sight; let us now take one from the sense of touch. Suppose that, with your eyes shut, you let your finger-tip press against a hard table. What is really happening? The physicist says that your finger-tip and the table consist, roughly speaking, of vast numbers of electrons and protons; more correctly, each electron and proton is to be thought of as a collection of processes of radiation, but we can ignore this for our present purposes. Although you think you are touching the table, no electron or proton in your finger ever really touches an electron or proton in the table, because this would develop an infinite force. When you press, repulsions are set up between parts of your finger and parts of the table. If you try to press upon a liquid or a gas, there is room in it for the parts that are repelled to get away. But if you press a hard solid, the electrons and protons that try to get away, because electrical forces from your finger repel them, are unable to do so, because they are jammed close to others which elbow them back to more or less their original position, like people in a dense crowd. Therefore the more you press the more they repel your finger. The repulsion consists of electrical forces, which set up in the nerves a current whose nature is not very definitely known. This current runs into the brain, and there has effects which, so far as the physiologist is concerned, are almost wholly conjectural. But there is one effect which is not conjectural, and that is the sensation of touch. This effect, owing to physiological inference or perhaps to a reflex, is associated by us with the finger-tip. But the sensation is the same if, by artificial means, the parts of the nerve nearer the brain are suitably stimulated – e.g. if your hand has been amputated and the right nerves are skilfully manipulated. Thus our confidence that touch affords evidence of the existence of bodies at the place which we think is being touched is quite misplaced. As a rule we are right, but we can be wrong; there is nothing of the nature of an infallible revelation about the matter. And even in the most favourable case, the perception of touch is something very different from the mad dance of electrons and protons trying to jazz out of each other's way, which is what physics maintains is really taking place at your finger-tip. Or, at least, it *seems* very different. But as we shall see, the knowledge we derive from physics is so abstract that we are not warranted in saying that what goes on in the physical world is, or is not, intrinsically very different from the events that we know through our own experiences.

Chapter 14

Perception and Physical Causal Laws

In an earlier chapter we saw the inadequacy of the traditional notion of cause, without adequately explaining the causal laws which are a substitute in the practice of science. The time has now come when it is possible to remedy this defect, and, in so doing, to fit perception into its place in the chain of physical causation and recapitulate the main points of previous arguments.

The old view was that an event A will always be followed by a certain event B, and that the problem of discovering causal laws is the problem, given an event B, of finding that event A which is its invariable antecedent or vice versa. At an early stage of a science this point of view is useful; it gives laws which are true usually, though probably not always, and it affords the basis for more exact laws. But it has no philosophical validity, and is superseded in science as soon as we arrive at genuine laws. Genuine laws, in advanced sciences, are practically always quantitative laws of *tendency*. I will try to illustrate by taking the simplest possible case in physics.

Imagine a hydrogen atom, in which the electron is revolving not in the minimum orbit, but in the next, which has four times the minimum radius. So long as this state continues, the atom has no external effects, apart from its infinitesimal gravitational action; we cannot, therefore, obtain any evidence of its existence except when it changes its state. In fact, our knowledge of atoms is like that which a ticket collector has of the population of his town: he knows nothing of those who stay quietly at home. Now at some moment, according to laws of which we have only statistical knowledge, the electron in our atom jumps to a smaller orbit, and the energy lost to the atom travels outward in a light-wave. We know no causal law as to when the electron will jump, though we know how far it will jump and exactly what will happen in the neighbourhood when it does. At least, when I say we know exactly what will happen, I ought to say that we know exactly the mathematical laws of what will happen. A series of events, having quantitative characteristics which obey certain equations, will travel outward in all directions from the electron, and will proceed quite regularly, like ripples on a pool, until other matter is encountered. We have here one important and apparently fundamental kind of causal law, the kind regulating the propagation of light *in vacuo*. This is summed up in Maxwell's equations, which enable us to calculate the diffusion of an electromagnetic disturbance starting from a source. So long as two such disturbances do not meet, the matter is exceedingly simple; but the equations also tell us what happens when they do meet. We then have, as always in traditional physics, two separate tendencies, which have a resultant compounded according to mathematical laws, of which the parallelogram law is the oldest and simplest. That is to say, each previous circumstance in the space–time neighbourhood contributes a tendency, and the resulting event is obtained by compounding these tendencies according to a mathematical law.

So far, we have been considering only electromagnetic phenomena in empty space. We have another set of facts about empty space, namely those upon which gravitation depends. These have to do with the structure of space–time, and show that this structure has singularities in the regions where there is matter, which spread with diminishing intensity as we get away from these regions. You may conceive the structure of space–time on the analogy of a pond with a fountain playing in it, so that wherever a spray falls from the fountain there is a little hill of water which flattens quickly as you get away from the spot where the spray falls. Here again the same sort of thing applies: to infer the structure in a small region of space–time from that in the neighbourhood, it will be necessary to superpose a number of tendencies according to mathematical rules. Thus philosophically this introduces no novelty.

But now consider what happens when the wave of light which started from our hydrogen atom comes in contact with matter. Various things may happen. The matter may absorb all or some of the energy of the light-ray; this is the interesting case from our point of view. The absorption may take the form of causing the electrons to move in larger orbits, in which case, later, when they return to their previous orbits, we get the phenomenon of fluorescence. Or the body may become heated; or it may visibly move, like a radiometer. The effects upon bodies depend upon the bodies as well as the light. Some of them can be individually predicted, others can only be calculated in statistical averages; this depends upon whether quantum considerations come in or not. Where they do, we can enumerate possibilities, and state the relative frequencies with which they will be realised, but we cannot tell which will be realised in any given case.

So far, we have considered the radiation of energy from matter into empty space, its propagation in empty space and its impact on matter from empty space. We have not considered the history of a given piece of matter, or the distinction between matter and empty space.

The essence of matter appears to be this: We can distinguish series of events in space–time which have a certain kind of close resemblance to each other, such that common sense regards them as manifestations of one 'thing'. But when we look closely at the question, it turns out that what physics offers is something more abstract than this. Take, e.g. the continued existence of a certain electron. This means to say that events in a certain neighbourhood will be such as can be calculated on the assumption that there is an electric charge of a certain standard magnitude in the middle of that neighbourhood; and that the neighbourhoods of which this is true form a tube in space–time.

So long as we stick to the standpoint of pure physics there is a certain air of taking in each other's washing about the whole business. Events in empty space are only known as regards their abstract mathematical characteristics; matter is only an abstract mathematical characteristic of events in empty space. This seems rather a cold world. But as a matter of fact we know some things that are a little more concrete. We know, e.g. what it feels like when we see things. From the point of view of physics, when our light-wave starts out through empty space, if it presently reaches our eye we know one link in the causal chain, namely the visual sensation, otherwise than as a term in an abstract mathematical formula. And it is this one term which forms the basis for our belief in all the rest. Seeing is believing.

At this point I propose to make a brief digression on the subject of our evidence for causal laws. The laws for which we first get evidence are such as do not hold always, but only as a general rule. As a rule, when you decide to move your arm, it moves: but sometimes it is paralysed and remains motionless. As a rule, when you say how-do-you-do to an old friend, he says the same to you; but he may have grown blind and deaf since you last say him, and not notice your words or gesture. As a rule, if you put a match to gunpowder, it explodes; but it may have got damp. It is such common but not invariable rules of sequence that we notice first. But science is always seeking to replace them by laws that may have no exceptions. We notice first that heavy bodies fall, then that some bodies do not fall. Then we generalise both sets of facts into the law of gravitation and the laws of resistance of the air. These more general laws do not state that anything will actually happen: they state a tendency, and lead to the conclusion that what actually happens is the resultant of a number of tendencies. We cannot know what the resultant will be unless we know a great deal about the neighbourhood concerned. For example, I might, within the next few seconds, be hit on the head by a meteorite; to know whether this is going to happen, I must know what matter is to be found in the neighbourhood of the earth. This illustrates that actual predictions based upon laws which are perfectly valid may always be falsified by some unknown fact of what we may call geography. Moreover, we can never be sure that our scientific laws are quite right; of this the Einsteinian modification of the law of gravitation has afforded a notable instance.

Let us now return to the relation between perception and the causal laws of physics.

Having realised the abstractness of what physics has to say, we no longer have any difficulty in fitting the visual sensation into the causal series. It used to be thought 'mysterious' that purely physical phenomena should end in something mental. That was because people thought they knew a lot about physical phenomena, and were sure they differed in quality from mental phenomena. We now realise that we know nothing of the intrinsic quality of physical phenomena except when they happen to be sensations, and that therefore there is no reason to be surprised that some are sensations, or to suppose that the others are totally unlike sensations. The gap between mind and matter has been filled in, partly by new views on mind, but much more by the realisation that physics tells us nothing as to the intrinsic character of matter.

I conceive what happens when we see an object more or less on the following lines. For the sake of simplicity, let us take a small self-luminous object. In this object, a certain number of atoms are losing energy and radiating it according to the quantum principle. The resulting light-waves become superposed according to the usual mathematical principles; each part of each light-wave consists of events in a certain region of space–time. On coming in contact with the human body, the energy in the light-wave takes new forms, but there is still causal continuity. At last it reaches the brain, and there one of its constituent events is what we call a visual sensation. This visual sensation is popularly called seeing the object from which the light-waves started – or from which they were reflected if the object was not self-luminous.

Thus what is called a perception is only connected with its object through the laws of physics. Its relation to the object is causal and mathematical; we cannot say whether or not it resembles the object in any intrinsic respect, except that both it and the object are brief events in space–time.

I think we may lay down the following universal characteristics of causal laws in an advanced science. Given any event, there are other events at neighbouring slightly later places in space–time which will occur if no other factors intervene; but in practice other factors almost always do intervene, and, in that case, the event which actually occurs at any point of space–time is a mathematical resultant of those which would have followed the various neighbouring events if they had been alone concerned. The equations of physics give the rules according to which events are connected, but all are of the above sort.

Formerly it was thought that the equations of physics suffice, theoretically, to determine the course of affairs in the physical world, given all the facts about some finite stretch of time, however short. Now it appears that this is not the case, so far as the known equations are concerned. The known equations suffice to determine what happens in empty space, and statistical averages as to what happens to matter; but they do not tell us when an individual atom will absorb or radiate energy. Whether there are laws, other than those of statistics, governing the behaviour of an individual atom in this respect, we do not know.

It should be observed that there are causal laws of a different sort from those of pure physics; such are the laws that light-waves 'cause' visual sensations and sound-waves 'cause' auditory sensations. All the empirical evidence for physics rests upon such laws, therefore nothing in physics can have a higher degree of certainty than such laws have. Let us stop a moment to ask what we mean by 'cause' in this connection.

The connection of light-waves and visual sensations looks a little different according as we start with physics or with psychology, though, of course, ultimately the result must be the same. Let us first start with physics. I say, then, that when a light-wave travels outwards from a body there are successive events at successive places, and that the corresponding event in a brain behind a normal eye is a visual sensation. This is the only event in the whole series about which I can say anything not purely abstract and mathematical.

Now let us start from the sensation. I say, then, that this sensation is one of a vast series of connected events, travelling out from a centre according to certain mathematical laws, in virtue of which the sensation enables me to know a good deal about events elsewhere. That is why the sensation is a source of physical knowledge.

It will be seen that, according to the view I have been advocating, there is no difficulty about interaction between mind and body. A sensation is merely one link in a chain of physical causation; when we regard the sensation as the end of such a chain, we have what would be regarded as an effect of matter on mind; when as the beginning, an effect of mind on matter. But mind is merely a cross-section in a stream of physical causation, and there is nothing odd about its being both an effect and a cause in the physical world. Thus physical causal laws are those that are fundamental.

There seems no reason to regard causation as *a priori*, though this question is not simple. Given certain very general assumptions as to the structure of space–time, there are bound to be what we have called causal laws. These general assumptions must really replace causality as our basic principles. But, general as they are, they cannot be taken as *a priori;* they are the generalisation and abstract epitome of the fact that there are causal laws, and this must remain merely an empirical fact, which is rendered probable, though not certain, by inductive arguments.

Chapter 15

The Nature of our Knowledge of Physics

In this chapter, we shall seek an answer to two questions: First, *how* do we know about the world dealt with in physics? Secondly, *what* do we know about it, assuming the truth of modern physics?

First: How do we know about the physical world? We have already seen that this question cannot have a simple answer, since the basis of inference is something that happens in our own heads, and our knowledge of anything outside our own heads must be more or less precarious. For the present, I shall take it for granted that we may accept testimony, with due precautions. In other words, I shall assume that what we hear when, as we believe, others are speaking to us does in fact have 'meaning' to the speaker, and not only to us; with a corresponding assumption as regards writing. This assumption will be examined at a later stage. For the present, I will merely emphasise that it *is* an assumption, and that it may possibly be false, since people seem to speak to us in dreams, and yet, on waking, we become persuaded that we invented the dream. It is impossible to prove, by a demonstrative argument, that we are not always dreaming; the best we can hope is a proof that this is improbable. But for the present let us leave this discussion on one side, and assume that the words we hear and read 'mean' what they would if we spoke or wrote them.

On this basis, we have reason to know that the worlds of different people are alike in certain respects and different in certain others. Take, for example, the audience at a theatre: they all, we say, hear the same words and see the same gestures, which, moreover, are those that the actors wish them to hear and see. But those who are near the stage hear the words more loudly than those further off; they also hear them somewhat earlier. And those who sit on the right do not see quite what is seen by those who sit on the left or in the centre. These differences are of two sorts: on the one hand, some people can see something invisible to others; on the other hand, when two people, as we say, see the 'same' thing, they see it differently owing to effects of perspective and of the way the light is reflected. All this is a question of physics, not of psychology; for if we place a camera in an empty seat in the theatre, the perspective in the resultant photograph is intermediate between the perspectives that are seen by persons sitting on either side; indeed the whole matter of perspective is determined by quite simple geometrical laws. These laws show also what is common to the shapes that two people see when they see the 'same' thing from different points of view: what is common is what is studied by projective geometry, which is concerned with what is independent of measurement in geometrical figures. All the differences in appearance due to perspective have to be learned in learning to draw: for this purpose, it is necessary to learn to see things as they really seem, and not as they seem to seem.

But, it will be said, what can you mean by how things 'really' seem and how they 'seem' to seem? We come here upon an important fact about learning. When, in early infancy, we are learning to correlate sight and touch, we acquire the habit of reacting to a visual stimulus in a manner which is more 'objective' than that in which a camera reacts. When we see a coin not directly in front of us, we judge it to be circular, although the camera would show it as oval, and a man would have to make it oval in a picture of a scene which contained it. We learn, therefore, to react to a visual shape in a manner corresponding to how it would appear if it were in the centre of the field of vision, provided we do not immediately focus upon it, which is what we naturally do when anything visible interests us. As a matter of fact, we are constantly looking in different directions, and, as a rule, only noticing what, at the moment, is in the centre of our field of vision. Thus our visual world consists rather of a synthesis of things viewed directly in succession than of things seen simultaneously while the centre of the field is kept fixed. This is one reason why the rules of perspective have to be learned, although a picture which ignores them makes an impression of being 'wrong'.

Another reason for the objectivity of the impressions we derive from sight is correlation with other senses, especially touch. Through this correlation we soon get to 'know' that a man twenty yards away is 'really' just as big as a man one yard away. When children are learning to draw, they find it very difficult to make distant objects sufficiently small, because they know that they are not 'really' small. We soon learn to judge the distance of a visual object, and to react to it according to the size that it would have if touched – or travelled over, in the case of very large objects such as mountains. Our sense of size is not derived from sight, but from such sources as touch and locomotion; our metrical judgments, when the stimulus is only visual, are a result of previous experience.

By the time a child can speak well, he has had a great deal of this kind of experience. Consequently our verbal reactions contain a great deal more objectivity than they would if they came at an earlier stage of infancy. The result is that a number of people can view a scene simultaneously, and use exactly the same words about it. The words which we naturally use in describing what we see are those describing features that will also be evident to others in our neighbourhood. We say 'There is a man', not 'There is a coloured shape whose visual dimensions are such-and-such an angle vertically, and such another horizontally'. The inference is a physiological inference, and only subsequent reflection makes us aware that it has taken place. We can, however, become aware of it through occasional mistakes; a dot on the window-pane may be mistaken for a man in a distant field. In this case, we can discover our error by opening the window, or by moving the head. In general, however, physiological inferences of this sort are correct, since they have resulted from correlations which are very common, and are likely to be present on a given occasion. Consequently our words tend to conceal what is private and peculiar in our impressions, and to make us believe that different people live in a common world to a greater extent than is in fact the case.

We have been using the word 'objectivity' in the preceding pages, and it is time to consider exactly what we mean by it. Suppose some scene – say in a theatre – is simultaneously seen by a number of people and photographed by a number of cameras. The impression made upon a person or a camera is in some respects like that made upon other persons and cameras, in other respects different. We shall call the elements which are alike 'objective' elements in the impression, and those which are peculiar we shall call 'subjective'. Thus those features of shapes which are considered in projective geometry will be objective, whereas those considered in metrical geometry (where lengths and angles are measured) cannot be made objective through sight alone, but demand the use of other senses. In the photographs, a man on the stage will be longer if the camera is near the stage than if it is far off, assuming all the cameras to be alike. But if four actors are standing in a row in one photograph, they will be standing in a row in another; this is an 'objective' feature of the impression. And the differences in the visual impressions of a number of spectators with normal eyesight are exactly analogous to the differences in the photographs; so also are the likenesses. Thus the 'subjectivity' that we are speaking about at present is something belonging to the physical world, not to psychology. It marks the fact that the stimulus, whether to an eye or to a camera, is not exactly the same wherever the eye or the camera may be placed; there are features of the stimulus which are constant (within limits), but there are others which are different from any two different points of view.

The tendency of our perceptions is to emphasise increasingly the objective elements in an impression, unless we have some special reason, as artists have, for doing the opposite. This tendency begins before speech, is much accentuated after speech has been acquired, and is prolonged by scientific physics. The theory of relativity is only the last term, so far, in the elimination of subjective elements from impressions. But it must not be supposed that the subjective elements are any less 'real' than the objective elements; they are only less important. They are less important because they do not point to anything beyond themselves as the others do. We want our senses to give us information, i.e. to tell us about something more than our own momentary impression. We acquire information through our senses if we attend to the objective elements in the impression and ignore the others; but the subjective elements are just as truly part of the actual impression. This is obvious as soon as we realise that the camera is as subjective as we are.

Such considerations lead irresistibly to the scientific view that, when an object can be seen or photographed from a number of points of view, there is a connected set of events (light-waves) travelling outward from a centre; that, moreover, there are some respects in which all these events are alike, and others in which they differ one from another. We must not think of a light-wave as a 'thing', but as a connected group of rhythmical events. The mathematical characteristics of such a group can be inferred by physics, within limits; but the intrinsic character of the component events cannot be inferred. The events constituting light-waves are only known through their effects upon our eyes, optic nerves, and brains, and these effects are not themselves light-waves, as is obvious from the fact that nerves and brains are not transparent. Light in the physical world, therefore, must consist of events which are in some way different from the events which happen when we see; but we cannot say more than this as to the intrinsic quality of these external events. Moreover, when a number of people, as we say, 'see the same thing', what we have reason to believe is that light-waves emanating from a certain region have reached the eyes of all these people. As to what is in the region from which the light-waves come, we cannot tell.

But – so the plain man is tempted to argue – we can tell quite well, because we can touch objects that we see, and discover that there is something hard and solid in the place from which the light-waves come. Or, again, we may find that there is something there which, though not solid, is very hot, and burns us when we try to touch it. We all feel that touch gives more evidence of 'reality' than sight; ghosts and rainbows can be seen but not touched. One reason for this greater sense of reality is that our spatial relation to an object when we touch it with our finger-tips is given, and therefore an object does not give such different impressions of touch to different people as it does of sight. Another reason is that there are a number of objects that can be seen but not touched – reflections, smoke, mist, etc. – and that these objects are calculated to surprise the inexperienced. None of these facts, however, justify the plain man in supposing that touch makes him know real things as they are, though we are verbally forced to admit that it brings him into 'contact' with them.

We have seen on an earlier occasion how complex is the physical and physiological process leading from the object to the brain when we touch something; and we have seen that illusions of touch can be produced artificially. What we experience when we have a sensation of touch is, therefore, no more a revelation of the real nature of the object touched than what we experience when we look at it. As a matter of fact, if modern physics is to be believed, sight, prudently employed, gives us a more delicate knowledge concerning objects than touch can ever do. Touch, as compared with sight, is gross and massive. we can photograph the path of an individual electron. We perceive colours, which indicate the changes happening in atoms. We can see faint stars even though the energy of the light that reaches us from them is inconceivably minute. Sight may deceive the unwary more than touch, but for accurate scientific knowledge it is incomparably superior to any of the other senses.

It is chiefly through ideas derived from sight that physicists have been led to the modern conception of the atom as a centre from which radiations travel. We do not know what happens in the centre. The idea that there is a little hard lump there, which *is* the electron or proton, is an illegitimate intrusion of common-sense notions derived from touch. For aught we know, the atom may consist entirely of the radiations which come out of it. It is useless to argue that radiations cannot come out of nothing. We know that they come, and they do not become any more really intelligible by being supposed to come out of a little lump.

Modern physics, therefore, reduces matter to a set of events which proceed outward from a centre. If there is something further in the centre itself, we cannot know about it, and it is irrelevant to physics. The events that take the place of matter in the old sense are inferred from their effect on eyes, photographic plates, and other instruments. What we know about them is not their intrinsic character, but their structure and their mathematical laws. Their structure is inferred chiefly through the maxim 'same cause, same effect'. It follows from this maxim that if the effects are different, the causes must be different; if, therefore, we see red and blue side by side, we are justified in inferring that in the direction where we see red something different is happening from what is happening in the direction where we see blue. By extensions of this line of argument we arrive at the mathematical laws of the physical world. Physics is mathematical, not because we know so much about the physical world, but because we know so little: it is only its mathematical properties that we can discover. For the rest, our knowledge is negative. In places where there are no eyes or ears or brains there are no colours or sounds, but there are events having certain characteristics which lead them to cause colours and sounds in places where there are eyes and ears and brains. We cannot find out what the world looks like from a place where there is nobody, because if we go to look there will be somebody there; the attempt is as hopeless as trying to jump on one's own shadow.

Matter as it appears to common sense, and as it has until recently appeared in physics, must be given up. The old idea of matter was connected with the idea of 'substance', and this, in turn, with a view of time that the theory of relativity shows to be untenable. The old view was that there is one cosmic time, and that, given any two events in any two parts of the universe, either they are simultaneous, or the first is earlier than the second, or the second earlier than the first. It was thought that the time–order of the two events must always be objectively definite, although *we* might be unable to determine it. We now find that this is not the case. Events which can be regarded as all in one place, or all parts of the history of one piece of matter, still have a definite time–order. So do events in different places if a person situated where the second takes place can see the first before the second happens, or, more exactly, if light can travel from the place of the one to the place of the other so as to reach the other place before the second event. (Here we mean by a 'place' the position of a given piece of matter: however the matter may move relatively to other matter, it is always in the same 'place' from its own point of view.) But if light travelling from the place of the one event to the place of the other event arrives at the place of the other event after the other event has taken place, and conversely, then there is no definite objective time–order of the two events, and there is no reason for regarding either as earlier than the other, nor yet for regarding the two as simultaneous; ideally careful observers will judge differently according to the way in which they are moving. Thus time is not cosmic, but is to some extent individual and personal for each piece of matter.

What do we mean by a 'piece of matter' in this statement? We do not mean something that preserves a simple identity throughout its history, nor do we mean something hard and solid, nor even a hypothetical thing-in-itself known only through its effects. We mean the 'effects' themselves, only that we no longer invoke an unknowable cause for them. We find that energy in various forms spreads outwards from various centres; we find also that such centres have a certain degree of persistence, though this persistence is not absolute – the modern physicist faces cheerfully the possibility that an electron and a proton may mutually annihilate each other, and even suggests that this may be the main source of the radiant energy of the stars, because when it happens it makes an explosion. What is asserted may be put as follows: When energy radiates from a centre, we can describe the laws of its radiation conveniently by imagining something in the centre, which we will call an electron or a proton according to circumstances, and for certain purposes it is convenient to regard this centre as persisting, i.e. as not a single point in space–time but a series of such points, separated from each other by time-like intervals. All this, however, is only a convenient way of describing what happens elsewhere, namely the radiation of energy away from the centre. As to what goes on in the centre itself, if anything, physics is silent.

What Dr. Whitehead calls the 'pushiness' of matter disappears altogether on this view. 'Matter' is a convenient formula for describing what happens where it isn't. I am talking physics, not metaphysics; when we come to metaphysics, we may be able, tentatively, to add something to this statement, but science alone can hardly add to it. Materialism as a philosophy becomes hardly tenable in view of this evaporation of matter. But those who would formerly have been materialists can still adopt a philosophy which comes to much the same thing in many respects. They can say that the type of causation dealt with in physics is fundamental, and that all events are subject to physical laws. I do not wish, as yet, to consider how far such a view should be adopted; I am only suggesting that it must replace materialism as a view to be seriously examined.

PART III MAN FROM WITHIN

Chapter 16

Self-observation

It will be remembered that, throughout Part I, we agreed to consider only those facts about a man which can be discovered by external observation, and we postponed the question whether this excluded any genuine knowledge or not. The usual view is that we know many things which could not be known without self-observation, but the behaviourist holds that this view is mistaken. I might be inclined to agree wholly with the behaviourist but for the considerations which were forced upon us in Part II, when we were examining our knowledge of the physical world. We were then led to the conclusion that, assuming physics to be correct, the data for our knowledge of physics are infected with subjectivity, and it is impossible for two men to observe the same phenomenon except in a rough and approximate sense. This undermines the supposed objectivity of the behaviourist method, at least in principle; as a matter of degree, it may survive to some extent. Broadly speaking, if physics is true and if we accept a behaviourist definition of knowledge such as that of Chapter 8, we ought, as a rule, to know more about things that happen near the brain than about things that happen far from it, and most of all about things that happen in the brain. This *seemed* untrue because people thought that what happens in the brain is what the physiologist sees when he examines it; but this, according to the theory of Chapter 12, happens in the brain of the physiologist. Thus the *a priori* objection to the view that we know best what happens in our brains is removed, and we are led back to self-observation as the most reliable way of obtaining knowledge. This is the thesis which is to be expanded and sustained in the present chapter.

As everyone knows, the certainty of self-observation was the basis of Descartes' system, with which modern philosophy began. Descartes, being anxious to build his metaphysic only upon what was absolutely certain, set to work, as a preliminary, to doubt anything that he could make himself doubt. He succeeded in doubting the whole external world, since there might be a malicious demon who took pleasure in presenting deceitful appearances to him. (For that matter, dreams would have supplied a sufficient argument.) But he could not manage to doubt his own existence. For, said he, I am really doubting; whatever else may be doubtful, the fact that I doubt is indubitable. And I could not doubt if I did not exist. He summed up the argument in his famous formula: *I think, therefore I am.* And having arrived at this certainty, he proceeded to build up the world again by successive inferences. Oddly enough, it was very like the world in which he had believed before his excursion into scepticism.

It is instructive to contrast this argument with Dr. Watson's. Dr. Watson, like Descartes, is sceptical of many things which others accept without question; and, like Descartes, he believes that there are some things so certain that they can be safely used as the basis of a startling philosophy. But the things which Dr. Watson regards as certain are just those which Descartes regarded as doubtful, and the thing which Dr. Watson most vehemently rejects is just what Descartes regarded as absolutely unquestionable. Dr. Watson maintains that there is no such thing as thinking. No doubt he believes in his own existence, but not because he thinks he can think. The things that strike him as absolutely indubitable are rats in mazes, time-measurements, physiological facts about glands and muscles, and so on. What are we to think when two able men hold such opposite views? The natural inference would be that *everything* is doubtful. This may be true, but there are degrees of doubtfulness, and we should like to know which of these two philosophers, if either, is right as to the region of minimum doubtfulness.

Let us begin by examining Descartes' view. 'I think, therefore I am' is what he says, but this won't do as it stands. What, from his own point of view, he should profess to know is not '*I* think', but 'there is thinking'. He finds doubt going on, and says: There is doubt. Doubt is a form of thought, therefore there is thought. To translate this into '*I* think' is to assume a great deal that a previous exercise in scepticism ought to have taught Descartes to call in question. He would say that thoughts imply a thinker. But why should they? Why should not a thinker be simply a certain series of thoughts, connected with each other by causal laws? Descartes believed in 'substance', both in the mental and in the material world. He thought that there could not be motion unless something moved, nor thinking unless someone thought. No doubt most people would still hold this view; but in fact it springs from a notion – usually unconscious – that the categories of grammar are also the categories of reality. We have already seen that 'matter' is merely a name for certain strings of sets of events. It follows that what we call motion of matter really means that the centre of such a set of events at one time does not have the same spatial relations to other events as the connected centre at another time has to the connected other events. It does not mean that there is a definite entity, a piece of matter, which is now in one place and now in another. Similarly, when we say, 'I think first this and then that', we ought not to mean that there is a single entity 'I' which 'has' two successive thoughts. We ought to mean only that there are two successive thoughts which have causal relations of the kind that makes us call them parts of one biography, in the same sort of way in which successive notes may be parts of one tune; and that these thoughts are connected with the body which is speaking in the way (to be further investigated) in which thoughts and bodies are connected. All this is rather complicated, and cannot be admitted as part of any ultimate certainty. What Descartes really felt sure about was a certain occurrence, which he described in the words 'I think'. But the words were not quite an accurate representation of the occurrence; indeed, words never can escape from certain grammatical and social requirements which make them say at once more and less than we really mean. I think we ought to admit that Descartes was justified in feeling sure that there was a certain occurrence, concerning which doubt was impossible; but he was not justified in bringing in the word 'I' in describing this occurrence, and it remains to be considered whether he was justified in using the word 'think'.

In using a general word such as 'think', we are obviously going beyond the datum, from a logical point of view. We are subsuming a particular occurrence under a heading, and the heading is derived from past experience. Now all words are applicable to many occurrences; therefore all words go beyond any possible datum. In this sense, it is impossible ever to convey in words the particularity of a concrete experience; all words are more or less abstract. Such, at least, is a plausible line of argument, but I am by no means sure that it is valid. For example, the sight of a particular dog may make the general word 'dog' come into your mind; you then know that it is a dog, but you may not notice what sort of dog it is. In this sense, the knowledge with which we start is abstract and general; that is to say, it consists of learned reaction to a stimulus of a certain sort. The reactions, at any rate in so far as they are verbal, are more uniform than the stimuli. A witness might be asked 'Did you see a dog?' 'Yes.' 'What sort of dog?' 'Oh just an ordinary dog; I don't remember more about it.' That is to say, the witness's reaction consisted of the generalised word 'dog' and no more. One is almost reminded of quantum phenomena in the atom. When light falls on a hydrogen atom, it may make the electron jump from the first orbit to the second, or to the third, or etc. Each of these is a generalised reaction to a stimulus which has no corresponding generality. So dogs and cats have each their individual peculiarities, but the ordinary inobservant person responds with the generalised reaction 'dog' or 'cat', and the particularity of the stimulus leads to no corresponding particularity in the knowledge-reaction.

To return to Descartes and his thinking: it is possible, according to what we have just said, that Descartes knew he was thinking with more certainty than he knew what he was thinking about. This possibility requires that we should ask what he meant by 'thinking'. And since, for him, thinking was the primitive certainty, we must not introduce any external stimulus, since he considered it possible to doubt whether anything external existed.

Descartes used the word 'thinking' somewhat more widely than we should generally do nowadays. He included all perception, emotion, and volition, not only what are called 'intellectual' processes. We may perhaps with advantage concentrate upon perception. Descartes would say that, when he 'sees the moon', he is more certain of his visual percept than he is of the outside object. As we have seen, this attitude is rational from the standpoint of physics and physiology, because a given occurrence in the brain is capable of having a variety of causes, and where the cause is unusual common sense will be misled. It would be theoretically possible to stimulate the optic nerve artificially in just the way in which light coming from the moon stimulates it; in this case, we should have the same experience as when we 'see the moon', but should be deceived as to its external source. Descartes was influenced by an argument of this sort, when he brought up the possibility of a deceitful demon. Therefore what he felt certain about was not what he had initially felt certain about, but what remained certain after an argument as to the causes of perception. This brings us to a distinction which is important, but difficult to apply: the distinction between what we in fact do not doubt, and what we should not doubt if we were completely rational. We do not in fact question the existence of the sun and moon, though perhaps we might teach ourselves to do so by a long course of Cartesian doubt. Even then, according to Descartes, we could not doubt that we have the experiences which we have hitherto called 'seeing the sun' and 'seeing the moon', although we shall need different words if we are to describe these experiences correctly.

The question arises: Why should we not doubt everything? Why should we remain convinced that we have these experiences? Might not a deceitful demon perpetually supply us with false memories? When we say 'a moment ago I had the experience which I have hitherto called seeing the sun', perhaps we are deceived. In dreams we often remember things that never happened. At best, therefore, we can be sure of our present momentary experience, not of anything that happened even half a minute ago. And before we can so fix our momentary experience as to make it the basis of a philosophy, it will be past, and therefore uncertain. When Descartes said 'I think', he may have had certainty; but by the time he said 'therefore I am', he was relying upon memory, and may have been deceived. This line of argument leads to complete scepticism about everything. If we are to avoid such a result, we must have some new principle.

In actual fact, we start by feeling certainty about all sorts of things, and we surrender this feeling only where some definite argument has convinced us that it is liable to lead to error. When we find any class of primitive certainties which never leads to error, we retain our convictions in regard to this class. That is to say, wherever we feel initial certainty, we require an argument to make us doubt, not an argument to make us believe. We may therefore take, as the basis of our beliefs, any class of primitive certainties which cannot be shown to lead us into error. This is really what Descartes does, though he is not clear about it himself.

Moreover, when we have found an error in something of which we were previously certain, we do not as a rule abandon entirely the belief which misled us, but we seek, if we can, to modify it so that it shall no longer be demonstrably false. This is what has happened with perception. When we think we see an external object, we may be deceived by a variety of causes. There may be a mirage or a reflection; in this case, the source of the error is in the external world, and a photographic plate would be equally deceived. There may be a stimulus to the eye of the sort that makes us 'see stars', or we may see little black dots owing to a disordered liver, in which case, the source of the error is in the body but not in the brain. We may have dreams in which we seem to see all sorts of things; in this case, the source of the error is in the brain. Having gradually discovered these possibilities of error, people have become somewhat wary as to the objective significance of their perceptions; but they have remained convinced that they really have the perceptions they thought they had, although the common-sense interpretation of them is sometimes at fault. Thus, while retaining the conviction that they are sure of *something*, they have gradually changed their view as to what it is that they are sure of. Nothing is known that tends to show error in the view that we really have the percepts we think we have, so long as we are prudent in interpreting them as signs of something external. That is the valid basis for Descartes' view that 'thought' is more certain than external objects. When 'thought' is taken to mean the experiences which we usually regard as percepts of objects, there are sound reasons for accepting Descartes' opinion to this extent.

Let us now take up Dr. Watson's view. We shall find, if I am not mistaken, that his position also is to a very large extent valid. That being so, we shall seek to find an intermediate opinion, accepting what seems valid and rejecting what seems doubtful in the contentions of both protagonists.

Dr. Watson's view as to what is most certain is one which is in entire accordance with common sense. All psychological matters the plain man regards as more or less open to question, but he has no doubts about his office, his morning train, the tax-collector, the weather, and the other blessings of this life. It may amuse him, in an idle hour, to listen to someone playing with the idea that life is a dream, or suggesting that the thoughts of the people in the train are more real than the train. But unless he is a philosophical lecturer, he does not countenance such notions in business hours. Who can imagine a clerk in an office conceiving metaphysical doubts as to the existence of his boss? Or would any railroad president regard with favour the theory that his railroad is only an idea in the minds of the shareholders? Such a view, he would say, though it is often sound as regards gold-mines, is simply silly when it comes to a railroad: anybody can see it, and can get himself run over if he wanders on the tracks under the impression that they do not exist. Belief in the unreality of matter is likely to lead to an untimely death, and that, perhaps, is the reason why this belief is so rare, since those who entertained it died out. We cannot dismiss the common-sense outlook as simply silly, since it succeeds in daily life; if we are going to reject it in part, we must be sure that we do so in favour of something equally tough as a means of coping with practical problems.

Descartes says: I think, therefore I am. Watson says: There are rats in mazes, therefore I don't think. At least, a parodist might thus sum up his philosophy. What Watson really says is more like this: (1) The most certain facts are those which are public, and can be confirmed by the testimony of a number of observers. Such facts form the basis of the physical sciences: physics, chemistry, biology, anatomy, physiology, to mention only those that are relevant to the matter in question. (2) The physical sciences are capable of affording an explanation of all the publicly observable facts about human behaviour. (3) There is no reason to suppose that there are any facts about human beings that can be known only in some other way. (4) In particular, 'introspection', as a means of discovering by self-observation things that are in principle undiscoverable by observation of others, is a pernicious superstition, which must be swept away before any really sound knowledge of man becomes possible. (5) And, as a corollary, there is no reason to believe in the existence of 'thought' as opposed to speech and other bodily behaviour.

I have numbered the above propositions, as it is important to keep them separate. On the whole, (1), (2), and (3) seem to me to be true, but (4) and (5) seem to me to be false. Behaviourists, I think, incline to the view that (4) and (5) follow from (1), (2), and (3); but this view I attribute to what I should regard as errors concerning the basis of physics. That is why it was necessary to discuss physics before coming to a decision on this question of self-observation. But let us examine each of the above propositions in turn.

(1) It is true that the facts upon which the physical sciences are based are all of them public, in the sense that many men can observe them. If a phenomenon is photographed, any number of people can inspect the photograph. If a measurement is made, not only may several people be present, but others can repeat the experiment. If the result does not confirm the first observer, the supposed fact is rejected. The publicity of physical facts is always regarded as one of the greatest assets of physics. On a common-sense basis, therefore, the first of the propositions in which we have summed up the behaviourist philosophy must be admitted.

There are, however, some very important provisos which must be mentioned. In the first place, a scientific observer is not expected to note his integral reaction to a situation, but only that part of it which experience leads him to regard as 'objective', i.e. the same as the reaction of any other competent observer. This process of learning to note only 'objective' features in our reaction is, as we have seen, begun in infancy; training in science only carries it further. A 'good' observer does not mention what is peculiar to himself in his reaction. He does not say: 'A boring speck of light danced about, causing me eye-fatigue and irritation; finally it settled at such-and-such a point.' He says simply: 'The reading was such-and-such.' All this objectivity is a result of training and experience. One may say, in fact, that very few men have the 'right' reaction to a scientific situation. Therefore an immense amount of theory is mixed up with what passes in science as pure observation. The nature and justification of this theory is a matter requiring investigation.

In the second place, we must not misinterpret the nature of the publicity in the case of physical phenomena. The publicity consists in the fact that a number of people make closely similar reactions at a given moment. Suppose, for example, that twelve men are told to watch a screen for the appearance of a bright light, and to say 'now' when it appears. Suppose the experimenter hears them all just when he himself sees the light; then he has good reason to believe that they have each had a stimulus similar to his. But physics compels us to hold that they have had twelve separate stimuli, so that when we say they have all seen the same light we can only legitimately mean that their twelve stimuli had a common causal origin. In attributing our perceptions to a normal causal origin outside ourselves, we run a certain risk of error, since the origin may be unusual: there may be reflection or refraction on the way to the eye, there may be an unusual condition of the eye or optic nerve or brain. All these considerations give a certain very small probability that, on a given occasion, there is not such an outside cause as we suppose. If, however, a number of people concur with us, i.e. simultaneously have reactions which they attribute to an outside cause that can be identified with the one we had inferred, then the probability of error is enormously diminished. This is exactly the usual case of concurrent testimony. If twelve men, each of whom lies every other time that he speaks, independently testify that some event has occurred, the odds in favour of their all speaking the truth are 4095 to 1. The same sort of argument shows that our public senses, when confirmed by others, are probably speaking the truth, except where there are sources of collective illusion such as mirage or suggestion.

In this respect, however, there is no *essential* difference between matters of external observation and matters of self-observation.

Suppose, for example, that, for the first time in your life, you smell assafoetida. You say to yourself 'That is a most unpleasant smell'. Now unpleasantness is a matter of self-observation. It may be *correlated* with physiological conditions which can be observed in others, but it is certainly not identical with these, since people knew that things were pleasant and unpleasant before they knew about the physiological conditions accompanying pleasure and its opposite. Therefore when you say 'That smell is unpleasant' you are noticing something that does not come into the world of physics as ordinarily understood. You are, however, a reader of psycho-analysis, and you have learned that sometimes hate is concealed love and love is concealed hate. You say to yourself, therefore: 'Perhaps I really like the smell of assafoetida, but am ashamed of liking it'. You therefore make your friends smell it, with the result that you soon have no friends. You then try children, and finally chimpanzees. Friends and children give verbal expression to their disgust: chimpanzees are expressive, though not verbal. All these facts lead you to state: 'The smell of assafoetida is unpleasant'. Although self-observation is involved, the result has the same kind of certainty, and the same kind of objective verification, as if it were one of the facts that form the empirical basis of physics.

(2) The second proposition, to the effect that the physical sciences are capable of affording an explanation of all the publicly observable facts about human behaviour, is one as to which it is possible to argue endlessly. The plain fact is that we do not yet know whether it is true or false. There is much to be said in its favour on general scientific grounds, particularly if it is put forward, not as a dogma, but as a methodological precept, a recommendation to scientific investigators as to the direction in which they are to seek for solution of their problems. But so long as much of human behaviour remains unexplained in terms of physical laws, we cannot assert dogmatically that there is no residue which is theoretically inexplicable by this method. We may say that the trend of science, so far, seems to render such a view improbable, but to say even so much is perhaps rash, though, for my part, I should regard it as still more rash to say that there certainly is such a residue. I propose, therefore, as a matter of argument, to admit the behaviourist position on this point, since my objections to behaviourism as an ultimate philosophy come from quite a different kind of consideration.

(3) The proposition we are now to examine may be stated as follows: 'All facts that can be known about human beings are known

by the same method by which the facts of physics are known'. This I hold to be true, but for a reason exactly opposite to that which influences the behaviourist. I hold that the facts of physics, like those of psychology, are obtained by what is really self-observation, although common sense mistakenly supposes that it is observation of external objects. As we saw in Chapter 13, your visual, auditory, and other percepts are all in your head, from the standpoint of physics. Therefore, when you 'see the sun', it is, strictly speaking, an event in yourself that you are knowing: the inference to an external cause is more or less precarious, and is on occasion mistaken. To revert to the assafoetida: it is by a number of self-observations that you know that the smell of assafoetida is unpleasant, and it is by a number of self-observations that you know that the sun is bright and warm. There is no essential difference between the two cases. One may say that the data of psychology are those private facts which are not very directly linked with facts outside the body, while the data of physics are those private facts which have a very direct causal connection with facts outside the body. Thus physics and psychology have the same method; but this is rather what is commonly taken to be the special method of psychology than what is regarded as the method of physics. We differ from the behaviourist in assimilating physical to psychological method, rather than the opposite.

(4) Is there a source of knowledge such as is believed in by those who appeal to 'introspection'? According to what we have just been saying, all knowledge rests upon something which might, in a sense, be called 'introspection'. Nevertheless, there may be some distinction to be discovered. I think myself that the only distinction of importance is in the degree of correlation with events outside the body of the observer. Suppose, for example, that a behaviourist is watching a rat in a maze, and that a friend is standing by. He says to the friend 'Do you see that rat?' If the friend says yes, the behaviourist is engaged in his normal occupation of observing physical occurrences. But if the friend says no, the behaviourist exclaims, 'I must give up this bootlegged whiskey'. In that case, if his horror still permits him to think clearly, he will be obliged to say that in watching the imaginary rat he was engaged in introspection. There was certainly something happening, and he could still obtain knowledge by observing what was happening, provided he abstained from supposing that it had a cause outside his body. But he cannot, without outside testimony or some other extraneous information, distinguish between the 'real' rat and the 'imaginary' one. Thus in the case of the 'real' rat also, his

primary datum ought to be considered introspective, in spite of the fact that it does not seem so; for the datum in the case of the 'imaginary' rat also does not *seem* to be merely introspective.

The real point seems to be this: some events have effects which radiate all round them, and can therefore produce reactions in a number of observers; of these, ordinary speech is an illustration. But other events produce effects which travel linearly, not spherically; of these, speech into a telephone from a sound-proof telephone box may serve as an illustration. This can be heard by only one person beside the speaker; if instead of a speaker we had an instrument at the mouthpiece, only one person could hear the sound, namely the person at the other end of the telephone. Events which happen inside a human body are like the noise in the telephone: they have effects, in the main, which travel along nerves to the brain, instead of spreading out in all directions equally. Consequently, a man can know a great deal about his own body which another man can only know indirectly. Another man can see the hole in my tooth, but he cannot feel my toothache. If he infers that I feel toothache, he still does not have the very same knowledge that I have; he may use the same words, but the stimulus to his use of them is different from the stimulus to mine, and I can be acutely aware of the pain which is the stimulus to my words. In all these ways a man has knowledge concerning his own body which is obtained differently from the way in which he obtains knowledge of other bodies. This peculiar knowledge is, in one sense, 'introspective', though not quite in the sense that Dr. Watson denies.

(5) We come now to the real crux of the whole matter, namely to the question: Do we think? This question is very ambiguous, so long as 'thinking' has not been clearly defined. Perhaps we may state the matter thus: Do we know events in us which would not be included in an absolutely complete knowledge of physics? I mean by a complete knowledge of physics a knowledge not only of physical laws, but also of what we may call geography, i.e. the distribution of energy throughout space–time. If the question is put in this way, I think it is quite clear that we do know things not included in physics. A blind man could know the whole of physics, but he could not know what things look like to people who can see, nor what is the difference between red and blue as seen. He could know all about wave-lengths, but people knew the difference between red and blue as seen before they knew anything about wave-lengths. The person who knows physics and can see knows that a certain wave-length will give him a sensation of red, but this knowledge is not part of physics. Again, we

know what we mean by 'pleasant' and 'unpleasant', and we do not know this any better when we have discovered that pleasant things have one kind of physiological effect and unpleasant things have another. If we did not already know what things are pleasant and what unpleasant, we could never have discovered this correlation. But the knowledge that certain things are pleasant and certain others unpleasant is no part of physics.

Finally, we come to imaginations, hallucinations, and dreams. In all these cases, we may suppose that there is an external stimulus, but the cerebral part of the causal chain is unusual, so that there is not in the outside world something connected with what we are imagining in the same way as in normal perception. Yet in such cases we can quite clearly know what is happening to us; we can for example, often remember our dreams. I think dreams must count as 'thought', in the sense that they lie outside physics. They may be accompanied by movements, but knowledge of them is not knowledge of these movements. Indeed all knowledge as to movements of matter is inferential, and the knowledge which a scientific man should take as constituting his primary data is more like our knowledge of dreams than like our knowledge of the movements of rats or heavenly bodies. To this extent, I should say, Descartes is in the right as against Watson. Watson's position seems to rest upon naïve realism as regards the physical world, but naïve realism is destroyed by what physics itself has to say concerning physical causation and the antecedents of our perceptions. On these grounds, I hold that self-observation can and does give us knowledge which is not part of physics, and that there is no reason to deny the reality of 'thought'.

Chapter 17

Images

In this chapter we shall consider the question of images. As the reader doubtless knows, one of the battle-cries of behaviourism is 'death to images'. We cannot discuss this question without a good deal of previous clearing of the ground.

What are 'images' as conceived by their supporters? Let us take this question first in the sense of trying to know some of the phenomena intended, and only afterwards in the sense of seeking a formal definition.

In the ordinary sense, we have visual images if we shut our eyes and call up pictures of scenery or faces we have known; we have auditory images when we recall a tune without actually humming it; we have tactual images when we look at a nice piece of fur and think how pleasant it would be to stroke it. We may ignore other kinds of images, and concentrate upon these, visual, auditory, and tactual. There is no doubt that we have such experiences as I have suggested by the above words; the only question is as to how these experiences ought to be described. Then we have another set of experiences, namely dreams, which feel like sensations at the moment, but do not have the same kind of relation to the external world as sensations have. Dreams, also, indubitably occur, and again it is a question of analysis whether we are to say that they contain 'images' or not.

The behaviourist does not admit images, but he equally does not admit sensations and perceptions. Although he does not say so quite definitely, he may be taken to maintain that there is nothing but matter in motion. We cannot, therefore, tackle the question of images by contrasting them with sensations or perceptions, unless we have first clearly proved the existence of these latter and defined their characteristics. Now it will be remembered that in Chapter 5 we attempted a behaviourist definition of perception, and decided that its most essential feature was 'sensitivity'. That is to say, if a person always has a reaction of a certain kind B when he has a certain spatial relation to an object of a certain kind A, but not otherwise, then we say that the person is 'sensitive' to A. In order to obtain from this a definition of 'perception', it is necessary to take account of the law of association; but for the moment we will ignore this complication, and say that a person 'perceives' any feature of his environment, or of his own body, to which he is sensitive. Now, however, as a result of the discussion in Chapter 16, we can include in his reaction, not only what others can observe, but also what he alone can observe. This enlarges the known sphere of perception, practically if not theoretically. But it leaves unchanged the fact that the essence of perception is a causal relation to a feature of the environment which, except in astronomy, is approximately contemporaneous with the perception, though always at least slightly earlier, owing to the time taken by light and sound to travel and the interval occupied in transmitting a current along the nerves.

Let us now contrast with this what happens when you sit still with your eyes shut, calling up pictures of places you have seen abroad, and perhaps ultimately falling asleep. Dr. Watson, if I understand him aright, maintains that either there is actual stimulation of the retina, or your pictures are mere word-pictures, the words being represented by small actual movements such as would, if magnified and prolonged, lead to actual pronunciation of the words. Now if you are in the dark with your eyes shut, there is no stimulation of the retina from without. It may be that, by association, the eye can be affected through stimuli to other senses; we have already had an example in the fact that the pupil can be taught to contract at a loud noise if this has been frequently experienced along with a bright light. We cannot, therefore, dismiss the idea that a stimulus to one sense may, as a result of past events, have an effect upon the organs of another sense. 'Images' might be definable as effects produced in this way. It may be that, when you see a picture of Napoleon, there is an effect upon your aural nerves analogous to that of having the word 'Napoleon' pronounced in your presence, and that that is why, when you see the picture, the word 'Napoleon' comes into your head. And similarly, when you shut your eyes and call up pictures of foreign scenes, you may actually pronounce, completely or incipiently, the word 'Italy', and this may, through association, stimulate the optic nerve in a way more or less similar to that in which some actual place in Italy stimulated it on some former occasion. Thence association alone may carry you along through a series of journeys, until at last, when you fall asleep, you think you are actually making them at the moment. All this is quite possible, but so far as I know there is no reason to hold that it is more than possible, apart from an *a priori* theory excluding every other explanation.

What I think is clearly untenable is the view, sometimes urged by Dr. Watson, that when we are, as we think, seeing imaginary pictures with the eyes shut, we are really only using such words as would describe them. It seems to me as certain as anything can be that, when I visualise, something is happening which is connected with the sense of sight. For example, I can call up quite clear mental pictures of the house in which I lived as a child; if I am asked a question as to the furniture of any of the rooms in that house, I can answer it by first calling up an image and then looking to see what the answer is, just as I should look to see in an actual room. It is quite clear to me that the picture comes first and the words after; moreover, the words need not come at all. I cannot tell what is happening in my retina or optic nerve at these moments of visualisation, but I am quite sure that something is happening which has a connection with the sense of sight that it does not have with other senses. And I can say the same of aural and tactual images. If this belief were inconsistent with anything else that seems to me equally certain, I might be induced to abandon it. But so far as I can see, there is no such inconsistency.

It will be remembered that we decided in favour of perceptions as events distinct from those which they perceive, and only causally connected with them. There is, therefore, no reason why association should not work in this region as well as in the region of muscles and glands; in other words, there is no reason to deny what used to be called 'association of ideas', in spite of the fact that bodily changes can also be associated. If a physical basis is wanted, it can be assumed to exist in the brain. The state of the brain which causes us to hear the word 'Napoleon' may become associated with the state of the brain which causes us to see a picture of Napoleon, and thus the word and the picture will call each other up. The association *may* be in the sense-organs or nerves, but may equally well be in the brain. So far as I know, there is no conclusive evidence either way, nor even that the association is not purely 'mental'.

When we try to find a definition of the difference between a sensation and an image, it is natural to look first for intrinsic differences. But intrinsic differences between ordinary sensations and ordinary images, for example as to 'liveliness', are found to be subject to exceptions, and therefore unsuitable for purposes of definition. Thus we are brought to differences as to causes and effects.

It is obvious that, in an ordinary case, you perceive a table because (in some sense) the table is there. That is to say, there is a causal chain leading backwards from your perception to something outside your body. This alone, however, is hardly sufficient as a criterion. Suppose you smell peat smoke and think of Ireland, your thought can equally be traced to a cause outside your body. The only real difference is that the outside cause (peat smoke) would not have had the effect (images of Ireland) upon every normal person, but only upon such as had smelt peat smoke in Ireland, and not all of them. That is to say, the normal cerebral apparatus does not cause the given stimulus to produce the given effect except where certain previous experiences have occurred. This is a very vital distinction. Part of what occurs in us under the influence of a stimulus from without depends upon past experience; part does not. The former part includes images, the latter consists of pure sensations. This, however, as we shall see later, is inadequate as a definition.

Mental occurrences which depend upon past experience are called 'mnemic' occurrences, following Semon. Images are thus to be included among mnemic occurrences, at least so far as human experience goes. This, however, does not suffice to define them, since there are others, e.g. recollections. What further defines them is their similarity to sensations. This only applies strictly to simple images; complex ones may occur without a prototype, though all their parts will have prototypes among sensations. Such, at least, is Hume's principle, and on the whole it seems to be true. It must not, however, be pressed beyond a point. As a rule, an image is more or less vague, and has a number of similar sensations as its prototypes. This does not prevent the connection with sensation in general, but makes it a connection with a number of sensations, not with one only.

It happens that, when a complex of sensations has occurred at some time in a person's experience, the recurrence of part of the whole tends to produce images of the remaining parts or some of them. This is association, and has much to do with memory.

It is common to speak of images as 'centrally excited', as opposed to sensations, which are excited by a stimulus to some sense organ. In essence this is quite correct, but there is need of some caution in interpreting the phrase. Sensations also have *proximate* causes in the brain; images also may be due to some excitement of a sense-organ, when they are roused by a sensation through association. But in such cases there is nothing to explain their occurrence except the past experience and its effect on the brain. They will not be aroused by the same stimulus in a person with similar sense-organs but different past experience. The connection with past experience is clearly known; it is, however, an explanatory hypothesis, not directly verifiable in the present state of knowledge, to suppose that this connection works through an effect of the past experience on the brain. This hypothesis must be regarded as doubtful, but it will save circumlocution to adopt it. I shall therefore not repeat, on each occasion, that we cannot feel sure it is true. In general, where the causal connection with past experience is obvious, we call an occurrence 'mnemic', without implying this or that hypothesis as to the explanation of mnemic phenomena.

It is perhaps worth while to ask how we know that images are like the sensations which are their prototypes. The difficulty of this question arises as follows. Suppose you call up an image of Waterloo Bridge, and you are convinced that it is like what you see when you look at Waterloo Bridge. It would seem natural to say that you know the likeness because you remember Waterloo Bridge. But remembering is often held to involve, as an essential element, the occurrence of an image which is regarded as referring to a prototype. Unless you can remember without images, it is difficult to see how you can be sure that images resemble prototypes. I think that in fact you cannot be sure, unless you can find some indirect means of comparison. You might, for example, have photographs of Waterloo Bridge taken from a given place on two different days, and find them indistinguishable, showing that Waterloo Bridge has not changed in the interval. You might see Waterloo Bridge on the first of these days, remember it on the second, and immediately afterwards look at it. In looking at it, you might find every detail coming to you with a feeling of expectedness, or you might find some details coming with a feeling of surprise. In this case you would say that your image had been wrong as regards the details which were surprising. Or, again, you might make a picture of Waterloo Bridge on paper, from memory, and then compare it with the original or a photograph. Or you might content yourself by writing down a description of it in words, and verifying its accuracy by direct observation. Innumerable methods of this kind can be devised by which you can test the likeness of an image to its prototype. The result is that there is often a great likeness, though seldom complete accuracy. The belief in the likeness of an image to its prototype is, of course, not generated in this way, but only tested. The belief exists prior to evidence as to its correctness, like most of our beliefs. I shall have more to say on this subject in the next chapter, which will be concerned with memory. But I think enough has been said to show that it is not unreasonable to regard images as having a greater or less degree of resemblance to their prototypes. To claim more is hardly justifiable.

We can now reach a definite conclusion about perception, sensation, and images. Let us imagine a number of people placed, as far as possible, in the same environment; we will suppose that they sit successively in a certain chair in a dark room, in full view of illuminated pictures of two eminent politicians of opposite parties whose names are written underneath them. We will suppose that all of them have normal eyesight. Their reactions will be partly similar, partly different. If any of these observers are babies too young to have learnt to focus, they will not see sharp outlines, but a mere blurr, not from an optical defect, but from a lack of cerebral control over muscles. In this respect, experience has an effect even upon what must count as pure sensation. But this difference is really analogous to the difference between having one's eyes open and having them shut; the difference is in the sense-organ, although it may be due to a difference in the brain. We will therefore assume that all the spectators know how to adjust the eyes so as to see as well as possible, and all try to see. We shall then say that, if the spectators differ as widely as is possible for normal human beings, what is common to the reactions of all of them is sensation, provided it is connected with the sense of sight, or, more correctly, provided it has that quality which we observe to be common and peculiar to visual objects. But probably all of them, if they are over three months old, will have tactile images while they see the pictures. And if they are more than about a year old, they will interpret them as pictures, which represent three-dimensional objects; before that age, they may see them as coloured patterns, not as representations of faces. Most animals, though not all, are incapable of interpreting pictures as representations. But in an adult human being this interpretation is not deliberate; it has become automatic. It is, I think, mainly a question of tactile images: the images you have in looking at a picture are not those appropriate to a smooth flat surface, but those appropriate to the object represented. If the object represented is a large one, there will also be images of movement – walking round the object, or climbing up it, or what not. All these are obviously a product of experience, and therefore do not count as part of the sensation. This influence of experience is still more obvious when it comes to reading the names of the politicians, considering whether they are good likenesses, and feeling what a fine fellow one of them looks and what unmitigated villainy is stamped upon the features of the other. None of this counts as sensation, yet it is part of a man's spontaneous reaction to an outside stimulus.

It is evidently difficult to avoid a certain artificiality in distinguishing between the effects of experience and the rest in a man's reaction to a stimulus. Perhaps we could tackle the matter in a slightly different way. We can distinguish stimuli of different sorts: to the eye, the ear, the nose, the palate, etc. We can also distinguish elements of different sorts in the reaction: visual elements, auditory elements, etc. The latter are defined, not by the stimulus, but by their intrinsic quality. A visual sensation and a visual image have a common quality which neither shares with an auditory sensation or an auditory image. We may then say: a visual image is an occurrence having the visual quality but not due to a stimulus to the eye, i.e. not having as a direct causal antecedent the incidence of light-waves upon the retina. Similarly an auditory image will be an occurrence having the auditory quality but not due to sound-waves reaching the ear, and so on for the other senses. This means a complete abandonment of the attempt to distinguish psychologically between sensations and images; the distinction becomes solely one as to physical antecedents. It is true that we can and do arrive at the distinction without scientific physics, because we find that certain elements in our integral reactions have the correlations that make us regard them as corresponding to something external while others do not – correlations both with the experience of others and with our own past and future experiences. But when we refine upon this common-sense distinction and try to make it precise, it becomes the distinction in terms of physics as stated just now.

We might therefore conclude that an image is an occurrence having the quality associated with stimulation by some sense-organ, but not due to such stimulation. In human beings, images seem to depend upon past experience, but perhaps in more instinctive animals they are partly due to innate cerebral mechanisms. In any case dependence upon experience is not the mark by which they are to be defined. This shows how intimate is the dependence of traditional psychology upon physics, and how difficult it is to make psychology into an autonomous science.

There is, however, still a further refinement necessary. Whatever is included under our present definition is an image, but some things not included are also images. The sight of an object may bring with it a visual image of some other object frequently associated with it. This latter is called an image, not a sensation, because, though also visual, it is not appropriate to the stimulus in a certain sense: it would not appear in a photograph of the scene, or in a photograph of the retina. Thus we are forced to say: the sensational element in the reaction to a stimulus is that part which enables you to draw inferences as to the nature of the extra-cerebral event (if any) which was the stimulus[1]; the rest is images. Fortunately, images and sensations *usually* differ in intrinsic quality; this makes it possible to get an approximate idea of the external world by using the usual intrinsic differences, and to correct it afterwards by means of the strict causal definition. But evidently the matter is difficult and complicated, depending upon physics and physiology, not upon pure psychology. This is the main thing to be realised about images.

The above discussion has suggested a definition of the word 'image'. We might have called an event an 'image' when it is recognisably of the same kind as a 'percept', but does not have the stimulus which it would have if it were a percept. But if this definition is to be made satisfactory, it will be necessary to substitute a different word in place of 'percept'. For example, in the percept of a visible object it would be usual to include certain associated tactual elements, but these must, from our point of view, count as images. It will be better to say, therefore, that an 'image' is an occurrence recognisably visual (or auditory or etc., as the case may be), but not caused by a stimulus which is of the nature of light (or sound or etc., as the case may be), or at any rate only indirectly so caused as a result of association. With this definition, I do not myself feel any doubt as to the existence of images. It is clear that they constitute most of the material of dreams and day-dreams, that they are utilised by composers in making music, that we employ them when we get out of a familiar room in the dark (though here the rats in mazes make a different explanation possible), and that they account for the shock of surprise we have when we take salt thinking it is sugar or (as happened to me recently) vinegar thinking it is coffee. The question of the physiological causation of images – i.e. whether it is in the brain or in other parts of the body – is not one which it is necessary to our purposes to decide, which is fortunate, since, so far as I know, there is not at present any adequate evidence on the point. But the existence of images and their resemblance to perceptions *is* important, as we shall see in the next chapter.

Images come in various ways, and play various parts. There are those that come as accretions to a case of sensation, which are not recognised as images except by the psychologist; these form, for example, the tactual quality of things we only see, and the visual quality of things we only touch. I think dreams belong, in part, to

---

[1] i.e. the immediate stimulus, not the 'physical object'.

this class of images: some dreams result from misinterpreting some ordinary stimulus, and in these cases the images are those suggested by a sensation, but suggested more uncritically than if we were awake. Then there are images which are not attached to a present reality, but to one which we locate in the past; these are present in memory, not necessarily always, but sometimes. Then there are images not attached to reality at all so far as our feeling about them goes: images which merely float into our heads in reverie or in passionate desire. And finally there are images which are called up voluntarily, for example, in considering how to decorate a room. This last kind has its importance, but I shall say nothing more about it at present, since we cannot profitably discuss it until we have decided what we are to mean by the word 'voluntary'. The first kind, which comes as an accretion to sensation, and gives to our feeling of objects a certain rotundity and full-bloodedness which the stimulus alone would hardly warrant, has been considered already. Therefore what remains for the present is the use of images in memory and imagination; and of these two I shall begin with memory.

Chapter 18

Imagination and Memory

In this chapter we have to consider the two topics of imagination and memory. The latter has already been considered in Chapter 6, but there we viewed it from outside. We want now to ask ourselves whether there is anything further to be known about it by taking account of what is only perceptible to the person remembering.

As regards the part played by images, I do not think this is essential. Sometimes there are memory-images, sometimes not; sometimes when images come in connection with memory, we may nevertheless know that the images are incorrect, showing that we have also some other and more reliable source of memory. Memory *may* depend upon images, as in the case mentioned above, of the house where I lived as a child. But it may also be purely verbal. I am a poor visualiser, except for things I saw before I was ten years old; when now I meet a man and wish to remember his appearance, I find that the only way is to describe him in words while I am seeing him, and then remember the words. I say to myself: 'This man has blue eyes and a brown beard and a small nose; he is short, with a rounded back and sloping shoulders.' I can remember these words for months, and recognise the man by means of them, unless two men having these characteristics are present at once. In this respect, a visualiser would have the advantage of me. Nevertheless, if I had made my verbal inventory sufficiently extensive and precise, it would have been pretty sure to answer its purpose. I do not think there is anything in memory that absolutely demands images as opposed to words. Whether the words we use in 'thought' are themselves sometimes images of words, or are always incipient movements (as Watson contends), is a further question, as to which I offer no opinion, since it ought to be capable of being decided experimentally.

The most important point about memory is one which has nothing to do with images, and is not mentioned in Watson's brief discussion. I mean the reference to the past. This reference to the past is not involved in mere habit memory, e.g. in skating or in repeating a poem formerly learned. But it is involved in recollection of a past incident. We do not, in this case, merely repeat what we did before: then, we felt the incident as present, but now we feel it as past. This is shown in the use of the past tense. We say to ourselves at the time 'I *am having* a good dinner', but next day we say 'I *did have* a good dinner'. Thus we do not, like a rat in a maze, repeat our previous performance: we alter the verbal formula. Why do we do so? What constitutes this reference of a recollection to the past[1]?

Let us take up the question first from the point of view of sensitivity. The stimulus to a recollection is, no doubt, always something in the present, but our reaction (or part of it) is more intimately related to a certain past event than to the present stimulus. This, in itself, can be paralleled in inanimate objects, for example, in a gramophone record. It is not the *likeness* of our reaction to that called forth on a former occasion that concerns us at the moment; it is its *un-likeness*, in the fact that now we have the feeling of pastness, which we did not have originally. You cannot sing into a dictaphone 'I love you', and have it say five days hence 'I loved you last Wednesday'; yet that is what we do when we remember. I think, however, that this feature of memory is probably connected with a feature of reactions due to association when the association is cerebral: I think also that this is connected with the difference in quality that exists usually, though not always, between images and sensations. It would seem that, in such cases, the reaction aroused through association is usually different from that which would have been aroused directly, in certain definite ways. It is fainter, and has, when attended to, the sort of quality that makes us call it 'imaginary'. In a certain class of cases, we come to know that we can make it 'real' if we choose; this applies, e.g. to the tactual images produced by visible objects that we can touch. In such cases, the image is attached by us to the object, and its 'imaginary' character fails to be noticed. These are the cases in which the association is not due to some accident of our experience, but to a collocation which exists in nature. In other cases, however, we are perfectly aware, if we reflect, that the association depends upon some circumstance in our private lives. We may, for instance, have had a very interesting conversation at a certain spot, and always think of this conversation when we find ourselves in this place. But we know that the conversation does not actually take place again when we go back to where it happened. In such a case, we notice the intrinsic difference between the event as a sensible fact in the present and the event as

[1]On this subject, cf. Broad, *The Mind and its Place in Nature*, p. 264 ff., in his chapter on 'Memory'.

merely revived by association. I think this difference has to do with our feeling of pastness. The difference which we can directly observe is not, of course, between our present recollection and the past conversation, but between our present recollection and present sensible facts. This difference, combined with the inconsistency of our recollection with present facts if our recollection were placed in the present, is perhaps a cause of our referring memories to the past. But I offer this suggestion with hesitation; and, as we shall find when we have examined imagination, it cannot be the whole truth, though it may be part of it.

There are some facts that tend to support the above view. In dreams when our critical faculty is in abeyance, we may live past events over again under the impression that they are actually happening; the reference of recollections to the past must, therefore, be a matter involving a somewhat advanced type of mental activity. Conversely, we sometimes have the impression that what is happening now really happened in the past; this is a well-known and much discussed illusion. It happens especially when we are profoundly absorbed in some inward struggle or emotion, so that outer events only penetrate faintly. I suggest that, in these circumstances, the quality of sensations approximates to that of images, and that this is the source of the illusion.

If this suggestion is right, the feeling of pastness is really complex. Something is suggested by association, but is recognisably different from a present sensible occurrence. We therefore do not suppose that this something is happening now; and we may be confirmed in this by the fact that it is inconsistent with something that is happening now. We may then either refer the something to the past, in which case we have a recollection, though not necessarily a correct one; or we may regard the something as purely imaginary, in which case we have what we regard as pure imagination. It remains to inquire why we do sometimes the one and sometimes the other, which brings us to the discussion of imagination. I think we shall find that memory is more fundamental than imagination, and that the latter consists merely of memories of different dates assembled together. But to support this theory will demand first an analysis of imagination and then, in the light of this analysis, an attempt to give further precision to our theory of memory.

Imagination is not, as the word might suggest, essentially connected with images. No doubt images are often, even usually, present when we imagine, but they need not be. A man can improvise on the piano without first having images of the music he is going to make; a poet might write down a poem without first making it up in his head. In talking, words suggest other words, and a man with sufficient verbal associations may be successfully carried along by them for a considerable time. The art of talking without thinking is particularly necessary to public speakers, who must go on when once they are on their feet, and gradually acquire the habit of behaving in private as they do before an audience. Yet the statements they make must be admitted to be often imaginative. The essence of imagination, therefore, does not lie in images.

The essence of imagination, I should say, is the absence of belief together with a novel combination of known elements. In memory, when it is correct, the combination of elements is not novel; and whether correct or not, there is belief. I say that in imagination there is 'a novel combination of known elements', because, if nothing is novel, we have a case of memory, while if the elements, or any of them, are novel, we have a case of perception. This last I say because I accept Hume's principle that there is no 'idea' without an antecedent 'impression'. I do not mean that this is to be applied in a blind and pedantic manner, where abstract ideas are concerned. I should not maintain that no one can have an idea of liberty until he has seen the Statue of Liberty. The principle applies rather to the realm of images. I certainly do not think that, in an image, there can be any element which does not resemble some element in a previous perception, in the distinctive manner of images.

Hume made himself an unnecessary difficulty in regard to the theory that images 'copy' impressions. He asked the question: Suppose a man has seen all the different shades of colour that go to make up the spectrum, except just one shade. To put the thing in modern language, suppose he has never seen light of a certain small range of wave-lengths, but has seen light of all other wave-lengths. Will he be able to form an image of the shade he has never seen? Hume thinks he will, although this contradicts the principle. I should say that images are always more or less vague copies of impressions, so that an image might be regarded as a copy of any one of a number of different impressions of slightly different shades. In order to get a test case for Hume's question, we should have to suppose that there was a broad band of the spectrum that the man had never seen – say the whole of the yellow. He would then, one may suppose, be able to form images which, owing to vagueness, might be applicable to orange–yellow, and others applicable to green–yellow, but none applicable to a yellow midway between orange and green. This is an example of an unreal puzzle manufactured by forgetting vagueness. It is analogous to the following profound problem: A man formerly hairy is now bald; he lost his hairs one by one; therefore there must have been just one hair that made the difference, so that while he had it he was not bald but when he lost it he was. Of course 'baldness' is a vague conception; and so is 'copying', when we are speaking of the way in which images copy prototypes.

What causes us, in imagination, to put elements together in a new way? Let us think first of concrete instances. You read that a ship has gone down on a route by which you have lately travelled; very little imagination is needed to generate the thought 'I might have gone down'. What happens here is obvious: the route is associated both with yourself and with shipwreck, and you merely eliminate the middle term. Literary ability is largely an extension of the practice of which the above is a very humble example. Take, say:

> And all our yesterdays have lighted fools
> The way to dusty death. Out, out, brief candle!
> Life's but a walking shadow, a poor player
> Who struts and frets his hour upon the stage,
> And then is heard no more. It is a tale
> Told by an idiot, full of sound and fury
> Signifying nothing.

I do not pretend to explain all the associations which led Shakespeare to think of these lines, but some few are obvious. 'Dusty death' is suggested by Genesis iii. 19: 'Dust thou art, and unto dust shalt thou return'. Having spoken of 'lighting fools the way', it is natural to think of a 'candle', and thence of a 'walking shadow' being lighted by the candle along the way. From shadows to players was a well-established association in Shakespeare's mind; thus in *Midsummer Night's Dream* he says of players: 'The best in this kind are but shadows, and the worst are no worse, if imagination amend them'. From a 'poor player' to a 'tale told by an idiot' is no very difficult transition for a theatre-manager; and 'sound and fury' no doubt often formed part of the tales to which he had to listen in spite of their 'signifying nothing'. If we knew more about Shakespeare, we could explain more of him in this sort of way.

Thus exceptional imaginative gifts appear to depend mainly upon associations that are unusual and have an emotional value owing to the fact that there is a certain uniform emotional tone about them. Many adjectives are suitable to death: in a mood quite different from Macbeth's, it may be called 'noble, puissant and mighty'. A Chancellor of the Exchequer, thinking of the Death Duties, might feel inclined to speak of 'lucrative death'; nevertheless he would not, like Vaughan, speak of 'dear, beauteous death'. Shakespeare also would not have spoken of death in such terms, for his view of it was pagan; he speaks of 'that churl death'. So a man's verbal associations may afford a key to his emotional reactions, for often what connects two words in his mind is the fact that they rouse similar emotions.

The absence of belief that accompanies imagination is a somewhat sophisticated product; it fails in sleep and in strong emotional excitement. Children invent terrors for fun, and then begin to believe in them. The state of entertaining an idea without believing it is one involving some tension, which demands a certain level of intellectual development. It may be assumed that imagination, at first, always involved belief, as it still does in dreams. I am not concerned at the moment to define 'belief', but a criterion is influence on action. If I say 'Suppose there were a tiger outside your front door', you will remain calm; but if I say, with such a manner as to command belief, 'There is a tiger outside your front door', you will stay at home, even if it involves missing your train to the office. This illustrates what I mean when I say that imagination, in its developed form, involves absence of belief. But this is not true of its primitive forms. And even a civilised adult, passing through a churchyard on a dark night, may feel fear if his imagination turns in the direction of ghosts.

When imagination passes into belief, it does not, as a rule, become a belief about the past. Generally we place the imagined object in the present, but not where it would be perceptible to our senses. If we place it in the past, it is because the past has some great emotional significance for us. If a person we love has been in great danger, and we do not know whether he has come through safely, imagination of his death may lead us to believe that he has been killed. And often imagination leads us to believe that something is going to happen. What is common to all such cases is the emotional interest: this first causes us to imagine an event, and then leads us to think that it has happened, is happening, or will happen, according to the circumstances. Hope and fear have this effect equally; wish-fulfilment and dread-fulfilment are equally sources of dreams and day-dreams. A great many beliefs have a source of this kind. But, in spite of psycho-analysis, there are a great many that have a more rational foundation. I believe that Columbus first crossed the ocean in 1492, though 1491 or 1493 would have suited me just as well. I cannot discover that there is any emotional element in this belief, or in the belief that Semipalatinsk is in Central Asia. The view that all our beliefs are irrational is perhaps somewhat overdone nowadays, though it is far more nearly true than the views that it has displaced.

We must now return to the subject of memory. Memory proper does not, like imagination, involve a re-arrangement of elements derived from past experience; on the contrary, it should restore such elements in the pattern in which they occurred. This is the vital difference between memory and imagination; belief, even belief involving reference to the past, may, as we have seen, be present in what is really imagination though it may not seem to be so to the person concerned. That being so, we still have to consider what constitutes the reference to the past, since the view tentatively suggested before we had considered imagination turns out to be inadequate.

There is one possible view, suggested, though not definitely adopted, by Dr. Broad in his chapter on 'Memory' already referred to. According to this view, we have to start from temporal succession as perceived within what is called the 'specious present', i.e. a short period of time such that the events that occur throughout it can be perceived together. (I shall return to this subject presently.) For example, you can see a quick movement as a whole; you are not merely aware that the object was first in one place and then in another. You can see the movement of the second-hand of a watch, but not of the hour-hand or minute-hand. When you see a movement in this sense, you are aware that one part of it is earlier than another. Thus you acquire the idea 'earlier', and you can mean by 'past' 'earlier than this', where 'this' is what is actually happening. This is a logically possible theory, but it seems nevertheless somewhat difficult to believe. I do not know, however, of any easier theory, and I shall therefore adopt it provisionally while waiting for something better.

For the understanding of memory, it is a help to consider the links connecting its most developed forms with other occurrences of a less complex kind. True recollection comes at the end of a series of stages. I shall distinguish five stages on the way, so that recollection becomes the sixth in gradual progress. The stages are as follows:

1. *Images* – As we have seen, images, at any rate in their simpler parts, in fact copy past sensations more or less vaguely, even when they are not known to do so. Images are 'mnemic' phenomena, in the

sense that they are called up by stimuli formerly associated with their prototypes, so that their occurrence is a result of past experience according to the law of association. But obviously an image which in fact copies a past occurrence does not constitute a recollection unless it is *felt* to be a copy.

2. *Familiarity* – Images and perceptions may come to us, and so may words or other bodily movements, with more or less of the feeling we call 'familiarity'. When you recall a tune that you have heard before, either by images or by actually singing it, part of what comes to you may feel familiar, part unfamiliar. This may lead you to judge that you have remembered the familiar part rightly and the unfamiliar part wrongly, but this judgment belongs to a later stage.

3. *Habit-Memory* – We have already discussed this in Chapter 6. People say they remember a poem if they can repeat it correctly. But this does not necessarily involve any recollection of a past occurrence; you may have quite forgotten when and where you read the poem. This sort of memory is mere habit, and is essentially like knowing how to walk although you cannot remember learning to walk. This does not deserve to be called memory in the strict sense.

4. *Recognition* – This has two forms. (*a*) When you see a dog, you can say to yourself 'there is a dog', without recalling any case in which you have seen a dog before, and even without reflecting that there have been such cases. This involves no knowledge about the past; essentially it is only an associative habit. (*b*) You may know 'I saw this before', though you do not know when or where, and cannot recollect the previous occurrence in any way. In such a case there is knowledge about the past, but it is very slight. When you judge: 'I saw *this* before', the word 'this' must be used vaguely, because you did not see exactly what you see now, but only something very like this. Thus all that you are really knowing is that, on some past occasion, you saw something very like what you are seeing now. This is about the minimum of knowledge about the past that actually occurs.

5. *Immediate Memory* – I come now to a region intermediate between sensation and true memory, the region of what is sometimes called 'immediate memory'. When a sense-organ is stimulated, it does not, on the cessation of the stimulus, return at once to its unstimulated condition; it goes on (so to speak) vibrating, like a piano-string, for a short time. For example, when you see a flash of lightning, your sensation, brief as it is, lasts much longer than the lightning as a physical occurrence. There is a period during which a sensation is fading: it is then called an 'acoleuthic' sensation. It is owing to this

fact that you can see a movement as a whole. As observed before, you cannot see the minute-hand of a watch moving, but you can see the second-hand moving. That is because it is in several appreciably different places within the short time that is required for one visual sensation to fade, so that you do actually, at one moment, see it in several places. The fading sensations, however, feel different from those that are fresh, and thus the various positions which are all sensibly present are placed in a series by the degree of fading, and you acquire the perception of movement as a process. Exactly the same considerations apply to hearing a spoken sentence.

Thus not only an instant, but a short finite time, is sensibly present to you at any moment. This short finite time is called the 'specious present'. By the felt degree of fading, you can distinguish earlier and later in the specious present, and thus experience temporal succession without the need of true memory. If you see me quickly move my arm from left to right, you have an experience which is quite different from what you would have if you now saw it at the right and remembered that a little while ago you saw it at the left. The difference is that, in the quick movement, the whole falls within the specious present, so that the entire process is sensible. The knowledge of something as in the immediate past, though still sensible, is called 'immediate memory'. It has great importance in connection with our apprehension of temporal processes, but cannot count as a form of true memory.

6. *True Recollection* – We will suppose, for the sake of definiteness, that I am remembering what I had for breakfast this morning. There are two questions which we must ask about this occurrence: (a) What is happening now when I recollect? (b) What is the relation of the present happening to the event remembered? (a) As to what is happening now, my recollection may involve either images or words; in the latter case, the words themselves may be merely imagined. I will take the case in which there are images without words, which must be the more primitive, since we cannot suppose that memory would be impossible without words.

The first point is one which seems so obvious that I should be ashamed to mention it, but for the fact that many distinguished philosophers think otherwise. The point is this: whatever may be happening now, the event remembered is *not* happening. Memory is often spoken of as if it involved the actual persistence of the past which is remembered; Bergson, e.g. speaks of the interpenetration of the present by the past. This is mere mythology; the event which occurs when I remember is quite different from the event remembered. People who are starving can remember their last meal, but the recollection does not appease their hunger. There is no mystic survival of the past when we remember; merely a new event having a certain relation to the old one. What this relation is, we shall consider presently.

It is quite clear that images are not enough to constitute recollection, even when they are accurate copies of a past occurrence. One may, in a dream, live over again a past experience; while one is dreaming, one does not seem to be recalling a previous occurrence, but living through a fresh experience. We cannot be said to be remembering, in the strict sense, unless we have a belief referring to the past. Images which, like those in dreams, feel as if they were sensations, do not constitute recollection. There must be some feeling which makes us refer the images to a past prototype. Perhaps familiarity is enough to cause us to do so. And perhaps this also explains the experience of trying to remember something and feeling that we are not remembering it right. Parts of a complex image may feel more familiar than other parts, and we then feel more confidence in the correctness of the familiar parts than in that of the others. The conviction that the image we are forming of a past event is wrong might seem to imply that we must be knowing the past otherwise than by images, but I do not think this conclusion is really warranted, since degrees of familiarity in images suffice to explain this experience.

(*b*) What is the relation of the present happening to the event remembered? If we recollect correctly, the several images will have that kind of resemblance of quality which images can have to their prototypes, and their structure and relations will be identical with those of their prototypes. Suppose, for instance, you want to remember whether, in a certain room, the window is to the right or left of the door as viewed from the fireplace. You can observe your image of the room, consisting (*inter alia*) of an image of the door and an image of the window standing (if your recollection is correct) in the same relation as when you are actually seeing the room. Memory will consist in attaching to this complex image the sort of belief that refers to the past; and the correctness of memory consists of similarity of quality and identity of structure between the complex image and a previous perception.

As for the trustworthiness of memory, there are two things to be said. Taken as a whole, memory is one of the independent sources of our knowledge; that is to say, there is no way of arriving at the things we know through memory by any argument wholly derived from things known otherwise. But no single memory is obliged to stand alone, because it fits, or does not fit, into a system of knowledge about the past based upon the sum-total of memories. When what is remembered is a perception by one or more of the public senses, other people may corroborate it. Even when it is private, it may be confirmed by other evidence. You may remember that you had a toothache yesterday, and that you saw the dentist today; the latter fact may be confirmed by an entry in your diary. All these make a consistent whole, and each increases the likelihood of the other. Thus we can test the truth of any particular recollection, though not of memory as a whole. To say that we cannot test the truth of memory as a whole is not to give a reason for doubting it, but merely to say that it is an independent source of knowledge, not wholly replaceable by other sources. We know that our memory is fallible, but we have reason to distrust it on the whole after sufficient care in verification has been taken.

The causation of particular acts of recollection seems to be wholly associative. Something in the present is very like something in the past, and calls up the context of the past occurrence in the shape of images or words; when attention falls upon this context, we believe that it occurred in the past, not as mere images, and we then have an act of recollection.

There are many difficult problems connected with memory which I have not discussed, because they have an interest which is more purely psychological than philosophical. It is memory as a source of knowledge that specially concerns the philosopher.

Chapter 19

The Introspective Analysis of Perception

We have considered perception already from the behaviourist standpoint, and also from that of physics. In the present chapter we are to consider if from the standpoint of self-observation, with a view to discovering as much as we can about the intrinsic character of the event in us when we perceive. I shall begin with certain traditional doctrines as to mental events, and shall thence pass to the doctrines that I wish to advocate.

The words 'mind' and 'matter' are used glibly, both by ordinary people and by philosophers, without any adequate attempt at definition. Philosophers are much to blame for this. My own feeling is that there is not a sharp line, but a difference of degree; an oyster is less mental than a man, but not wholly un-mental. And I think 'mental' is a character, like 'harmonious' or 'discordant', that cannot belong to a single entity in its own right, but only to a system of entities. But before defending this view, I wish to spend some time on the theories that have been current in the past.

Traditionally, there are two ways of becoming aware that something exists, one by the senses, the other by what is called 'introspection', or what Kant called the 'inner sense'. By means of introspection, it is maintained, we become aware of occurrences quite different in kind from those perceived through the outer senses. Occurrences known through introspection are traditionally called 'mental' and so are any other occurrences which intrinsically resemble them.

Mental occurrences are traditionally of three main types, called knowing, willing, and feeling. 'Feeling', in this connection, means pleasure and unpleasure – we do not say 'pleasure and pain', because 'pain' is an ambiguous word: it may stand for a painful sensation, as when you say 'I have a pain in my tooth', or it may stand for the unpleasant character of the sensation. Roughly, pleasure is a quality which makes you want an experience to continue, and unpleasure is the opposite quality which makes you want an experience to stop.

However, I am not concerned to enlarge upon feeling at present.

As for the other two kinds of mental occurrence, 'knowing' and 'willing' are recognised as too narrow to describe what is meant. Philosophers wish to include not only knowledge but also error, and not only the sort of knowledge that is expressed in beliefs but also the sort that occurs in perception. The word 'cognition' or 'cognitive state' is used to cover everything that could possibly be described as either knowledge or error; perception is *prima facie* included, but pure sensation is more debatable.

'Willing', again, is too narrow a term. A term is required which will include desire and aversion, and generally those states of mind which lead up to action. These are all included under the head of 'conation', a technical term invented for this special purpose.

Cognition and conation both have, in the orthodox theory, the property of being directed to an *object*. What you perceive or believe, what you desire or will, is something different from your state of mind. To take instances: you remember a past event, but your remembering occurs now; therefore your remembering is a different occurrence from what you remember. You will to move your arm, but the movement is a physical occurrence, and therefore obviously different from your volition. Many psychologists have taken this relation to an object as the essential characteristic of mind – notably the two Austrians Brentano and Meinong. Sometimes feeling also is regarded as having an object: it is held that we are pleased or displeased *at* something. This view, however, has never won general acceptance, whereas the view that cognition and conation are directed to objects may be regarded as orthodox.

It is undeniable that this characteristic of being directed to objects is, in some sense, a property of cognition and conation, but there is room for great difference of opinion as to the proper analysis of the property. I think we cannot hope to understand the word 'mental' until we have undertaken this analysis, and I shall therefore proceed to address myself to it. I shall confine myself to cognition, which is more important for our present purposes than conation.

As regards cognition, though philosophers have disagreed widely, I think that, until recently, most would have assented to at least the following paragraph:

Cognition is of various sorts. Take, as important kinds, perception, memory, conception, and beliefs involving concepts. Perception is the ordinary awareness of sensible objects: seeing a table, hearing a piano, and so on. Memory is awareness of a past occurrence, when this awareness is direct, not inferred or derived from testimony. Conception is more difficult to characterise. One may say, as a way of pointing out what is intended, that we 'conceive' whenever we understand the meaning of an abstract word, or think of that which is in fact the meaning of the word. If you see a white patch of snow, or recall it by means of images, you do not have a concept; but if you think about whiteness, you have a concept. Similarly if, after seeing a number of coins, you think about roundness as a common characteristic of all of them, you have a concept. The object of your thought, in such a case, is a *universal* or a Platonic idea. Every sentence must contain at least one word expressing a concept, and therefore every belief that can be expressed in words contains concepts.

Each of these kinds of cognitive attitude involves its own problems. In the present chapter we are concerned with perception. This has to be treated both introspectively and causally; it is the introspective treatment that we have now to undertake.

When you have the experience called 'seeing a table', there is a certain amount of difference between your unreflecting judgment and what careful examination reveals as to the nature of your experience. You judge that the table is rectangular, but the patch of colour in your visual field is not a rectangle; when you learn to draw, you have to draw the table as it really seems and not as it seems to seem. You have images of sensations of touch; if you were to try to touch the table and it turned out to be an optical illusion, you would get a violent shock of surprise. You have also expectations of a certain degree of permanence and weight. If you went to lift the table, you would find your muscles quite wrongly adjusted if the table were much lighter than it looked. All these elements must be included in the perception, though not in the sensation.

'Sensation', as opposed to perception, is more or less hypothetical. It is supposed to be the core, in the perception, which is solely due to the stimulus and the sense-organ, not to past experience. When you judge that the table is rectangular, it is past experience that enables and compels you to do so; if you had been born blind and just operated upon, you could not make this judgment. Nor would you have expectations of hardness, etc. But none of this can be discovered by introspection. From an introspective point of view, the elements due to past experience are largely indistinguishable from those due to the stimulus alone. One supposes that past experience modifies the brain, and thereby modifies the mental occurrence due to the stimulus. The notion of sensation as opposed to perception belongs, therefore, to the causal study of perception, not to the introspective study.

There is, however, a distinction to be made here. You can discover by mere self-observation that visual objects are accompanied by expectations or images of touch; and similarly if you touch an object in the dark you will probably be led to form some visual image of it. Here you can arrive at a certain degree of analysis of your perception through the fact that images, as a rule, *feel* different from the immediate results of a sensory stimulus. On the other hand, no amount of introspection alone will reveal such things as the blind spot. The filling in of a sensation by elements belonging to the same sense is much less discoverable by introspection than the filling in by associated images belonging to other senses. Thus although by introspection alone we could discover *part* of the influence of experience on perception, there is another part which we cannot discover in this way.

Remaining in the introspective attitude, it is evident that the contents of our minds at any given moment are very complex. Throughout our normal waking life we are always seeing, hearing, and touching, sometimes smelling and tasting, always having various bodily sensations, always feeling pleasant or unpleasant feelings (usually both), always having desires or aversions. We are not normally aware of all these items, but we can become aware of any of them by turning our attention in the right direction. I am not at present discussing 'unconscious mental states', because they, obviously, can only be known causally, and we are now considering what can be known introspectively. There may be any number of perceptions that cannot be known by introspection; the point for us, at the moment, is that those that can be discovered by introspection at any one time are many and various.

I do not wish, just now, to discuss the nature of attention; I wish only to point out that it enables us to take the first steps in abstraction. Out of the whole multiplicity of objects of sense; it enables us to single out a small selection, which is an indispensable preliminary to abstraction. For example, attention will enable us to discriminate a coloured pattern which we are seeing, and to separate it from the other things we see and from images and other objects of sense and thoughts which may exist simultaneously. For the sake of simplicity, let us suppose that we discriminate a black and white pattern in the form of a triangle. Within this pattern we can further discriminate sides and angles and an inside and outside – of course the sides are not mathematical lines nor the angles mathematical points.

We now come to a question of very great importance, upon which our views of the relations of mind and matter largely depend. The question is this:

What difference is there between the propositions 'There is a triangle' and 'I see a triangle'?

Both these statements seem as certain as any statement can be – at least if rightly interpreted. As always happens in such cases, we are quite certain of something, but not quite certain what it is that we are certain of. I want to ask whether this something that we are certain of is really different in the above two statements, or whether the difference between them is only as to surroundings of which we are not certain. Most philosophers hold that there is a difference in what we are certain of; Mach, James, Dewey, the American realists, and I hold that the difference is in the uncertain context. Let us examine this question.

The *suggestions* of the two statements 'I see a triangle' and 'There is a triangle' are obviously different. The first states an event in my life, and suggests its possible effects upon me. The second aims at stating an event in the world, supposed to be equally discoverable by other people. You might say 'There is a triangle' if you had seen it a moment ago but now had your eyes shut; in this case you would not say 'I see a triangle'. On the other hand, one sometimes, under the influence of indigestion or fatigue, sees little black dots floating in the air; in such circumstances you would say 'I see a black dot', but not 'There is a black dot'. This illustration shows that when you say 'There is a black dot' you are making a stronger assertion than when you say 'I see a black dot'. In the other case, when you say 'There is a triangle' because you saw it a moment ago, though not now, you have three stages: First, memory assures you of the proposition 'I saw a triangle', and then you pass on to 'There was a triangle', and then, further, to 'There is a triangle, because nothing can have happened to destroy it so quickly'. Here we have obviously passed far beyond the region of immediate certainty.

It seems clear, therefore, that, of our two statements, the one which comes nearest to expressing the fact of which we are immediately certain is 'I see a triangle', because the other makes inferences to something public, and thus goes beyond the bare datum. This is on the assumption that we should not say 'There is a black dot' when we see a black dot which we attribute to eye-trouble and therefore suppose that no one else can see. Let us therefore concentrate upon 'I see a triangle', and ask ourselves whether the whole of this, or only part, can be accepted as a primitive certainty.

A moment's reflection shows that both 'I' and 'see' are words which take us beyond what the momentary event reveals. Take 'I' to begin with. This is a word whose meaning evidently depends upon memory and expectation. 'I' means the person who had certain remembered experiences and is expected to have certain future experiences. We might say 'I see a triangle now and I saw a square a moment ago'. The word 'I' has exactly the same meaning in its two occurrences in this sentence, and therefore evidently has a meaning dependent upon memory. Now it is our object to arrive at the contribution to your knowledge which is made by seeing the triangle at the moment. Therefore, since the word 'I' takes you beyond this contribution, we must cut it out if we want to find a correct verbal expression for what is added to our knowledge by seeing the triangle. We will say 'A triangle is being seen'. This is at any rate one step nearer to what we are seeking.

But now we must deal with the word 'seen'. As ordinarily used, this is a causal word, suggesting something dependent upon the eyes. In this sense, it obviously involves a mass of previous experience; a new-born baby does not know that what it sees depends upon its eyes. However, we could eliminate this. Obviously all objects of sight have a common quality, which no objects of touch or hearing have; a visual object is different from an auditory object, and so on. Therefore instead of saying 'A triangle is being seen', we should say 'There is a visual triangle'. Of course the meanings of the words 'visual' and 'triangle' can only be learnt by experience, but they are not *logically* dependent upon experience. A being could be imagined which would know the words at birth; such a being could express its datum in the words 'There is a visual triangle'. In any case, the problems remaining belong to the study of concepts; we will therefore ignore them at present.

Now in English the words 'there is' are ambiguous. When I used them before, saying 'There is a triangle', I meant them in the sense of *voilà* or *da ist*. Now I mean them in the sense of *il y a* or *es giebt*. One might express what is meant by saying 'A visual triangle exists, but the word 'exist' has all sorts of metaphysical connotations that I wish to avoid. Perhaps it is best to say 'occurs'.

We have now arrived at something which is just as true when your perception is illusory as when it is correct. If you say 'A visual black dot is occurring', you are speaking the truth, if there is one in your field of vision. We have eliminated the suggestion that others could see it, or that it could be touched, or that it is composed of matter in the sense of physics. All these suggestions are present when one says, in ordinary conversation, 'There is a black dot'; they are intended to be eliminated by the addition of the word 'visual' and the substitution of 'is occurring' for 'there is'. By these means we have arrived at what is indubitable and intrinsic in the addition to your knowledge derived from a visual datum.

We must now ask ourselves once more: Is there still a distinction, within what is immediate and intrinsic, between the occurrence of a visual datum and the cognition of it? Can we say, on the basis of immediate experience, not only 'A visual black dot occurs', but also 'A visual black dot is cognised'? My feeling is that we cannot. When we say that it is cognised, we seem to me to mean that it is part of an experience, that is to say, that it can be remembered, or can modify our habits, or, generally, can have what are called 'mnemic' effects. All this takes us beyond the immediate experience into the realm of its causal relations. I see no reason to think that there is any duality of subject and object in the occurrence itself, or that it can properly be described as a case of 'knowledge'. It gives rise to knowledge, through memory, and through conscious or unconscious inferences to the common correlates of such data. But in itself it is not knowledge, and has no duality. The datum is a datum equally for physics and for psychology; it is a meeting point of the two. It is neither mental nor physical, just as a single name is neither in alphabetical order nor in order of precedence; but it is part of the raw material of both the mental and the physical worlds. This is the theory which is called 'neutral monism', and is the one that I believe to be true.

Chapter 20

Consciousness?

Twenty-three years have elapsed since William James startled the world with his article entitled 'Does "consciousness" exist?' In this article, reprinted in the volume called *Essays in Radical Empiricism,* he set out the view that 'there is only one primal stuff or material in the world', and that the word 'consciousness' stands for a function, not an entity. He holds that there are 'thoughts', which perform the function of 'knowing', but that thoughts are not made of any different 'stuff' from that of which material objects are made. He thus laid the foundations for what is called 'neutral monism', a view advocated by most American realists. This is the view advocated in the present volume. In this chapter, we have to ask ourselves whether there is anything that we can call 'consciousness' in any sense involving a peculiar kind of stuff, or whether we can agree with William James that there is no 'inner duplicity' in the stuff of the world as we know it, and that the separation of it into knowing and what is known does not represent a fundamental dualism.

There are two very different meanings attached to the word 'consciousness' by those who use it. On the one hand, we are said to be 'conscious of' something; in this sense, 'consciousness' is a relation. On the other hand, 'consciousness' may be regarded as a quality of mental occurrences, not consisting in their relation to other things. Let us take the first view first, since, in discussing it, we shall find reasons for rejecting the second view.

What is the relation we call being 'conscious of' something? Take the difference between a person awake and a person asleep. The former reacts to all kinds of stimuli to which the latter does not react; we therefore say that the latter is not 'conscious of' what is happening in his neighbourhood. But even if the sleeper does react in a fashion, for example, by turning away from the light, such a reaction does not fall within what is commonly regarded as 'knowledge' or 'awareness'; we should say that the sleeper turned over 'unconsciously'. If he wakes up sufficiently to speak intelligently, for instance to address the disturber by name, we consider him 'conscious'. So we do if we find that he remembers the incident next morning. But common sense does not regard any and every bodily movement in response to a stimulus as evidence of 'consciousness'. There is no doubt, I think, that common sense regards certain kinds of response as evidence of some 'mental' process caused by the stimulus, and regards the 'consciousness' as residing in the inferred 'mental' occurrence.

Sometimes, however, as in hypnotism and sleep-walking, people refuse to admit 'consciousness' even where many of the usual marks of it are present. For this there are certain reasons. One of them is subsequent lack of memory; another is lack of intelligence in what is being done. If you offer a hypnotised patient a drink of ink, telling him it is port wine, and he drinks it up with every sign of enjoyment, you say that he is not 'conscious', because he does not react normally to the nasty taste. It would seem better, however, to say that he is conscious of the hypnotist and what he commands, though not of other things of which he would be conscious in a normal condition. And lack of subsequent memory is a very difficult criterion, since we normally forget many things that have happened to us, and the sleep-walker's forgetting is only unusually complete. This is obviously a matter of degree. Take next morning's memories in the case of a man who was drunk overnight. They become more and more vague as he reviews the later hours of the evening, but there is no sharp line where they cease abruptly. Thus, if memory is a test, consciousness must be a matter of degree. I think that here, again, common sense regards a certain amount of memory as necessary evidence to prove that there were 'mental' processes at the time of the acts in question, acts in sleep being regarded as not involving 'mind', and other acts in certain abnormal conditions being supposed to resemble those of sleep in this respect.

It follows that, if we are to find out what is commonly meant by 'consciousness', we must ask ourselves what is meant by a 'mental' occurrence. Not every mental occurrence, however, is in question. The only kinds concerned are those which seem to have relation to an 'object'. A feeling of pleasant drowsiness would commonly count as 'mental', but does not involve 'consciousness' of an 'object'. It is this supposed peculiar relation to an 'object' that we have to examine.

We may take, as the best example, an ordinary act of perception. I see, let us say, a table, and I am convinced that the table is outside me, whereas my seeing of it is a 'mental' occurrence, which is inside me. In such a case I am 'conscious' of the table – so at least common sense would say. And since I cannot see without seeing something, this relation to an 'object' is of the very essence of seeing. The same essential relation to an 'object', it would be said, is characteristic of every kind of consciousness.

But when we begin to consider this view more closely, all sorts of difficulties arise. We have already seen that, on grounds derived from physics, the table itself, as a physical thing, cannot be regarded as the object of our perception, if the object is something essential to the existence of the perception. In suitable circumstances, we shall have the same perception although there is no table. In fact, there is no event outside the brain which *must* exist whenever we 'see a table'. It seems preposterous to say that when we think we see a table we really see a motion in our own brain. Hence we are led to the conclusion that the 'object' which is essential to the existence of an act of perception is just as 'mental' as the perceiving. In fact, so this theory runs, the mental occurrence called 'perceiving' is one which contains within itself the relation of perceiver and perceived, both sides of the relation being equally 'mental'.

Now, however, there seems no longer any reason to suppose that there is any essentially relational character about what occurs in us when we perceive. The original reason for thinking so was the naïvely realistic view that we see the actual table. If what we see is as mental as our seeing, why distinguish between the two? The coloured pattern that we see is not really 'out there', as we had supposed; it is in our heads, if we are speaking of physical space. True, more than a coloured pattern occurs when we 'see a table'. There are tactual expectations or images: there is probably belief in an external object; and afterwards there may be memory or other 'mnemic' effects. All this may be taken as representing what the above theory took to be the 'subject' side of an act of perception, while the coloured pattern is what the theory took to be the 'object' side. But both sides are on a level as regards being 'mental'. And the relation between the two sides is not of such a kind that the existence of the one logically demands the existence of the other; on the contrary, the relation between the two sides is causal, being dependent upon experience and the law of association.

If this is correct, what really happens when, as common sense would say, we are conscious of a table, is more or less as follows. First there is a physical process external to the body, producing a stimulus to the eye which occurs rarely (not never) in the absence of an actual physical table. Then there is a process in the eye, nerves, and brain, and finally there is a coloured pattern. This coloured pattern, by the law of association, gives rise to tactual and other expectations and images; also, perhaps, to memories and other habits. But everything in this whole series consists of a causally continuous chain of events in space–time, and we have no reason to assert that the events in us are so very different from the events outside us – as to this, we must remain ignorant, since the outside events are only known as to their abstract mathematical characteristics, which do not show whether these events are like 'thoughts' or unlike them.

It follows that 'consciousness' cannot be defined either as a peculiar kind of relation or as an intrinsic character belonging to certain events and not to others. 'Mental' events are not essentially relational, and we do not know enough of the intrinsic character of events outside us to say whether it does or does not differ from that of 'mental' events. But what makes us call a certain class of events 'mental' and distinguish them from other events is the combination of sensitivity with associative reproduction. The more markedly this combination exists, the more 'mental' are the events concerned; thus mentality is a matter of degree.

There is, however, a further point which must be discussed in this connection, and that is 'self-consciousness', or awareness of our own 'mental' events. We already had occasion to touch on this in Chapter 16 in connection with Descartes' 'I think, therefore I am'. But I want to discuss the question afresh in connection with 'consciousness'.

When the plain man 'sees a table' in the presence of a philosopher, the plain man can be driven, by the arguments we have repeatedly brought forward, to admit that he cannot have complete certainty as to anything outside himself. But if he does not lose his head or his temper, he will remain certain that there is a coloured pattern, which may be in him, but indubitably exists. No argument from logic or physics even tends to show that he is mistaken in this; therefore there is no reason why he should surrender his conviction. The argument about knowledge in Chapter 8, showed that, accepting the usual views of physicists as to causal laws, our knowledge becomes more certain as the causal chain from object to reaction is shortened, and can only be quite certain when the two are in the same place in space–time, or at least contiguous. Thus we should expect that the highest grade of certainty would belong to knowledge as to what happens in our own heads. And this is exactly what we have when we are aware of our own 'mental' events, such as the existence of a coloured pattern when we thought we were seeing a table.

We might, therefore, if we were anxious to preserve the word 'mental', define a 'mental' event as one that can be known with the highest grade of certainty, because, in physical space–time, the event and the knowing of it are contiguous. Thus 'mental' events will be certain of the events that occur in heads that have brains. They will not be *all* events that occur in brains, but only such as cause a reaction of the kind that can be called 'knowledge'.

There are, however, still a number of difficult questions, to which, as yet, a definitive answer cannot be given. When we 'know' a thought of our own, what happens? And do we know the thought in a more intimate way than we know anything else? Knowledge of external events, as we have seen, consists of a certain sensitivity to their presence, but not in having in or before our minds anything similar to them, except in certain abstract structural respects. Is knowledge of our own minds equally abstract and indirect? Or is it something more analogous to what we ordinarily imagine knowledge to be?

Take first the question: What happens when we 'know' a thought of our own? Taking the definition of 'knowing' that we adopted in Chapter 8, we shall say: We 'know' a thought of our own when an event in our brain causes a characteristic reaction which is present when the event occurs and not otherwise. In this sense, whenever we say, 'I see a table', we are knowing a thought, since an event in our brain is the only invariable antecedent of such a statement (assuming it to be made truthfully). We may *think* we are knowing a table, but this is an error.

Thus the difference between introspective and other knowledge is only in our intention and in the degree of certainty. When we say, 'I see a table', we may intend to know an external object, but if so we may be mistaken; we are, however, actually knowing the occurrence of a visual percept. When we describe the same occurrence in the words 'A certain coloured pattern is occurring', we have changed our intention and are much more certain of being right. Thus all that differentiates our reaction when it gives introspective knowledge from our reaction when it gives knowledge of another kind is the elimination of a possible source of error.

I come now to the question: Do we know our own thoughts in a more intimate way than we know anything else? This is a question to which it is difficult to give precision; it describes something that one *feels* to be a problem without being able to say exactly what the problem is. However, some things can be said which may serve to clear up our feelings, if not our ideas.

Suppose you are asked to repeat after a man whatever he says, as a test of your hearing. He says 'How do you do?' and you repeat 'How do you do?' This is your knowledge-reaction, and you hear yourself speaking. You can perceive that what you hear when you speak is closely similar to what you hear when the other man speaks. This makes you feel that your reaction reproduces accurately what you heard. Your knowledge-reaction, in this case, is the cause of an occurrence closely similar to the occurrence that you are knowing. Moreover, our inveterate naïve realism makes us think that what we said was what we heard while we were speaking. This is, of course, an illusion, since an elaborate chain of physical and physiological causation intervenes between speaking and hearing oneself speak; nevertheless, the illusion re-enforces our conviction that our knowledge, in such a case, is very intimate. And it is, in fact, as intimate as it can hope to be, when our knowledge-reaction reproduces the very event we are knowing, or at least an event extremely similar to it. This *may* be the case on other occasions, but we can only know, with any certainty, that it is the case when what is known is a percept. This accounts for the fact that our most indubitable and complete knowledge is concerning percepts, not concerning other mental events or events in the external world. Our reaction to a sound can be to make a similar sound, and if we are clever enough we can paint something very like what we see. But we cannot show our knowledge of a pleasure by creating for ourselves another very similar pleasure, nor of a desire by creating a similar desire. Thus percepts are known with more accuracy and certainty than anything else either in the outer world or in our own minds.

The conclusion we have reached in this chapter is that William James was right in his views on 'consciousness'. No mental occurrence has, in its own intrinsic nature, that sort of relational character that was implied in the opposition of subject and object, or of knower and known. Nevertheless we can distinguish 'mental' events from others, and our most indubitable knowledge is concerned with a certain class of mental events. We have arrived at this result by following out to its logical conclusion the behaviourist definition of knowledge which we gave in Chapter 8. We have had to modify considerably the point of view which originally led us to that definition, the modification having been forced upon us by the physical knowledge which, starting from a common-sense realism, has been gradually driven, through the causal theory of perception, to a view of cognition far more subjective than that from which physicists, like the rest of mankind, originally set out. But I do not see how there can be any escape from this development.

Chapter 21

Emotion, Desire, and Will

Hitherto, in our investigation of man from within, we have considered only the cognitive aspect, which is, in fact, the most important to philosophy. But now we must turn our attention to the other sides of human nature. If we treat them more briefly than the cognitive side, it is not because they are less important, but because their main importance is practical and our task is theoretical. Let us begin with the emotions.

The theory of the emotions has been radically transformed by the discovery of the part played by the ductless glands. Cannon's *Bodily Changes in Pain, Hunger, Fear and Rage* is a book whose teaching has come to be widely known, though not more so than its importance warrants. It appears that certain secretions from the glands into the blood are the essential physiological conditions of the emotions. Some people say that the physiological changes correlated with these secretions *are* the emotions. I think this view must be received with some caution. As every one knows, the adrenal glands secrete adrenin, which produces the bodily symptoms of fear or rage. On one occasion my dentist injected a considerable amount of this substance into my blood, in the course of administering a local anæsthetic. I turned pale and trembled, and my heart beat violently; the bodily symptoms of fear were present, as the books said they should be, but it was quite obvious to me that I was not actually feeling fear. I should have had the same bodily symptoms in the presence of a tyrant about to condemn me to death, but there would have been something extra which was absent when I was in the dentist's chair. What was different was the cognitive part: I did not feel fear because I knew there was nothing to be afraid of. In normal life, the adrenal glands are stimulated by the perception of an object which is frightful or enraging; thus there is already a cognitive element present. The fear or rage attaches itself to the object which has stimulated the glands, and the full emotion arises. But when adrenin is artificially administered, this cognitive element is absent, and the emotion in its entirety fails to arise. Probably if it were administered in sleep it would produce a dream of terror, in which the dreamer's imagination would supply an object for fear. The same thing might happen in waking life with animals or young children. But with an adult of average rationality, the knowledge that there is nothing to be afraid of inhibits the full development of the emotion. Fear and rage are both active emotions, demanding a certain kind of behaviour towards an object; when this behaviour is obviously not called for, it is impossible to feel either emotion fully.

There are, however, other emotions, such as melancholy, which do not demand an object. These, presumably, can be caused in their entirety by administering the proper secretions. A disordered liver may cause melancholy which is not relieved by knowledge of its source. The emotions which do not require an object are those which do not call for any appropriate line of action.

Emotions are subject to 'conditioning', so that the stimuli which call them out become more various as a result of experience. Dr. Watson has found only two original stimuli to fear in young infants, namely loud noises, and lack of support; but anything associated with either of these may become terrifying.

The separation of an emotional element in our integral reaction to a situation is more or less artificial. No doubt there is a definite physiological concomitant, namely stimulation of a gland; but fear, for example, involves a mode of action towards an object, for which mode of action the secretion of adrenin is helpful. There is, however, something in common among a number of occasions that have a given emotional tone; this may be seen from the fact that they are associated. When we are feeling some emotion strongly, we tend to think of other occasions when we have had similar feelings. Association by means of emotional similarity is a characteristic of a great deal of poetry. And this accounts for the fact that, if our blood is in a state usually associated with terror, we shall, if our critical faculty is in abeyance, be very likely to imagine some cause of fear so vividly as to believe that it is really present:

> In the night, imagining some fear,
> How easy is a bush supposed a bear.

But in a rational man, if he is not drunk or sleepy, other associations are too strong for this production of imaginary terrors. That is why it is possible to show the physical symptoms of fear under the influence of adrenin, without actually feeling the emotion.

The emotions are what makes life interesting, and what makes us feel it important. From this point of view, they are the most valuable element in human existence. But when, as in philosophy, we are trying to understand the world, they appear rather as a hindrance. They generate irrational opinions, since emotional associations seldom correspond with collocations in the external world. They cause us to view the universe in the mirror of our moods, as now bright, now dim, according to the state of the mirror. With the sole exception of curiosity, the emotions are on the whole a hindrance to the intellectual life, though the degree of vigour required for successful thinking is likely to be correlated with a considerable susceptibility to emotion. If I say little about the emotions in this book, it is not from underestimating their human importance, but solely because the task upon which we are engaged is theoretical rather than practical: to understand the world, not to change it. And if emotion determines the ends we shall pursue, knowledge is what gives us the power to realise them. Even from the practical point of view, the advancement of knowledge is more useful than anything else that lies within human power.

I come now to the subject of *desire,* which we considered from a behaviourist standpoint in Chapter 3. I want now to ask whether there is anything to be added from an introspective point of view.

Let us again remind ourselves that there is something of artificiality in isolating elements within the one process leading from stimulus to reaction. Whenever a stimulus produces a reaction, we may consider the reaction as the effect of the stimulus, or as the cause of further effects. The former is the natural way of viewing the reaction when we are concerned with knowledge; the latter is the natural way when we are concerned with desire and will. In desire, we wish to change something in ourselves or in our environment or both. The question is: What can we discover introspectively about desire?

I think that here, as in the case of knowledge, the purely behaviouristic account is more important causally than the introspective account, and applies over a much wider range. Desire as a characteristic of behaviour, as considered in Chapter 3, begins very low in the scale of evolution, and remains, even in human beings, the whole of what can be discovered in a large number of instances. The Freudian 'unconscious' desires give a formula which is useful as explaining causally a number of acts, but these desires do not exist as anything except ways of behaving. Some desires, on the other hand, are conscious and explicit. What, exactly, is added in these last that is not present in the others?

Let us take some stock instance, say, Demosthenes desiring to become a great orator. This was a desire of which he was conscious, and in accordance with which he deliberately moulded his actions. One may suppose, to begin with, a merely behaviouristic tendency to do such things as seemed likely to impress his companions. This is a practically universal characteristic of human nature, which is displayed naïvely by children. Then come attempts, just like those of rats in mazes, to reach the goal; wrong turnings, leading to derision; right turnings, leading to a brief nibble at the cheese of admiration. Self-observation, still of a behaviourist kind, may lead to the formula: I want to be admired. At this point the desire has become 'conscious'. When this point has been reached, knowledge can be brought to bear on the problem of achieving the desired end. By association, the means come to be desired also. And so Demosthenes arrives at the decision to subject himself to a difficult training as an orator, since this seems the best way of achieving his end. The whole development is closely analogous to that of explicit knowledge out of mere sensitivity; it is, indeed, part of the very same evolution. We cannot, in our integral reaction to a situation, separate out one event as knowledge and another as desire; both knowledge and desire are features which characterise the reaction, but do not exist in isolation.

In explicit conscious desire there is always an object, just as there is in explicit conscious perception; we desire some event or some state of affairs. But in the primitive condition out of which explicit desire is evolved this is not the case. We have a state of affairs which may be said to involve discomfort, and activities of various sorts until a certain different state of affairs is achieved, or fatigue supervenes, or some other interest causes a distraction. These activities will be such as to achieve the new state of affairs quickly if there has been previous experience of a revelant kind. When we reach the level of explicit conscious desire, it seems as if we were being attracted to a goal, but we are really still pushed from behind. The attraction to the goal is a short-hand way of describing the effects of learning together with the fact that our efforts will continue till the goal is achieved, provided the time required is not too long. There are feelings of various kinds connected with desire, and in the case of familiar desires, such as hunger, these feelings become associated with what we know will cause the desire to cease. But I see no more reason in the case of desire than in the case of knowledge to admit an *essentially* relational occurrence such as many suppose desire to be.

Only experience, memory and association – so I should say – confer objects upon desire, which are initially blind tendencies to certain kinds of activity.

It remains to say a few words about 'will'. There is a sense in which will is an observable phenomena, and another in which it is a metaphysical superstition. It is obvious that I can say, 'I will hold my breath for thirty seconds', and proceed to do so; that I can say, 'I will go to America', and proceed to do so; and so on. In this sense, will is an observable phenomenon. But as a faculty, as a separable occurrence, it is, I think, a delusion. To make this clear, it will be necessary to examine the observable phenomenon.

Very young infants do not appear to have anything that could be called 'will'. Their movements, at first, are reflexes, and are explicable, where they first cease to be reflexes, by the law of conditioned reflexes. One observes, however, something that looks very like will when the child learns control over fingers and toes. It seems clear, in watching this process, that, after some experience of involuntary movements, the child discovers how to think of a movement first and then make the movement, and that this discovery is exceedingly pleasurable. We know that, in adult life, a deliberate movement is one which we think of before we make it. Obviously we cannot think of a movement unless we have previously made it; it follows that no movement can be voluntary unless it has previously been involuntary. I think that, as William James suggested, a voluntary movement is merely one which is preceded by the thought of it, and has the thought of it as an essential part of its cause.

When I say this, I do not mean to take any particular view as to what constitutes 'thinking'. It may consist almost entirely of talking, as Dr. Watson holds; or it may be something more. That is not the point at present. The point is that, whatever philosophy one may adopt, there certainly is an occurrence which is described by ordinary people as 'thinking of getting up in the morning', or 'thinking of' any other bodily movement. Whatever the analysis of this occurrence may be, it is an essential part of the cause of any movement which can be attributed to the 'will'.

It is true, of course, that we may think of a movement without performing it. This is analogous to imagining a state of affairs without believing in it; each is a rather sophisticated and late development. Each will only happen when we think of several things at once, and one of them interferes with another. It may, I think, be assumed that, whenever we think of a possible movement, we have a tendency to perform it, and are only restrained, if at all, by some thought, or other circumstance, having a contrary tendency.

If this is the case, there is nothing at all mysterious about the will. Whatever may constitute 'thinking of' a movement, it is certainly something associated with the movement itself; therefore, by the usual law of learned reactions we should expect that thinking of a movement would tend to cause it to occur. This, I should say, is the essence of will.

Emphatic cases of volition, where we decide after a period of deliberation, are merely examples of conflicting forces. You may have both pleasant and unpleasant associations with some place that you are thinking of going to; this may cause you to hesitate, until one or other association proves the stronger. There may be more than this in volition, but I cannot see any good ground for believing that there is.

Chapter 22

Ethics

Ethics is traditionally a department of philosophy, and that is my reason for discussing it. I hardly think myself that it ought to be included in the domain of philosophy, but to prove this would take as long as to discuss the subject itself, and would be less interesting.

As a provisional definition, we may take ethics to consist of general principles which help to determine rules of conduct. It is not the business of ethics to say how a person should act in such and such specific circumstances; that is the province of casuistry. The word 'casuistry' has acquired bad connotations, as a result of the Protestant and Jansenist attacks on the Jesuits. But in its old and proper sense it represents a perfectly legitimate study. Take, say, the question: In what circumstances is it right to tell a lie? Some people, unthinkingly, would say: Never! But this answer cannot be seriously defended. Everybody admits that you should lie if you meet a homicidal maniac pursuing a man with a view to murdering him, and he asks you whether the man has passed your way. It is admitted that lying is a legitimate branch of the art of warfare; also that priests may lie to guard the secrets of the confessional, and doctors to protect the professional confidences of their patients. All such questions belong to casuistry in the old sense, and it is evident that they are questions deserving to be asked and answered. But they do not belong to ethics in the sense in which this study has been included in philosophy.

It is not the business of ethics to arrive at actual rules of conduct, such as: 'Thou shalt not steal'. This is the province of morals. Ethics is expected to provide a basis from which such rules can be deduced. The rules of morals differ according to the age, the race, and the creed of the community concerned, to an extent that is hardly realised by those who have neither travelled nor studied anthropology. Even within a homogeneous community differences of opinion arise. Should a man kill his wife's lover? The Church says no, the law says no, and common sense says no; yet many people would say yes, and juries often refuse to condemn. These doubtful cases arise when a moral rule is in process of changing. But ethics is concerned with something more general than moral rules, and less subject to change. It is true that, in a given community, an ethic which does not lead to the moral rules accepted by that community is considered immoral. It does not, of course, follow that such an ethic is in fact false, since the moral rules of that community may be undesirable. Some tribes of head-hunters hold that no man should marry until he can bring to the wedding the head of an enemy slain by himself. Those who question this moral rule are held to be encouraging licence and lowering the standard of manliness. Nevertheless, we should not demand of an ethic that it should justify the moral rules of head-hunters.

Perhaps the best way to approach the subject of ethics is to ask what is meant when a person says: 'You *ought* to do so-and-so' or 'I *ought* to do so-and-so'. Primarily, a sentence of this sort has an emotional content; it means 'this is the act towards which I feel the emotion of approval'. But we do not wish to leave the matter there; we want to find something more objective and systematic and constant than a personal emotion. The ethical teacher says: 'You ought to approve acts of such-and-such kinds.' He generally gives reasons for this view, and we have to examine what sorts of reasons are possible. We are here on very ancient ground. Socrates was concerned mainly with ethics; Plato and Aristotle both discussed the subject at length; before their time, Confucius and Buddha had each founded a religion consisting almost entirely of ethical teaching, though in the case of Buddhism there was afterwards a growth of theological doctrine. The views of the ancients on ethics are better worth studying than their views on (say) physical science; the subject has not yet proved amenable to exact reasoning, and we cannot boast that the moderns have as yet rendered their predecessors obsolete.

Historically, virtue consisted at first of obedience to authority, whether that of the gods, the government, or custom. Those who disobeyed authority suffered obvious penalties. This is still the view of Hegel, to whom virtue consists in obedience to the state. There are, however, different forms of this theory, and the objections to them are different. In its more primitive form, the theory is unaware that different authorities take different views as to what constitutes virtue, and it therefore universalises the practice of the community in which the theoriser lives. When other ages and nations are found to have different customs, these are condemned as abominations. Let us consider this view first.

The view we are now to examine is the theory that there are certain rules of conduct – e.g. the Decalogue – which determine virtue in all situations. The person who keeps all the rules is perfectly virtuous; the person who fails in this is wicked in proportion to the frequency of his failures. There are several objections to this as the basis of ethics. In the first place, the rules can hardly cover the whole field of human conduct; e.g. there is nothing in the Decalogue to show whether we ought to have a gold standard or not. Accordingly those who hold this view regard some questions as 'moral issues', while others have not this character. That means, in practice, that in regard to 'moral issues' we ought to act in a certain way, regardless of consequences, while in other matters we ought to consider which course will do the most good. Thus in effect we are driven to adopt two different ethical systems, one where the code has spoken, the other where it is silent. This is unsatisfactory to a philosopher.

The second objection to such a view is suggested by the first. We all feel that certain results are desirable, and others undesirable; but a code of conduct which takes no account of circumstances will have sometimes the sort of consequences we think desirable, and sometimes the sort we think undesirable. Take, e.g. the precept 'Thou shalt not kill'. All respectable people hold that this does not apply when the State orders a person to kill; on this ground among others, the New York School Board recently refused to sanction the teaching of the Decalogue in schools.

A third objection is that it may be asked how the moral rules are known. The usual answer, historically, is that they are known by revelation and tradition. But these are extra-philosophical sources of knowledge. The philosopher cannot but observe that there have been many revelations, and that it is not clear why he should adopt one rather than another. To this it may be replied that conscience is a personal revelation to each individual, and invariably tells him what is right and what is wrong. The difficulty of this view is that conscience changes from age to age. Most people nowadays consider it wrong to burn a man alive for disagreeing with them in metaphysics, but formerly this was held to be a highly meritorious act, provided it was done in the interests of the right metaphysics. No one who has studied the history of moral ideas can regard conscience as invariably right. Thus we are driven to abandon the attempt to define virtue by means of a set of rules of conduct.

There is, however, another form of the view that virtue consists in obedience to authority. This may be called 'the administrator's ethic'. A Roman or Anglo-Indian pro-consul would define virtue as obedience to the moral code of the community to which a man happens to belong.

No matter how moral codes may differ, a man should always obey that of his own time and place and creed. A Mohammedan, for instance, would not be regarded as wicked for practising polygamy, but an Englishman would, even if he lived in a Mohammedan country. This view makes social conformity the essence of virtue; or, as with Hegel, regards virtue as obedience to the government. The difficulty of such theories is that they make it impossible to apply ethical predicates to authority: we cannot find any meaning for the statement that a custom is good or that the government is bad. The view is appropriate to despots and their willing slaves; it cannot survive in a progressive democracy.

We come a little nearer to a correct view when we define right conduct by the motive or state of mind of the agent. According to this theory, acts inspired by certain emotions are good, and those inspired by certain other emotions are bad. Mystics hold this view, and have accordingly a certain contempt for the letter of the law. Broadly speaking, it would be held that acts inspired by love are good, and those inspired by hate are bad. In practice, I hold this view to be right; but philosophically I regard it as deducible from something more fundamental.

All the theories we have hitherto considered are opposed to those which judge the rightness or wrongness of conduct by its consequences. Of these the most famous is the utilitarian philosophy, which maintained that happiness is the good, and that we ought to act so as to maximise the balance of happiness over unhappiness in the world. I should not myself regard happiness as an adequate definition of the good, but I should agree that conduct ought to be judged by its consequences. I do not mean, of course, that in every practical exigency of daily life we should attempt to think out the results of this or that line of conduct, because, if we did, the opportunity for action would often be past before our calculations were finished. But I do mean that the received moral code, in so far as it is taught in education and embodied in public opinion or the criminal law, should be carefully examined in each generation, to see whether it still serves to achieve desirable ends, and, if not, in what respects it needs to be amended. The moral code, in short, like the legal code, should adapt itself to changing circumstances, keeping the public good always as its motive. If so, we have to consider in what the public good consists.

According to this view, 'right conduct' is not an autonomous concept, but means 'conduct calculated to produce desirable results'.

It will be right, let us say, to act so as to make people happy and intelligent, but wrong to act so as to make them unhappy and stupid. We have to ask ourselves how we can discover what constitutes the ends of right conduct.

There is a view, advocated, e.g. by Dr. G. E. Moore, that 'good' is an indefinable notion, and that we know *a priori* certain general propositions about the kinds of things that are good on their own account. Such things as happiness, knowledge, appreciation of beauty, are known to be good, according to Dr. Moore; it is also known that we ought to act so as to create what is good and prevent what is bad. I formerly held this view myself, but I was led to abandon it, partly by Mr. Santayana's *Winds of Doctrine*. I now think that good and bad are derivative from desire. I do not mean quite simply that the good is the desired, because men's desires conflict, and 'good' is, to my mind, mainly a social concept, designed to find an issue from this conflict. The conflict, however, is not only between the desires of different men, but between incompatible desires of one man at different times, or even at the same time, and even if he is solitary, like Robinson Crusoe. Let us see how the concept of 'good' emerges from reflection on conflicts of desires.

We will begin with Robinson Crusoe. In him there will be conflicts, for example, between fatigue and hunger, particularly between fatigue at one time and foreseen hunger at another. The effort which he will require in order to work when he is tired with a view to providing food on another occasion has all the characteristics of what is called a moral effort: we think better of a man who makes the effort than of one who does not, and the making of it requires self-control. For some reason, this sort of thing is called, not morals, but 'morale'; the distinction, however, seems to me illusory. Robinson Crusoe is bound to realise that he has many desires, each of which is stronger at one time than at another, and that, if he acts always upon the one that is strongest at the moment, he may defeat others that are stronger in the long run. So far, only intelligence is involved; but one may assume that, with the progress of intelligence, there goes a growing desire for a harmonious life, i.e. a life in which action is dominated by consistent quasi-permanent desires. Again: some desires, in addition to the desire for a harmonious life, are more likely to lead to harmony than certain other desires. Intellectual curiosity, e.g. affords a mild diffused satisfaction, whereas drugs provide ecstasy followed by despair. If we arrive unexpectedly in Robinson Crusoe's island and find him studying botany, we shall think better of him than if we find him dead drunk on his last bottle of whiskey. All this belongs to morals, although it is purely self-regarding.

When we come to considering men in society, moral questions become both more important and more difficult, because conflicts between the desires of different persons are harder to resolve than internal conflicts among the desires of one person. There are some distinctions to be made. First, there is the difference between the point of view of the neutral authority contemplating a squabble in which it is not interested, and the point of view of the disputants themselves. Then there is the distinction between what we wish people to *do*, and what we wish them to *feel* in the way of emotions and desires.

The view of authority everywhere is that squabbles to which it is not a party are undesirable, but that in the squabbles to which it is a party virtue consists in promoting the victory of authority. In the latter respect, it is acting, not as an authority, but merely as a combination of quarrelsome individuals who think it more profitable to quarrel with outsiders than with each other; we will therefore ignore this aspect of authority, and consider its action only when it is a neutral. In this case, it aims at preventing quarrels by punishing those who begin them, or sometimes by punishing both parties. Monsieur Huc, the Jesuit missionary who wrote a fascinating account of his travels in China, Tartary, and Tibet about eighty years ago, relates an amusing conversation he had with a mandarin. Monsieur Huc had remarked that Chinese justice was dilatory, expensive, and corrupt. The mandarin explained that it had been made so in obedience to an Imperial edict, setting forth that the subjects of the Son of Heaven had become too much addicted to litigation, and must be led to abandon this practice. The rescript then proceeded to suggest to magistrates and judges the desirability of the above defects as a means of diminishing the number of law-suits. It appeared that the Emperor's commands had been faithfully obeyed in this respect – more so than in some others.

Another method adopted by public authorities to prevent the impulse towards internal quarrels is the creation of *esprit de corps*, public spirit, patriotism, etc., i.e. a concentration of quarrelsome impulses on persons outside the group over which it rules. Such a method, obviously, is partial and external; it would not be open to a world-wide democratic authority, should this ever come into existence. Such an authority would have to adopt better methods of producing harmony; it would also have a higher claim to the obedience of citizens than some authorities have at present.

What can we say from the point of view of the disputants themselves? It is of course obvious that there will be a greater *total* satisfaction when two people's desires harmonise than when they conflict, but that is not an argument which can be used to people who in fact hate each other. One can argue that the one who is going to be beaten would do well to give way, but each will think that he himself is going to be victorious. One can argue that there is more happiness to be derived from love than from hate, but people cannot love to order, and there is no satisfaction to be derived from an insincere love. Nor is it always true in an individual case that love brings more happiness than hate. During and immediately after the war, those who hated the Germans were happier than those who still regarded them as human beings, because they could feel that what was being done served a good purpose. I think, therefore, that certain departments of morals, and those the most important, cannot be inculcated from a personal point of view, but only from the point of view of a neutral authority. That is why I said that ethics is mainly social.

The attitude of a neutral authority would, it seems to me, be this: Men desire all sorts of things, and in themselves all desires, taken singly, are on a level, i.e. there is no reason to prefer the satisfaction of one to the satisfaction of another. But when we consider not a single desire but a group of desires, there is this difference, that sometimes all the desires in a group can be satisfied, whereas in other cases the satisfaction of some of the desires in the group is incompatible with that of others. If A and B desire to marry each other, both can have what they want, but if they desire to kill each other, at most one can succeed, unless they are Kilkenny cats. Therefore the former pair of desires is socially preferable to the latter. Now our desires are a product of three factors: native disposition, education, and present circumstances. The first factor is difficult to deal with at present, for lack of knowledge. The third is brought into operation by means of the criminal law, economic motives, and social praise and blame, which make it on the whole to the interest of an individual in a community to promote the interests of the dominant group in that community. But this is done in an external way, not by creating good desires, but by producing a conflict of greed and fear in which it is hoped that fear will win. The really vital method is education, in the large sense in which it includes care of the body and habit-formation in the first few years. By means of education, men's desires can be changed, so that they act spontaneously in a social fashion. To force a man to curb his desires, as we do by the criminal law, is not nearly so satisfactory as to cause him genuinely to feel the desires which promote socially harmonious conduct.

And this brings me to the last point with which we are concerned, namely, the distinction between feeling and doing. No doubt, from a social point of view the important thing is what a man does, but it is impossible to cause a man to do the right things consistently unless he has the right desires. And the right desires cannot be produced merely by praising them or by desiring to have them; the technique of moral education is not one of exhortation or *explicit* moral instruction.

We can now state the ethic at which we have arrived in abstract terms. Primarily, we call something 'good' when we desire it, and 'bad' when we have an aversion from it. But our use of words is more constant than our desires, and therefore we shall continue to call a thing good even at moments when we are not actually desiring it, just as we always call grass green though it sometimes looks yellow. And the laudatory associations of the word 'good' may generate a desire which would not otherwise exist: we may want to eat caviare merely because we are told that it is good. Moreover the use of words is social, and therefore we learn only to call a thing good, except in rare circumstances, if most of the people we associate with are also willing to call it good. Thus 'good' comes to apply to things desired by the whole of a social group. It is evident, therefore, that there can be more good in a world where the desires of different individuals harmonise than in one where they conflict. The supreme moral rule should, therefore, be: *Act so as to produce harmonious rather than discordant desires.* This rule will apply wherever a man's influence extends: within himself, in his family, his city, his country, even the world as a whole, if he is able to influence it.

There will be two main methods to this end: first, to produce social institutions under which the interests of different individuals or groups conflict as little as possible; second, to educate individuals in such a way that their desires can be harmonised with each other and with the desires of their neighbours. As to the first method, I shall say nothing further, since the questions that arise belong to politics and economics. As to the second, the important period is the formative period of childhood, during which there should be health, happiness, freedom, and a gradual growth of self-discipline through opportunities for difficult achievement of a sort which is useful and yet satisfies the impulse towards mastery of the environment. The desire for power, which is present in most people and strongest in the most vigorous, should be directed towards power over things rather than over people.

It is clear that, if harmonious desires are what we should seek, love is better than hate, since, when two people love each other, both can be satisfied, whereas when they hate each other one at most can achieve the object of his desire. It is obvious also that desire for knowledge is to be encouraged, since the knowledge that a man acquires is not obtained by taking it away from some one else; but a desire for (say) large landed estates can only be satisfied in a small minority. Desire for power over other people is a potent source of conflict, and is therefore to be discouraged; a respect for the liberty of others is one of the things that ought to be developed by the right kind of education. The impulse towards personal achievement ought to go into such things as artistic creation or scientific discovery or the promotion of useful institutions – in a word, into activities that are creative rather than possessive. Knowledge, which may do positive harm where men's desires conflict (for example, by showing how to make war more deadly), will have only good results in a world where men's desires harmonise, since it tends to show how their common desires are to be realised.

The conclusion may be summed up in a single phrase: *The good life is one inspired by love and guided by knowledge*[1].

[1]Cf. *What I Believe*, by the present author – To-day and To-morrow Series.

PART IV THE UNIVERSE

Chapter 23

Some Great Philosophies of the Past

Our discussions, hitherto, have been concerned very largely with Man, but Man on his own account is not the true subject-matter of philosophy. What concerns philosophy is the universe as a whole; Man demands consideration solely as the instrument by means of which we acquire knowledge of the universe. And that is why it is human beings as capable of knowledge that have concerned us mainly in past chapters, rather than as centres of will or of emotion. We are not in the mood proper to philosophy so long as we are interested in the world only as it affects human beings; the philosophic spirit demands an interest in the world for its own sake. But since we apprehend the world through our own senses, and think about it with our own intellect, the picture that we acquire is inevitably coloured by the personal medium through which it comes to us. Consequently we have to study this medium, namely ourselves, in order to find out, if we can, what elements in our picture of the world are contributed by us, and what elements we may accept as representative of outside fact. Previous chapters have studied cognition, both as an outwardly observable reaction, and as it appears to introspection. In the chapters that remain, we shall be concerned with what we can know about the universe, in view of the nature of the instrument that we have to employ. I do not think we can know as much as many philosophers of the past have supposed, but I think it is worth while to have in our minds an outline of their systems. I shall therefore begin by setting forth a few typical philosophical constructions of earlier centuries.

Modern philosophy is generally taken as beginning with Descartes, who flourished in the first half of the seventeenth century. We have already had occasion, in Chapter 16 to consider his argument 'I think, therefore I am', but now we will deal with him somewhat more generally. He inaugurated two movements, one in metaphysics, one in theory of knowledge. In metaphysics, he emphasised the gulf between mind and matter, or between soul and body; in theory of knowledge he advocated a critical scrutiny of premisses. These two movements had different histories, each of them interesting. The science of dynamics was rapidly developing in Descartes' time, and seemed to show that the motions of matter could be calculated mathematically, given sufficient data. As the motions of matter include our bodily acts, even speaking and writing, it seemed as if the consequence must be a materialistic theory of human behaviour. This consequence, however, was distasteful to most philosophers, and they therefore invented various ways of escaping from it. Descartes himself thought that the will could have certain direct physical effects. He thought that the brain contains a fluid called the 'animal spirits', and that the will could influence the direction of its motion, though not the velocity. In this way he was still able to hold that the will is effective in the manner in which common sense supposes it to be. But this view did not fit in at all well with the rest of his philosophy. He held that, apart from the Supreme Substance, namely God, there are two created substances, mind and matter; that the essence of mind is thought, and that the essence of matter is extension. He made these two substances so different that interaction between them became difficult to understand, and his followers decided that there is never any effect either of mind on matter or of matter on mind.

The motives for this development were various; perhaps the most important was the development of physics immediately after Descartes' time. A law was discovered called the 'conservation of momentum'. This states that, if a system of bodies is in any sort of motion, and is free from outside influences, the amount of motion *in any direction* is constant. This showed that the kind of action of the will on the 'animal spirits' which Descartes had assumed was contrary to the principles of dynamics. It seemed to follow that mind cannot influence matter, and it was inferred that matter cannot influence mind, since the two were regarded as co-equal substances. It was held that each goes its own way, according to its own laws. The fact that our arm moves when we will it to move was regarded as analogous to the fact that two perfectly accurate clocks strike at the same moment, though neither has any effect upon the other. The series of mental events and the series of physical events were parallel, each going at the same rate as the other; therefore they continued to synchronise, in spite of their independence of each other.

Spinoza sought to make this parallelism less mysterious by denying that there are two separate substances, mind and matter. He maintained that there is only one substance, of which thought and extension are attributes. But there seemed still no good reason why the events belonging to the two attributes should develop along parallel lines. Spinoza is in many ways one of the greatest of philosophers, but his greatness is rather ethical than metaphysical. Accordingly he was regarded by contemporaries as a profound metaphysician but a very wicked man.

The notion of the impossibility of interaction between mind and body has persisted down to our own day. One still hears of 'psycho-physical parallelism', according to which to every state of the brain a state of mind *corresponds* and vice-versa, without either acting on the other. This whole point of view, though not exactly that of Descartes, derives from him. It has a number of sources, religious, metaphysical, and scientific; but there seems no ground whatever for regarding it as true.

Take, first, the rigid determinism of traditional physics, which was to have been avoided. Spinoza rightly perceived that this could not be avoided by such methods, and therefore accepted determinism in the psychical as in the physical realm. If everything we *say* is determined by physical causes, our thoughts are only free when we tell lies: so long as we say what we think, our thoughts also can be inferred from physics. The philosophy which I advocate escapes this consequence in several ways. In the first place, causality does not involve *compulsion*, but only a law of sequence: if physical and mental events run parallel, either may with equal justice be regarded as causing the other, and there is no sense in speaking of them as causally independent. Thus the Cartesian dualism does not have the pleasant consequences which were intended. In the second place, modern physics has become less deterministic than the physics of the past few centuries. We do not know, e.g. what makes a radio-active atom explode or an electron jump from a larger to a smaller orbit. In these matters we only know statistical averages.

Take next the view that mind and matter are quite disparate. This we have criticised already. It rests upon a notion that we know much more about matter than we do, and in particular upon the belief that the space of physics can be identified with the space of sensible experience. This belief is absent in Leibniz, who, however, never quite realised what his own view was. It is not absent in Kant, who realised that the space of sensible experience is subjective, and inferred that the space of physics is subjective. Since Kant, no one seems to have thought clearly about space until Einstein and Minkowski. The separation of physical and sensible space, logically carried out, shows the groundlessness of traditional views about mind and matter. This part of Descartes' philosophy, therefore, though it accelerated the progress of physics, must be regarded as metaphysically an aberration.

The other part of Descartes' philosophy, namely, the emphasis upon methodical doubt, and consequently upon theory of knowledge, has been more fruitful. The beginning of a philosophic attitude is the realisation that we do not know as much as we think we do, and to this Descartes contributed notably. We have seen that he set to work to doubt all he could, but found he could not doubt his own existence, which he therefore took as the starting-point of his constructive system. He supposed that the most certain fact in the world is 'I think'. This was unfortunate, since it gave a subjective bias to modern philosophy. As a matter of fact, 'I' seems to be only a string of events, each of which separately is more certain than the whole. And 'think' is a word which Descartes accepted as indefinable, but which really covers complicated relations between events. When is an event a 'thought'? Is there some intrinsic characteristic which makes it a thought? Descartes would say yes, and so would most philosophers. I should say no. Take, e.g. a visual and an auditory sensation. Both are 'thoughts' in Descartes' sense, but what have they in common? Two visual sensations *have* an indefinable common quality, viz. that which makes them visual. Two auditory sensations likewise. But a visual and an auditory sensation have in common, if I am not mistaken, no intrinsic property, but a certain capacity for being *known* without inference. This amounts to saying that they are mnemic causes of a certain kind of event, called a cognition, and that they have, moreover, a certain formal similarity to the cognition which they cause. Therefore, instead of taking the general 'I think' as our basis, we ought to take the particular occurrences which are known without inference, among which sensations (or rather 'perceptions') will be included. These occurrences, as we have already seen, may be regarded with equal justice as physical and mental: they are parts of chains of physical causation, and they have mnemic effects which are cognitions. The former fact makes us call them physical, the latter mental, both quite truly. It is the particular events which are certain, not the 'I think' which Descartes made the basis of his philosophy. It is not correct to regard the ultimate certainties as 'subjective', except in the sense that they are events in that part of space–time in which our body is – and our mind also, I should say.

A new turn was given to the Cartesian type of metaphysics by Leibniz (1646-1716), who, like Descartes, was supremely eminent both in mathematics and in philosophy. Leibniz rejected the view that there is only one substance, as Spinoza held, or only two other than God, as the orthodox followers of Descartes maintained. He also rejected the dualism of mind and matter, holding that there are innumerable substances all in a greater or less degree mental, and none in any degree material. He maintained that every substance is immortal, and that there is no interaction between one substance and another – this last being a view derived from the Cartesian independence of mind and matter. He also extended to his many substances the belief in parallelism which had existed for the two substances of the Cartesians. He called his substances 'monads', and maintained that every monad mirrors the universe, and develops along lines which correspond, point by point, with those along which every other monad is developing. A man's soul or mind is a single monad, while his body is a collection of monads, each mental in some degree, but less so than the monad which is his soul. Inferior monads mirror the world in a more confused way than higher ones do, but there is some element of confusion in the perceptions of even the most superior monads. Every monad mirrors the world from its own point of view, and the difference between points of view is compared to a difference of perspective. 'Matter' is a confused way of perceiving a number of monads; if we perceived clearly, we should see that there is no such thing as matter.

Leibniz's system had great merits and great demerits. The theory that 'matter' is a confused way of perceiving something non-material was an advance upon anything to be found in his predecessors. He had, though only semi-consciously, the distinction between physical and perceptual space: there is space in each monad's picture of the world, and there is also the assemblage or pattern of 'points of view'. The latter corresponds to what I have called 'physical space', the former to 'perceptual space'. Leibniz maintained, as against Newton, that space and time consists only of relations – a view which has achieved a definitive triumph in Einstein's theory of relativity. The weak point of his system was what he called the 'pre-established harmony', in virtue of which all the monads (so to speak) kept step, in spite of the fact that they were 'windowless' and never acted upon each other. Perception, for Leibniz, was not an effect of the object perceived, but a modification arising in the perceiving monad and running parallel with what was happening in the perceived object. This view would never have seemed plausible but for the anterior Cartesian theory of the mutual independence of mind and matter. And if Leibniz himself developed, as he believed, in complete independence of all other created things, it is not clear what good reasons he could have had for believing in the existence of anything except himself, since, by his own theory, his experiences would remain unchanged if everything else were annihilated. In fact, he was only able to refute this possibility by bringing in theological considerations, which, whether valid or not, are out of place in philosophy. For this reason, his doctrines, ingenious as they were, found little acceptance in France and England, though in Germany they prevailed, in a modified form, until the time of Kant.

The systems of Descartes, Spinoza and Leibniz have one very important characteristic in common, namely, that they all depend upon the category of 'substance'. This is a concept which has developed out of the common-sense notion of 'thing'. A 'substance' is that which has qualities, and is in general supposed to be indestructible, though it is difficult to see why. It acquired its hold over metaphysicians partly because both matter and the soul were held to be immortal, and partly through a hasty transference to reality of ideas derived from grammar. We say 'Peter is running', 'Peter is talking', 'Peter is eating', and so on. We think that there is one entity, Peter, who does all these things, and that none of them could be done unless there were someone to do them, but that Peter might quite well do none of them. Similarly we assign qualities to Peter: we say he is wise and tall and blond and so on. All these qualities, we feel, cannot subsist by themselves in the void, but only when there is a subject to which they belong; but Peter would remain Peter even if he became foolish and short and dyed his hair. Thus Peter, who is regarded as a 'substance', is self-subsistent as compared with his qualities and states, and he preserves his substantial identity throughout all sorts of changes. Similarly in the material world an atom is supposed (or rather was supposed until recently) to preserve its identity throughout all time, however it might move and whatever combinations it might form with other atoms. The concept of 'motion', upon which all physics seemed to depend, was only strictly applicable to a substance which preserves its identity while changing its spatial relations to other substances; thus 'substance' acquired an even firmer hold upon physics than upon metaphysics.

Nevertheless, the notion of 'substance', at any rate in any sense involving permanence, must be shut out from our thoughts if we are to achieve a philosophy in any way adequate either to modern physics or to modern psychology. Modern physics, both in the theory of relativity and in the Heisenberg–Schrödinger theories of atomic structure, has reduced 'matter' to a system of events, each of which lasts only for a very short time. To treat an electron or a proton as a single entity has become as wrong-headed as it would be to treat the population of London or New York as a single entity. And in psychology, equally, the 'ego' has disappeared as an ultimate conception, and the unity of a personality has become a peculiar causal nexus among a series of events. In this respect, grammar and ordinary language have been shown to be bad guides to metaphysics. A great book might be written showing the influence of syntax on philosophy; in such a book, the author could trace in detail the influence of the subject–predicate structure of sentences upon European thought, more particularly in this matter of 'substance'. And it must be understood that the same reasons which lead to the rejection of substance lead also to the rejection of 'things' and 'persons' as ultimately valid concepts. I say 'I sit at my table', but I ought to say: 'One of a certain string of events causally connected in the sort of way that makes the whole series that is called a 'person' has a certain spatial relation to one of another string of events causally connected with each other in a different way and having a spatial configuration of the sort denoted by the word "table" '. I do not say so, because life is too short; but that is what I should say if I were a true philosopher. Apart from any other grounds, the inadequacy of the notion of 'substance' would lead us to regard the philosophy of Descartes, Spinoza, and Leibniz as incompatible with modern science. There is of course in all three a great deal that does not depend upon 'substance', and that still has value; but 'substance' supplied the framework and a good deal of the argumentation, and therefore introduces a fatal defect into these three great systems.

I come now to the triad of British philosophers, Locke, Berkeley, and Hume – English, Irish, and Scotch respectively. Perhaps from patriotic bias or from community of national temperament, I find more that I can accept, and regard as still important, in the writings of these three than in the philosophy of their continental predecessors. Their constructions are less ambitious, their arguments more detailed, and their methods more empirical; in all these respects they show more kinship with the modern scientific outlook. On the other hand, Locke and Hume, if not Berkeley, approach philosophy too exclusively from the side of psychology, and are concerned to study Man rather than the universe.

Locke was a contemporary and friend of Newton; his great book, *An Essay concerning Human Understanding,* was published at almost the same moment as Newton's *Principia.* His influence has been enormous, greater, in fact, than his abilities would seem to warrant; and this influence was not only philosophical, but quite as much political and social. He was one of the creators of eighteenth-century liberalism: democracy, religious toleration, freedom of economic enterprise, educational progress, all owe much to him. The English Revolution of 1688 embodied his ideas; the American Revolution of 1776 and the French Revolution of 1789 expressed what had grown, in a century, out of his teaching. And in all these movements, philosophy and politics went hand in hand. Thus the practical success of Locke's ideas has been extraordinary.

When, knowing all this, one comes to read Locke himself, it is difficult to resist a feeling of disappointment. He is sensible, enlightened, minute, but uninspired and (to moderns) uninspiring. One has to remember that his contemporaries found common sense exhilarating after a century of wars of religion and a long struggle with obscurantism. Locke combated the doctrine of 'innate ideas', according to which we learned only certain things by experience, but possessed our abstract knowledge in virtue of our congenital constitution. He regarded the mind at birth as a wax tablet, upon which experience proceeded to write. Undoubtedly he was, in this matter, more in the right than his opponents, although the terms in which the controversy was waged are not such as a modern could employ. We should say that the innate apparatus of man consists of 'reflexes' rather than 'ideas'; also that our sense-organs, our glands, and our muscles lead to responses of certain kinds, in which our own organisation plays a part of the same importance as that played by the external stimulus. The element in our knowledge-responses that corresponds to our own bodily organisation might, perhaps, be regarded as representing what Locke's opponents meant by 'innate'. But it does not represent this at all accurately so far as our feelings towards it are concerned. The 'innate' ideas were the ideas to be proud of; they embraced pure mathematics, natural theology, and ethics. But nobody is proud of sneezing or coughing. And when Locke tried to show, in detail, how our knowledge is generated by experience, he was liberating philosophy from a great deal of useless lumber, even if his own doctrines were not altogether such as we can now accept.

Locke used his own principles only in ways consistent with common sense; Berkeley and Hume both pushed them to paradoxical conclusions. The philosophy of Berkeley, to my mind, has not received quite the attention and respect that it deserves – not that I agree with it, but that I think it ingenious and harder to refute than is often supposed. Berkeley, as everyone knows, denied the reality of matter, and maintained that everything is mental. In the former respect I agree with him, though not for his reasons; in the latter respect, I think his argument unsound and his conclusion improbable, though not certainly false. However, I will leave the development of my own views to a later chapter, and confine myself to Berkeley's argument.

Berkeley contended that when, for example, you 'see a tree', all that you really *know* to be happening is in you, and is mental. The colour that you see, as Locke had already argued, does not belong to the physical world, but is an effect upon you, produced, according to Locke, by a physical stimulus. Locke held that the purely spatial properties of perceived objects really belong to the objects, whereas such things as colour, softness, sound, etc. are effects in us. Berkeley went further, and argued that the spatial properties of perceived objects are no exception. Thus the object perceived is composed entirely of 'mental' constituents, and there is no reason to believe in the existence of anything not mental. He did not wish to admit that a tree ceases to exist when we do not look at it, so he maintained that it acquires permanence through being an idea in the mind of God. It is still only an 'idea', but not one whose existence depends upon the accidents of our perceptions.

The real objection to Berkeley's view is rather physical than metaphysical. Light and sound take time to travel from their sources to the percipient, and one must suppose that something is happening along the route by which they travel. What is happening along the route is presumably not 'mental', for, as we have seen, 'mental' events are those that have peculiar mnemic effects which are connected with living tissue. Therefore, although Berkeley is right in saying that the events we know immediately are mental, it is highly probable that he is wrong as to the events which we infer in places where there are no living bodies. In saying this, however, we are anticipating the results of a fuller discussion in a later chapter.

Hume, proceeding from a starting-point essentially similar to that of Locke and Berkeley, arrived at conclusions so sceptical that all subsequent philosophers have shied away from them. He denied the existence of the Self, questioned the validity of induction, and doubted whether causal laws could be applied to anything except our own mental processes. He is one of the very few philosophers not concerned to establish any positive conclusions. To a great extent, I think, we must admit the validity of his reasons for refusing to feel the usual certainties. As regards the Self, he was almost certainly right. As we have already argued, a person is not a single entity, but a series of events linked together by peculiar causal laws. As regards induction, the question is very difficult, and I shall devote a subsequent chapter to it. As regards causal laws, the question, as we shall find later, is the same as the question of induction. On both points Hume's doubts are not to be lightly dismissed.

The usual modern criticism of Locke, Berkeley, and Hume is that they were unduly 'atomistic'. They thought of the mind as a collection of 'ideas', each as hard and separate as a billiard-ball. They had not the conception of continuous change or of integral processes; their causal units were too small. As we have already seen in connection with *Gestaltpsychologie* and with sentences, the causal unit is often a configuration which cannot be broken up without losing its distinctive causal properties. In this sense, it is true that the traditional British philosophy was too atomistic. But in another sense I do not think it is true, and I think much modern philosophy is confused on this point. Although a configuration may lose its *causal* properties when broken up into its elements, it nevertheless does consist of these elements related in certain ways; analysis into 'atoms' is perfectly valid, so long as it is not assumed that the causal efficacy of the whole is compounded out of the separate effects of the separate atoms. It is because I hold this view that I call the philosophy which I advocate 'logical atomism'. And to this extent I regard Locke, Berkeley, and Hume as in the right as against their modern critics. But this also is a topic which will be resumed in a later chapter.

Hume's criticism of the notion of cause was what led Kant to his new departure. Kant's philosophy is difficult and obscure, and philosophers still dispute as to what he meant. Those who disagree with him are held by his supporters to have misunderstood him; I must therefore warn the reader that what follows is my view of what he meant, and that there is no agreed view.

Kant maintained that, in virtue of our mental constitution, we deal with the raw material of sense-impressions by means of certain 'categories' and by arranging it in space and time. Both the categories and the space–time arrangement are supplied by us, and do not belong to the world except as known by us. But since our mental constitution is a constant datum, all phenomena *as known* will be spatio-temporal and will conform to the categories. Among the latter, 'cause' is the most important. Thus although there may be no causes in the world as it is in itself (a point on which Kant was inconsistent in the interest of morals), yet phenomena, i.e. things as they seem to us, will always have other phenomena as their causes. And although there is no time in the real world, things as they appear to us will be some earlier and some later. Space, again, is supplied by us, and therefore geometry can be known *a priori*, without our having to study the outer world. Kant thought that Euclidean geometry was quite certainly true, although it could not be proved by logic alone, since Euclid's axioms could be denied without self-contradiction.

It was on this question of geometry that the weakness of Kant's system first became obvious. It was found that we have no grounds for regarding Euclidean geometry as quite true. Since Einstein, we have positive grounds for regarding it as not quite true. It appears that geometry is just as empirical as geography. We depend upon observation if we want to know whether the sum of the angles of a triangle is two right angles just as much as if we want to know how much land there is in the western hemisphere.

With regard to the 'categories' there are equally great difficulties. Let us take 'cause' as our illustration. We see lightning, and then we hear thunder; as phenomena, our seeing and hearing are connected as cause and effect. But we must not – if we are to take the subjectivity of 'cause' seriously – suppose that our seeing or our hearing has an outside cause. In that case, we have no reason to suppose that there is anything outside ourselves. Nay, more: what really happens when we see is not, according to Kant, what we perceive by introspection; what really happens is something without a date, without a position in space, without causes and without effects. Thus we do not know ourselves any better than we know the outside world. Space and time and the categories interpose a mirage of illusion which cannot be penetrated at any point. As an answer to Hume's scepticism, this seems a somewhat unsuccessful effort. And Kant himself, later, in the

Critique of Practical Reason, demolished much of his own edifice, because he thought that ethics at least must have validity in the 'real' world. This part of his philosophy, however, is usually ignored by his followers or apologetically minimised.

Kant gave a new turn to an old philosophical controversy, as to how far our knowledge is *a priori* and how far it is based on experience. Kant admitted that without experience we could know nothing, and that what we know is only valid within the realm of experience. But he held that the general framework of our knowledge is *a priori* in the sense that it is not proved by means of particular facts of experience, but represents the conditions to which phenomena have to conform in order to be capable of being experienced. Before his day, the tendency had been for continental philosophers to regard almost everything as *a priori* while British philosophers regarded almost everything as empirical. But both sides thought that what is *a priori* can be proved by logic, at least in theory, whereas Kant held that mathematics is *a priori* and yet 'synthetic', i.e. not capable of being proved by logic. In this he was misled by geometry. Euclidean geometry, considered as true, is 'synthetic' but not *a priori*; considered merely as deducing consequences from premises, it is *a prioi* but not 'synthetic'. The geometry of the actual world, as required by engineers, is empirical; the geometry of pure mathematics, which does not inquire into the truth of the axioms but merely shows their implications, is an exercise in pure logic.

It should be said, however, that, if the correct analysis of knowledge bears any resemblance at all to that which has been suggested in this book, the whole controversy between empiricists and apriorists becomes more or less unreal. All beliefs are *caused* by external stimuli; when they are as particular as the stimuli they are of the sort which an empiricist might regard as *proved* by experience, but when they are more general difficulties arise. A foreigner arrives in England and sees the customs-house officials, who lead him to the generalisation that all Englishmen are rude; but a few minutes later the porter upsets this induction in the hope of a tip. Thus sometimes a given belief will be caused by one event and destroyed by another. If all the events in a man's life, so far as they affect the belief in question, are such as to cause it, he counts the belief true. The more general a belief is, the more events are relevant to it, and therefore the more difficult it is for it to be such as a man will long consider true. Roughly speaking, the beliefs which count as *a priori* will be those which well might have been upset by subsequent events, but in fact were confirmed. Here as elsewhere we are driven to the view that theory of knowledge is not so fundamental as it has been considered since Kant.

There is one more traditional controversy which I wish to consider, namely, that between monists and pluralists. Is the universe one, or is it many? If many, how intimately are they interconnected? The monistic view is very old: it is already complete in Parmenides (fifth century BC). It is fully developed in Spinoza, Hegel, and Bradley. The pluralistic view, on the other hand, is found in Heraclitus, the atomists, Leibniz, and the British empiricists. For the sake of definiteness, let us take the monistic view as found in Bradley, who is in the main a follower of Hegel. He maintains that every judgment consists in assigning a predicate to Reality as a whole: the whole is the subject of every predicate. Suppose you start by saying 'Tommy has a cold in the head'. This may not *seem* to be a statement about the universe as a whole, but according to Bradley it is. If I may be allowed to set forth his argument in popular language which his followers might resent, I should put it something like this: First of all, who is Tommy? He is a person with a certain nature, distinguished from other persons by that nature; he may resemble others in many respects, but not in all, so that you cannot really explain who Tommy is unless you set forth all his characteristics. But when you try to do this, you are taken beyond Tommy: he is characterised by relations to his environment. He is affectionate or rebellious or thirsty, noisy or quiet, and so on; all of these qualities involve his relations to others. If you try to define Tommy without mentioning anything outside him, you will find this quite impossible; therefore he is not a self-subsistent being, but an unsubstantial fragment of the world. The same thing applies even more obviously to his nose and his cold. How do you know he has a cold? Because material substances of a certain kind pass from his nose to his handkerchief, which would not be possible if he alone existed. But now, when you take in the environment with a view to defining Tommy and his nose and his cold, you find that you cannot define his immediate environment without taking account of its environment, and so on, until at last you have been forced to include the whole world. Therefore Tommy's cold is in reality a property of the world, since nothing short of the world is sufficiently substantial to have properties.

We may put the argument in a more abstract form. Everything which is part of the world is constituted, in part, by its relations to other things; but relations cannot be real. Bradley's argument against relations is as follows. First he argues that, if there are relations, there must be qualities between which they hold. This part of the argument need not detain us. He then proceeds:

'But how the relation can stand to the qualities is, on the other side, unintelligible. If it is nothing to the qualities, then they are not related at all; and, if so, as we saw, they have ceased to be qualities, and their relation is a nonentity. But if it is to be something to them, then clearly we shall require a *new* connecting relation. For the relation hardly can be the mere adjective of one or both of its terms; or, at least, as such it seems indefensible. And, being something itself, if it does not itself bear a relation to the terms, in what intelligible way will it succeed in being anything to them? But here again we are hurried off into the eddy of a hopeless process, since we are forced to go on finding new relations without end. The links are united by a link, and this bond of union is a link which also has two ends; and these require each a fresh link to connect them with the old. The problem is to find how the relation can stand to its qualities, and this problem is insoluble.'

I cannot deal adequately with this argument without abstruse technicalities which would be out of place. I will, however, point out what seems to me the essential error. Bradley conceives a relation as something just as substantial as its terms, and not radically different in kind. The analogy of the chain with links should make us suspicious, since it clearly proves, if it is valid, that chains are impossible, and yet, as a fact they exist. There is not a word in his argument which would not apply to physical chains. The successive links are united not by another link, but by a spatial relation. I think Bradley has been misled, unconsciously, by a circumstance to which I alluded in an earlier chapter, namely, the fact that the *word* for a relation is as substantial as the *words* for its terms. Suppose A and B are two events, and A precedes B. In the proposition 'A precdes B', the word 'precedes' is just as substantial as the words 'A' and 'B'. The relation of the *two* events A and B is represented, in language, by the time or space order of the *three* words 'A', 'precedes', and 'B'. But this order is an actual relation, not a word for a relation. The first step in Bradley's regress does actually have to be taken in giving verbal expression to a relation, and the word for a relation does have to be related to the words for its terms. But this is a linguistic, not a metaphysical, fact, and the regress does not have to go any further.

It should be added that, as Bradley himself recognises, his difficulties break out afresh when he comes to consider the relation of subject and predicate when a character is assigned to Reality, and that he is therefore compelled to conclude that *no* truth is quite true. A conclusion of this sort, based upon an extremely abstract argument, makes it natural to suspect that there is some error in the argument.

Pluralism is the view of science and common sense, and is therefore to be accepted if the arguments against it are not conclusive. For my part, I have no doubt whatever that it is the true view, and that monism is derived from a faulty logic inspired by mysticism. This logic dominates the philosophy of Hegel and his followers; it is also the essential basis of Bergson's system, although it is seldom mentioned in his writings. When it is rejected, ambitious metaphysical systems such as those of the past are seen to be impossible.

Chapter 24

Truth and Falsehood

The question of truth and falsehood has been wrapped in unnecessary mystery owing to a number of causes. In the first place, people wish to think that their beliefs are more apt to be true than false, so that they seek a theory that will show that truth is normal and falsehood more or less accidental. In the second place, people are very vague as to what they mean by 'belief' or 'judgment', though persuaded that they know beliefs or judgments to be the objects to which the predicates 'true' or 'false' apply. In the third place, there is a tendency to use 'truth' with a big T in the grand sense, as something noble and splendid and worthy of adoration. This gets people into a frame of mind in which they become unable to think. But just as the grave-diggers in *Hamlet* became familiar with skulls, so logicians become familiar with truth. 'The hand of little employment hath the daintier sense,' says Hamlet. Therefore it is not from the logician that awe before truth is to be expected.

There are two questions in our present subject: (1) What are the objects to which the predicates 'true' and 'false' apply? (2) What is the difference between such as are true and such as are false? We will begin with the first of these questions.

Prima facie, 'true' and 'false' apply to statements, whether in speech or in writing. By extension, they are supposed to apply to the beliefs expressed in those statements, and also to hypotheses which are entertained without being believed or disbelieved. But let us first consider the truth and falsehood of statements, following our practice of going as far as we can with the behaviourists before falling back on introspection. We considered the meaning of words earlier; now we have to consider sentences. Of course a sentence may consist of a single word, or of a wink; but generally it consists of several words. In that case, it has a meaning which is a function of the meanings of the separate words and their order. A sentence which has no meaning is not true or false; thus it is only sentences as vehicles of a certain sort of meaning that have truth or falsehood. We have therefore to examine the meaning of a sentence.

Let us take some very humble example. Suppose you look in a time-table and find it there stated that a passenger train leaves King's Cross for Edinburgh at 10 AM. What is the meaning of this assertion? I shudder when I think of its complexity. If I were to try to develop the theme adequately, I should be occupied with nothing else till the end of the present volume, and then I should have only touched the fringe of the subject. Take first the social aspect: it is not essential that anybody but the engine-driver and stoker should travel by the train, though it is essential that others should be *able* to travel by it if they fulfil certain conditions. It is not essential that the train should reach Edinburgh: the statement remains true if there is an accident or breakdown on the way. But it is essential that the management of the railway should intend it to reach Edinburgh. Take next the physical aspect: it is not essential, or even possible, that the train should start *exactly* at ten; one might perhaps say that it must not start more than ten seconds before its time or more than fifty seconds after, but these limits cannot be laid down rigidly. In countries where unpunctuality is common they would be much wider. Then we must consider what we mean by 'starting', which no one can define unless he has learnt the infinitesimal calculus. Then we consider the definitions of 'King's Cross' and 'Edinburgh', both of which are more or less vague terms. Then we must consider what is meant by a 'train'. Here there will be first of all complicated legal questions; what constitutes fulfilment of a railway company's obligations in the way of running 'trains'? Then there are questions as to the constitution of matter, since evidently a train is a piece of matter; also of course there are questions as to methods of estimating Greenwich time at King's Cross. Most of the above points have to do with the meaning of single words, not with the meaning of the whole sentence. It is obvious that the ordinary mortal does not trouble about such complications when he uses the words: to him a word has a meaning very far from precise, and he does not try to exclude marginal cases. It is the search for precision that introduces complications. We think we attach a meaning to the word 'man', but we don't know whether to include Pithecanthropus Erectus. To this extent, the meaning of the word is vague.

As knowledge increases, words acquire meanings which are more precise and more complex; new words have to be introduced to express the less complex constituents which have been discovered. A word is intended to describe something in the world; at first it does so very badly, but afterwards it gradually improves. Thus single words embody knowledge, although they do not make assertions.

In an ideal logical language, there will be words of different kinds. First, proper names. Of these, however, there are no examples in actual language. The words which are *called* proper names describe collections, which are always defined by some characteristic; thus assertions about 'Peter' are really about everything that is 'Peterish'. To get a true proper name, we should have to get to a single particular or a set of particulars defined by enumeration, not by a common quality. Since we cannot acquire knowledge of actual particulars, the words we use denote, in the best language we can make, either adjectives or relations between two or more terms. In addition to these, there are words indicative of structure: e.g. in 'A is greater than B', the words 'is' and 'than' have no separate meaning, but merely serve to show the 'sense' of the relation 'greater', i.e. that it goes from A to B, not from B to A.

Strictly speaking, we are still simplifying. True adjectives and relations will require particulars for their terms; the sort of adjectives we can know, such as 'blue' and 'round', will not be applicable to particulars. They are therefore analogous to the adjective 'populous' applied to a town. To say 'this town is populous' means 'many people live in this town'. A similar transformation would be demanded by logic in all the adjectives and relations we can know empirically. That is to say, no word that we can understand would occur in a grammatically correct account of the universe.

Leaving on one side the vagueness and inaccuracy of words, let us ask ourselves; in what circumstances do we feel convinced that we know a statement to be true or false as the case may be? A present statement will be regarded as true if, e.g. it agrees with recollection or perception; a past statement, if it raised expectations now confirmed. I do not mean to say that these are the only grounds upon which we regard statements as true; I mean that they are simple and typical, and worth examining. If you say 'It was raining this morning', I may recollect that it was or that it wasn't. One may perhaps say that the words 'this morning' are associated for me with the word 'raining' or with the words 'not raining'. According to which occurs, I judge your statement true or false. If I have neither association, I do not judge your statement either true or false unless I have material for an inference; and I do not wish to consider inference yet. If you say 'The lights have gone out', when I can see the lights shining, I judge that you speak falsely, because my perception is associated with the words 'lights shining'. If you say 'The lights will go out in a minute', you produce a certain familiar kind of tension called 'expectation', and after a time you produce a judgment that you spoke falsely (if the lights do not go out). These are the ordinary *direct* ways of deciding on the truth or falsehood of statements about past, present, or future.

It is necessary to distinguish between direct and indirect grounds for accepting or rejecting statements. Pragmatism considers only indirect grounds. Broadly speaking, it considers a statement false when the consequences of accepting it are unfortunate. But this belongs to the region of inference. I ask you the way to the station, you tell me wrong, and I miss my train; I then *infer* that you told me wrong. But if you say 'The lights are out' when I see them shining, I reject your statement without inference. In this case, something in my present circumstances is associated with words different from yours, and different in ways which I have learnt to regard as involving incompatibility. The ultimate test of falsehood is *never*, so I think, the nature of the consequences of a belief, but the association between words and sensible or remembered facts. A belief is 'verified' when a situation arises which gives a feeling of expectedness in connection with it; it is falsified when the feeling is one of surprise. But this only applies to beliefs which await some future contingency for verification or refutation. A belief which is an immediate reaction to a situation – e.g. when you are waiting for a race to begin and presently you say 'They're off' – has no need of verification, but verifies other beliefs. And even where the confirmation of a belief is in the future, it is the expectedness, not the pleasantness, of the consequences that confirms the truth of the belief.

I think it is a mistake to treat 'belief' as one kind of occurrence, as is done in traditional psychology. The sort of belief which is based upon memory or perception alone differs from the sort which involves expectation. When you find in the time-table that a train leaves King's Cross at ten, your belief that this statement occurs in the time-table does not await future confirmation, but your belief about the train does: you may go to King's Cross and see the train start. A belief which concerns an event may be a recollection, a perception, or an expectation. It may be none of these, in the case of an event which you have not seen and do not expect to see – e.g. Cæsar crossing the Rubicon, or the abolition of the House of Lords. But such beliefs always involve inference. I do not at this stage consider logical and mathematical beliefs, some of which must be, *in a sense,* non-inferential. But I think we shall find that this sense is different from that in which memories and perceptions are non-inferential.

A belief, I should say, interpreted narrowly, is a form of words related to an emotion of one of several kinds. (I shall give a broader meaning later.) The emotion is different according as the belief embodies a reminiscence, a perception, an expectation, or something outside the experience of the believer. Moreover, a form of words is not essential. Where the emotion is present, and leads to action relevant to some feature of the environment, there may be said to be a belief. The fundamental test of a belief, of no matter what sort, is that it causes some event which actually takes place to arouse the emotion of expectedness or its opposite. I do not now attempt to decide what an emotion is. Dr. Watson gives a behaviouristic account of emotions, which would, if adopted, make my definition of 'belief' purely behaviouristic. I have framed the definition so as not to involve a decision on the question of introspection.

The subject of truth and falsehood may be subdivided as follows:

A. *Formal Theory* – Given the meanings of the component words, what decides whether a sentence is true or false?

B. *Causal Theory* – Can we distinguish between truth and falsehood by (*a*) their causes, (*b*) their effects?

C. *Individual and Social Elements* – A statement is a social occurrence, a belief is something individual. How can we define a belief, and what is it when not composed of words?

D. *Consistency and Truth* – Can we get outside the circle of beliefs or statements to something else which shows them true, not merely consistent? In other words, what possible relation is there between propositions and facts?

It is very hard to disentangle these questions. The first question, as to formal theories, leads to the fourth, as to the relation of propositions to facts. E.g. 'Brutus killed Cæsar' is true because of a certain fact; what fact? The fact that Brutus killed Cæsar. This keeps us in the verbal realm, and does not get us outside it to some realm of non-verbal fact by which verbal statements can be verified. Hence our fourth problem arises. But this leads us to our second problem, as to causes and effects of what is true or false, for it is here that we shall naturally look for the vital relation between propositions and facts. And here again we must distinguish between *thinking* truly and *speaking* truly. The former is an individual affair, the latter a social affair. Thus all our problems hang together.

I will begin with C, the difference between a belief and a statement. By a 'statement' I mean a form of words, uttered or written, with a view to being heard or read by some other person or persons, and not a question, interjection, or command, but such as we should call an assertion. As to the question what forms of words are assertions, that is one for the grammarian and differs from language to language. But perhaps we can say rather more than that. The distinction, however, between an assertion and an imperative is not sharp. In England, notices say 'Visitors are requested not to walk on the grass'. In America, they say 'Keep off! This means you'. Effectively, the two have the same meaning: yet the English notice consists only of a statement, while the American notice consists of an imperative followed by a statement which must be false if read by more than one person. In so far as statements are intended to influence the conduct of others, they partake of the nature of imperatives or requests. Their characteristic, however, is that they endeavour to effect their aim by producing a *belief* which may or may not exist in the mind of the speaker. Often, however, they *express* a belief, without stopping to consider the effect upon others. Thus a statement may be defined as a form of words which either expresses a belief or is intended to create one. Our next step, therefore, must be the definition of 'belief'.

'Belief' is a word which will be quite differently defined if we take an analytic point of view from the way in which we shall define it if we regard the matter causally. From the point of view of science, the causal point of view is the more important. Beliefs influence action in certain ways; what influences action in these ways may be called a belief, even if, analytically, it does not much resemble what would ordinarily be so called. We may therefore widen our previous definition of belief. Consider a man who goes to the house where his friend used to live, and, finding he has moved, says, 'I *thought* he still lived here', whereas he acted merely from habit without thought. If we are going to use words causally, we ought to say that this man had a 'belief' and therefore a 'belief' will be merely a characteristic of a string of actions. We shall have to say: A man 'believes' a certain proposition p if, whenever he is aiming at any result to which p is relevant, he acts in a manner calculated to achieve the result if p is true, but not otherwise. Sometimes this gives definite results, sometimes not. When you call a telephone number, it is clear that you believe that to be the number of the subscriber you want. But whether you believe in the conservation of energy or a future life may be harder to decide. You may hold a belief in some contexts and not in others; for we do not think in accordance with the so-called 'Laws of Thought'. 'Belief', like all the other categories of traditional psychology, is a notion incapable of precision.

This brings me to the question whether the truth or falsehood of a belief can be determined either by its causes or by its effects. There is, however, a preliminary difficulty. I said just now that A believes *p* if he acts in a way which will achieve his ends if *p* is *true*. I therefore assumed that we know what is meant by 'truth'. I assumed, to be definite, that we know what is meant by 'truth' as applied to a form of words. The argument was as follows: From observation of a person's acts, you infer his beliefs, by a process which may be as elaborate as the discovery of Kepler's Laws from the observed motions of the planets. His 'beliefs' are not assumed to be 'states of mind', but merely characteristics of series of actions. These beliefs, when ascertained by observation, can be expressed in words; you can say, e.g. 'This person believes that there is a train from King's Cross at 10 AM'. Having once expressed the belief in words of which the meaning is known, you have arrived at the stage where formal theories are applicable. Words of known meaning, put together according to a known syntax, are true or false in virtue of some fact, and their relation to this fact results logically from the meanings of the separate words and the laws of syntax. This is where logic is strong.

It will be seen that, according to what we have said, truth is applicable primarily to a form of words, and only derivatively to a belief. A form of words is a social phenomenon, therefore the fundamental form of truth must be social. A form of words is true when it has a certain relation to a certain fact. What relation to what fact? I think the fundamental relation is this: a form of words is true if a person who knows the language is led to that form of words when he finds himself in an environment which contains features that are the meanings of those words, and these features produce reactions in him sufficiently strong for him to use words which mean them. Thus 'a train leaves King's Cross at 10 AM' is true if a person can be led to say, 'It is now 10 AM, this is King's Cross, and I see a train starting'. The environment causes words, and words directly caused by the environment (if they are statements) are 'true'. What is called 'verification' in science consists in putting oneself in a situation where words previously used for other reasons result directly from the environment. Of course, given this basis, there are innumerable indirect ways of verifying statements, but all, I think, depend upon this direct way.

The above theory may be thought very odd, but it is partly designed to meet the fourth of our previous questions, namely, 'How can we get outside words to the facts which make them true or false?' Obviously we cannot do this within logic, which is imprisoned in the realm of words; we can only do it by considering the relations of words to our other experiences, and these relations, in so far as they are relevant, can hardly be other than causal. I think the above theory, as it stands, is too crude to be quite true. We must also bring in such things as expectedness, which we discussed earlier. But I believe that the definition of truth or falsehood will have to be sought along some such lines as I have indicated.

I want in conclusion to indulge in two speculations. The first concerns a possible reconciliation of behaviourism and logic. It is clear that, when we have a problem to solve, we do not always solve it as the rat does, by means of random movements; we often solve it by 'thinking', i.e. by a process in which we are not making any overt movements. The same thing was sometimes true of Köhler's chimpanzees. Now what is involved in the possibility of solving a problem by verbal thinking? We put words together in various ways which are not wholly random, but limited by previous knowledge of the *sort* of phrase that is likely to contain a solution of our problem. At last we hit upon a phrase which seems to give what we want. We then proceed to an overt action of the kind indicated by the phrase; if it succeeds, our problem is solved. Now this process is only intelligible if there is some connection between the laws of syntax and the laws of physics – using 'syntax' in a psychological rather than a grammatical sense. I think this connection is *assumed* in logic and ordinary philosophy, but it ought to be treated as a problem requiring investigation by behaviourist methods. I lay no stress on this suggestion, except as giving a hint for future investigations. But I cannot think that the behaviourist has gone far towards the solution of his problem until he has succeeded in establishing a connection between syntax and physics. Without this, the efficacy of 'thought' cannot be explained on his principles.

My second speculation is as to the limitations which the structure of language imposes upon the extent of our possible knowledge of the world. I am inclined to think that quite important metaphysical conclusions, of a more or less sceptical kind, can be drawn from simple considerations as to the relation between language and things. A spoken sentence consists of a temporal series of events; a written sentence is a spatial series of bits of matter. Thus it is not surprising that language can represent the course of events in the physical world; it can, in fact, make a map of the physical world, preserving its structure in a more manageable form, and it can do this because it consists of physical events. But if there were such a world as the mystic postulates, it would have a structure different from that of language, and would therefore be incapable of being verbally described. It is fairly clear that nothing verbal can confirm or confute this hypothesis.

A great deal of the confusion about relations which has prevailed in practically all philosophies comes from the fact that relations are indicated, not by relations, but by words which are as substantial as other words. Consequently, in thinking about relations, we constantly hover between the unsubstantiality of the relation itself and the substantiality of the word. Take, say, the fact that lightning precedes thunder. We saw earlier that to express this by a language closely reproducing the structure of the fact, we should have to say simply: 'lightning, thunder', where the fact that the first word precedes the second means that what the first word means precedes what the second word means. But even if we adopted this method for temporal order, we should still need words for all other relations, because we could not without intolerable ambiguity symbolise them also by the order of our words. When we say 'lightning precedes thunder', the word 'precedes' has a quite different relation to what it means from that which the words 'lightning' and 'thunder' have to what they respectively mean. Wittgenstein[1] says that what really happens is that we establish a relation between the word 'lighting' and the word 'thunder', namely the relation of having the word 'precedes' between them. In this way he causes relations to be symbolised by relations. But although this may be quite correct, it is sufficiently odd to make it not surprising that people have thought the word 'precedes' means a relation in the same sense in which 'lightning' means a kind of event. This view, however, must be incorrect. I think it has usually been held unconsciously, and has produced many confusions about relations which cease when it is exposed to the light of day – for example, those which lead Bradley to condemn relations.

In all this I have been considering the question of the relation between the structure of language and the structure of the world. It is clear that anything that can be said in an inflected language can be said in an uninflected language, therefore, everything that can be said in language can be said by means of a temporal series of

[1] *Tractatus Logico-Philosophicus* (Kegan Paul).

uninflected words. This places a limitation upon what can be expressed in words. It may well be that there are facts which do not lend themselves to this very simple schema; if so, they cannot be expressed in language. Our confidence in language is due to the fact that it consists of events in the physical world, and therefore shares the structure of the physical world, and therefore can express that structure. But if there be a world which is not physical, or not in space–time, it may have a structure which we can never hope to express or to know. These considerations might lead us to something like the Kantian *a priori,* not as derived from the structure of the mind, but as derived from the structure of language, which is the structure of the physical world. Perhaps that is why we know so much physics and so little of anything else. However, I have lapsed into mystical speculation, and will leave these possibilities, since, by the nature of the case, I cannot *say* anything true about them.

Chapter 25

The Validity of Inference

It is customary in science to regard certain facts as 'data', from which laws and also other facts are 'inferred'. We saw in Chapter 7 that the *practice* of inference is much wider than the theories of any logician would justify, and that it is nothing other than the law of association or of 'learned reactions'. In the present chapter, I wish to consider what the logicians have evolved from this primitive form of inference, and what grounds we have, as rational beings, for continuing to infer. But let us first get as clear a notion as we can of what should be meant by a 'datum'.

The conception of a 'datum' cannot be made absolute. Theoretically, it should mean something that we know without inference. But before this has any definite meaning, we must define both 'knowledge' and 'inference'. Both these terms have been considered in earlier chapters. For our present purpose it will simplify matters to take account only of such knowledge as is expressed in words. We considered in Chapter 24 the conditions required in order that a form of words may be 'true'; for present purposes, therefore, we may say that 'knowledge' means 'the assertion of a true form of words'. This definition is not quite adequate, since a man may be right by chance; but we may ignore this complication. We may then define a 'datum' as follows: A 'datum' is a form of words which a man utters as the result of a stimulus, with no intermediary of any learned reaction beyond what is involved in knowing how to speak. We must, however, permit such learned reactions as consist in adjustments of the sense-organs or in mere increase of sensitivity. These merely improve the receptivity to data, and do not involve anything that can be called inference.

If the above definition is accepted, all our data for knowledge of the external world must be of the nature of percepts. The belief in external objects is a learned reaction acquired in the first months of life, and it is the duty of the philosopher to treat it as an inference whose validity must be tested. A very little consideration shows that, logically, the inference cannot be demonstrative, but must be at best probable. It is not logically *impossible* that my life may be one long dream, in which I merely imagine all the objects that I believe to be external to me. If we are to reject this view, we must do so on the basis of an inductive or analogical argument, which cannot give complete certainty. We perceive other people behaving in a manner analogous to that in which we behave, and we assume that they have had similar stimuli. We may hear a whole crowd say 'Oh' at the moment when we see a rocket burst, and it is natural to suppose that the crowd saw it too. Nor are such arguments confined to living organisms. We can talk to a dictaphone and have it afterwards repeat what we said; this is most easily explained by the hypothesis that at the surface of the dictaphone events happened, while I was speaking, which were closely analogous to those that were happening just outside my ears. It remains *possible* that there is no dictaphone and I have no ears and there is no crowd watching the rocket; my percepts *may* be all that is happening in such cases. But, if so, it is difficult to arrive at any causal laws, and arguments from analogy are more misleading than we are inclined to think them. As a matter of fact, the whole structure of science, as well as the world of common sense, demands the use of induction and analogy if it is to be believed. These forms of inference, therefore, rather than deduction, are those that must be examined if we are to accept the world of science or any world outside our own dreams.

Let us take a simple example of an induction which we have all performed in practice. If we are hungry, we eat certain things we see and not others – it may be said that we infer edibility inductively from a certain visual and olfactory appearance. The history of this process is that children a few months old put everything into their mouths unless they are stopped; sometimes the result is pleasant, sometimes unpleasant; they repeat the former rather than the latter. That is to say: given that an object having a certain visual and olfactory appearance has been found pleasant to eat, an object having a very similar appearance will be eaten; but when a certain appearance has been found connected with unpleasant consequences when eaten, a similar appearance does not lead to eating next time. The question is: what logical justification is there for our behaviour? Given all our past experience, are we more likely to be nourished by bread than by a stone? It is easy to see why we think so, but can we, as philosophers justify this way of thinking?

It is, of course, obvious that unless one thing can be a sign of another both science and daily life would be impossible. More particularly, reading involves this principle. One accepts printed words as signs, but this is only justifiable by means of induction. I do not mean that induction is necessary to establish the existence of other people, though that also, as we have seen, is true. I mean something simpler. Suppose you want your hair cut, and as you walk along the street you see a notice 'hair-cutting, first floor'. It is only by means of induction that you can *establish* that this notice makes it in some degree probable that there is a hair-cutter's establishment on the first floor. I do not mean that you employ the principle of induction; I mean that you act in accordance with it, and that you would have to appeal to it if you were accompanied by a long-haired sceptical philosopher who refused to go upstairs till he was persuaded there was some point in doing so.

The principle of induction, *prima facie*, is as follows: Let there be two kinds of events, A and B (e.g. lightning and thunder), and let many instances be known in which an event of the kind A has been quickly followed by one of the kind B, and no instances of the contrary. Then either a sufficient number of instances of this sequence, or instances of suitable kinds, will make it increasingly probable that A is always followed by B, and in time the probability can be made to approach certainty without limit provided the right kind and number of instances can be found. This is the principle we have to examine. Scientific theories of induction generally try to substitute well-chosen instances for numerous instances, and represent number of instances as belonging to crude popular induction. But in fact popular induction depends upon the emotional interest of the instances, not upon their number. A child which has burnt its hand *once* in a candle-flame establishes an induction, but words take longer, because at first they are not emotionally interesting. The principle used in primitive practice is: Whatever, on a given occasion, immediately precedes something very painful or pleasant, is a sign of that interesting event. Number plays a secondary part as compared with emotional interest. That is one reason why rational thought is so difficult.

The logical problem of induction is to show that the proposition 'A is always accompanied (or followed) by B' can be rendered probable by knowledge of instances in which this happens, provided the instances are suitably chosen or very numerous. Far the best examination of induction is contained in Mr. Keynes's *Treatise on Probability*. There is a valuable doctor's thesis by the late Jean Nicod, *Le Problème logique de l'induction*, which is very ably reviewed by

R. B. Braithwaite in *Mind,* October 1925. A man who reads these three will know most of what is known about induction. The subject is technical and difficult, involving a good deal of mathematics, but I will attempt to give the gist of the results.

We will begin with the condition in which the problem had been left by J. S. Mill. He had four canons of induction, by means of which, given suitable examples, it could be demonstrated that A and B were causally connected, if the law of causation could be assumed. That is to say, given the law of causation, the scientific use of induction could be reduced to deduction. Roughly the method is this: We know that B must have a cause; the cause cannot be C or D or E or etc., because we find by experiment or observation that these may be present without producing B. On the other hand, we never succeed in finding A without its being accompanied (or followed) by B. If A and B are both capable of quantity, we may find further that the more there is of A the more there is of B. By such methods we eliminate all possible causes except A; therefore, since B must have a cause, that cause must be A. All this is not really induction at all; true induction only comes in in proving the law of causation. This law Mill regards as proved by mere enumeration of instances: we know vast numbers of events which have causes, and no events which can be shown to be uncaused; therefore, it is highly probable that all events have causes. Leaving out of account the fact that the law of causality cannot have quite the form that Mill supposed, we are left with the problem: Does mere number of instances afford a basis for induction? If not, is there any other basis? This is the problem to which Mr. Keynes addresses himself.

Mr. Keynes holds that an induction may be rendered more probable by number of instances, not because of their mere number, but because of the probability, if the instances are very numerous, that they will have nothing in common except the characteristics in question. We want, let us suppose, to find out whether some quality A is always associated with some quality B. We find instances in which this is the case; but it may happen that in all our instances some quality C is also present, and that it is C that is associated with B. If we can so choose our instances that they have nothing in common except the qualities A and B, then we have better grounds for holding that A is always associated with B. If our instances are very numerous, then, even if we do not *know* that they have no other common quality, it may become quite likely that this is the case. This, according to Mr. Keynes, is the sole value of many instances.

A few technical terms are useful. Suppose we want to establish inductively that there is some probability in favour of the generalisation: 'Everything that has the property *F* also has the property *f*'. We will call this generalisation *g*. Suppose we have observed a number of instances in which F and f go together, and no instances to the contrary. These instances may have other common properties as well; the sum-total of their common properties is called the *total positive analogy,* and the sum-total of their *known* common properties is called the *known positive analogy.* The properties belonging to some but not to all of the instances in question are called the *negative analogy*: all of them constitute the *total negative analogy,* all those that are known constitute the *known negative analogy.* To strengthen an induction, we want to diminish the positive analogy to the utmost possible extent; this, according to Mr. Keynes, is why numerous instances are useful.

On 'pure' induction, where we rely solely upon number of instances, without *knowing* how they affect the analogy, Mr. Keynes concludes (p. 236):

'We have shown that if each of the instances necessarily follows from the generalisation, then each additional instance increases the probability of the generalisation, so long as the new instance could not have been predicted with certainty from a knowledge of the former instances . . . The common notion, that each successive verification of a doubtful principle strengthens it, is formally proved, therefore without any appeal to conceptions of law or of causality. *But we have not proved* that this probability approaches certainty as a limit, or even that our conclusion becomes more likely than not, as the number of verifications or instances is indefinitely increased.'

It is obvious that induction is not much use unless, with suitable care, its conclusions can be rendered more likely to be true than false. This problem therefore necessarily occupies Mr. Keynes.

It is found that an induction will approach certainty as a limit if two conditions are fulfilled:

(1) If the generalisation is false, the probability of its being true in a new instance when it has been found to be true in a certain number of instances, however great that number may be, falls short of certainty by a finite amount.

(2) There is a finite *a priori* probability in favour of our generalisation.

Mr. Keynes uses 'finite' here in a special sense. He holds that not all probabilities are numerically measurable; a 'finite' probability is one which exceeds some numerically measurable probability however small. E.g. our generalisation has a finite *a priori* probability if it is less unlikely than throwing heads a billion times running.

The difficulty is, however, that there is no easily discoverable way of estimating the *a priori* probability of a generalisation. In examining this question, Mr. Keynes is led to a very interesting postulate which, if true, will, he thinks, give the required finite *a priori* probability. His postulate as he gives it is not quite correct, but I shall give his form first, and then the necessary modification.

Mr. Keynes supposes that the qualities of objects cohere in groups, so that the number of *independent* qualities is much less than the total number of qualities. We may conceive this after the analogy of biological species: a cat has a number of distinctive qualities which are found in all cats, a dog has a number of other distinctive qualities which are found in all dogs. The method of induction can, he says, be justified if we assume 'that the objects in the field, over which our generalisations extend, do not have an infinite number of independent qualities; that, in other words, their characteristics, however numerous, cohere together in groups of invariable connection, which are finite in number' (p. 256). Again (p. 258): 'As a logical foundation for Analogy, therefore, we seem to need some such assumption as that the amount of variety in the universe is limited in such a way that there is no one object so complex that its qualities fall into an infinite number of independent groups . . . or rather that none of the objects about which we generalise are as complex as this; or at least, that, though some objects may be infinitely complex, we sometimes have a finite probability that an object about which we seek to generalise is not infinitely complex'.

This postulate is called the 'principle of limitation of variety'. Mr. Keynes again finds that it is needed in attempts to establish laws by statistics; if he is right, it is needed for all our scientific knowledge outside pure mathematics. Jean Nicod pointed out that it is not quite sufficiently stringent. We need, according to Mr. Keynes, a finite probability that the object in question has only a finite number of independent qualities; but what we really need is a finite probability that the number of its independent qualities is less than some assigned finite number. This is a very different thing, as may be seen by the following illustration. Suppose there is some number of which we know only that it is finite; it is infinitely improbable that it will be less than a million, or a billion, or any other assigned finite number, because, whatever such number we take, the number of smaller numbers is finite and the number of greater numbers is infinite. Nicod requires us to assume that there is a finite number *n* such that there is a finite probability that the number of independent qualities of our object is less than *n*. This is a much stronger assumption than Mr. Keynes's, which is merely that the number of independent qualities is finite. It is the stronger assumption which is needed to justify induction.

This result is very interesting and very important. It is remarkable that it is in line with the trend of modern science. Eddington has pointed out that there is a certain finite number which is fundamental in the universe, namely the number of electrons. According to the quantum theory, it would seem that the number of possible arrangements of electrons may well also be finite, since they cannot move in all possible orbits, but only in such as make the action in one complete revolution conform to the quantum principle. If all this is true, the principle of limitation of variety may well also be true. We cannot, however, arrive at a proof of our principle in this way, because physics uses induction, and is therefore presumably invalid unless the principle is true. What we can say, in a general way, is that the principle does not refute itself, but, on the contrary, leads to results which confirm it. To this extent, the trend of modern science may be regarded as increasing the plausibility of the principle.

It is important to realise the fundamental position of probability in science. At the very best, induction and analogy only give probability. Every inference worthy of the name is inductive, therefore all inferred knowledge is at best probable. As to what is meant by probability, opinions differ. Mr. Keynes takes it as a fundamental logical category: certain premisses may make a conclusion more or less probable, without making it certain. For him, probability is a relation between a premiss and a conclusion. A proposition does not have a definite probability on its own account; in itself, it is merely true or false. But it has probabilities of different amounts in regard to different premisses. When we speak, elliptically, of *the* probability of a proposition, we mean its probability in relation to all our relevant knowledge. A proposition in probability cannot be refuted by mere observation: improbable things may happen and probable things may fail to happen. Nor is an estimate of probability relevant to given evidence proved wrong when further evidence alters the probability.

For this reason the inductive principle cannot be proved or disproved by experience. We might prove validly that such and such a conclusion was enormously probable, and yet it might not happen.

We might prove invalidly that it was probable, and yet it might happen. What happens affects the probability of a proposition, since it is relevant evidence; but it never alters the probability relative to the previously available evidence. The whole subject of probability, therefore, on Mr. Keynes's theory, is strictly *a priori* and independent of experience.

There is however another theory, called the 'frequency theory', which would make probability not indefinable, and would allow empirical evidence to affect our estimates of probability relative to given premisses. According to this theory in its crude form, the probability that an object having the property F will have the property f is simply the proportion of the objects having both properties to all those having the property F. For example, in a monogamous country the probability of a married person being male is exactly a half. Mr. Keynes advances strong arguments against all forms of this theory that existed when his book was written. There is however an article by R. H. Nisbet on 'The Foundations of Probability' in *Mind* for January 1926, which undertakes to rehabilitate the frequency theory. His arguments are interesting, and suffice to show that the controversy is still an open one, but they do not, in my opinion, amount to decisive proof. It is to be observed, however, that the frequency theory, if it could be maintained, would be preferable to Mr. Keynes's, because it would get rid of the necessity for treating probability as indefinable, and would bring probability into much closer touch with what actually occurs. Mr. Keynes leaves an uncomfortable gap between probability and fact, so that it is far from clear why a rational man will act upon a probability. Nevertheless, the difficulties of the frequency theory are so considerable that I cannot venture to advocate it definitely. Meanwhile, the details of the discussion are unaffected by the view we may take on this fundamental philosophical question. And on either view the principle of limitation of variety will be equally necessary to give validity to the inferences by induction and analogy upon which science and daily life depend.

Chapter 26

Events, Matter, and Mind

Everything in the world is composed of 'events'; that, at least, is the thesis I wish to maintain. An 'event', as I understand it, is something having a small finite duration and a small finite extension in space; or rather, in view of the theory of relativity, it is something occupying a small finite amount of space–time. If it has parts, these parts, I say, are again events, never something occupying a mere point or instant, whether in space, in time, or in space–time. The fact that an event occupies a finite amount of space–time does not prove that it has parts. Events are not impenetrable, as matter is supposed to be; on the contrary, every event in space–time is overlapped by other events. There is no reason to suppose that any of the events with which we are familiar are infinitely complex; on the contrary, everything known about the world is compatible with the view that every complex event has a finite number of parts. We do not know that this is the case, but it is an hypothesis which cannot be refuted and is simpler than any other possible hypothesis. I shall therefore adopt it as a working hypothesis in what follows.

When I speak of an 'event' I do not mean anything out of the way. Seeing a flash of lightning is an event; so is hearing a tyre burst, or smelling a rotten egg, or feeling the coldness of a frog. These are events that are 'data' in the sense of Chapter 15; but, on the principles explained in that chapter, we infer that there are events which are not data and happen at a distance from our own body. Some of these are data to other people, others are data to no one. In the case of the flash of lightning, there is an electromagnetic disturbance consisting of events travelling outward from the place where the flash takes place, and then when this disturbance reaches the eye of a person or animal that can see, there is a percept, which is causally continuous with the events between the place of the lightning and the body of the percipient. Percepts afford the logical premisses for all inferences to events that are not percepts, wherever such inferences are logically justifiable. Particular colours and sounds and so on are events; their causal antecedents in the inanimate world are also events.

If we assume, as I propose to do, that every event has only a finite number of parts, then every event is composed of a finite number of events that have no parts. Such events I shall call 'minimal events'. It will simplify our discussion to assume them, but by a little circumlocution this assumption could be eliminated. The reader must not therefore regard it as an essential part of what follows.

A minimal event occupies a finite region in space–time. Let us take time alone for purposes of illustration. The event in question may overlap in time with each of two others, although the first of these others wholly precedes the second; for example, you may hear a long note on the violin while you hear two short notes on the piano. (It is not necessary to suppose that these are really minimal events; I merely want to illustrate what is meant.) I assume that every event is contemporaneous with events that are not contemporaneous with each other; this is what is meant by saying that every event lasts for a finite time, as the reader can easily convince himself if he remembers that time is wholly relational. If we look away from the world of physics for a moment, and confine ourselves to the world of one man's experience, we can easily define an 'instant' in his life. It will be a group of events, all belonging to his experience, and having the following two properties: (1) any two of the events overlap; (2) no event outside the group overlaps with every member of the group. By a slightly more complicated but essentially similar method, we can define a point-instant in space–time as a group of events having two properties analogous to those used just now in defining an 'instant' in one biography[1]. Thus the 'points' (or point-instants) that the mathematician needs are not simple, but are structures composed of events, made up for the convenience of the mathematician. There will be many 'points' of which a given minimal event is a member; all these together make up the region of space–time occupied by that event. Space–time order, as well as space–time points, results from the relations between events.

A piece of matter, like a space–time point, is to be constructed out of events, but the construction is considerably more complicated, and in the end is only an approximation to what the physicist supposes to be really taking place. There are, at the moment, two somewhat different views of matter, one appropriate to the study of atomic structure, the other to the general theory of relativity as affording an explanation of gravitation. The view appropriate to atomic structure

---

[1] See *The Analysis of Matter*, by the present author, chap. xxviii.

has itself two forms, one derived from Heisenberg, the other from De Broglie and Schrödinger. These two forms, it is true, are mathematically equivalent, but in words they are very different. Heisenberg regards a piece of matter as a centre from which radiations travel outward; the radiations are supposed really to occur, but the matter at their centre is reduced to a mere mathematical fiction. The radiations are, for example, such as constitute light; they are all avowedly systems of events, not changes in the conditions or relations of 'substances'. In the De Broglie-Schrödinger system, matter consists of wave motions. It is not necessary to the theory to postulate anything about these wave-motions except their mathematical characteristics, but, obviously, since they are to explain matter they cannot serve their purpose if they consist of motions of matter. In this system also, therefore, we are led to construct matter out of systems of events, which just happen, and do not happen 'to' matter or 'to' anything else.

Gravitation, as explained by the general theory of relativity, is reduced to 'crinkles' in space–time. Space–time being, as we have already seen, a system constructed out of events, the 'crinkles' in it are also derived from events. There is no reason to suppose that there is a 'thing' at the place where the 'crinkle' is most crinkly. Thus in this part of physics, also, matter has ceased to be a 'thing' and has become merely a mathematical characteristic of the relations between complicated logical structures composed of events.

It was traditionally a property of substance to be permanent, and to a considerable extent matter has retained this property in spite of its loss of substantiality. But its permanence now is only approximate, not absolute. It is thought that an electron and a proton can meet and annihilate each other; in the stars this is supposed to be happening on a large scale[1]. And even while an electron or a proton lasts, it has a different kind of persistence from that formerly attributed to matter. A wave in the sea persists for a longer or shorter time: the waves that I see dashing themselves to pieces on the Cornish coast may have come all the way from Brazil, but that does not mean that a 'thing' has travelled across the Atlantic; it means only that a certain process of change has travelled. And just as a wave in the sea comes to grief at last on the rocks, so an electron or a proton may come to grief when it meets some unusual state of affairs.

Thus 'matter' has very definitely come down in the world as a result of recent physics. It used to be the cause of our sensations: Dr.

[1] See Eddington's *Stars and Atoms*, pp. 102 ff.

Johnson 'disproved' Berkeley's denial of matter by kicking a stone. If he had known that his foot never touched the stone, and that both were only complicated systems of wave-motions, he might have been less satisfied with his refutation. We cannot say that 'matter' is the cause of our sensations. We can say that the events which cause our sensations usually belong to the sort of group that physicists regard as material; but that is a very different thing. Impenetrability used to be a noble property of matter, a kind of Declaration of Independence; now it is a merely tautological result of the way in which matter is defined. The events which are the real stuff of the world are not impenetrable, since they can overlap in space–time. In a word 'matter' has become no more than a convenient shorthand for stating certain causal laws concerning events.

But if matter has fared badly, mind has fared little better. The adjective 'mental' is one which is not capable of any exact significance. There is, it is true, an important group of events, namely percepts, all of which may be called 'mental'. But it would be arbitrary to say that there are no 'mental' events except percepts, and yet it is difficult to find any principle by which we can decide what other events should be included. Perhaps the most essential characteristics of mind are introspection and memory. But memory in some of its forms is, as we have seen, a consequence of the law of conditioned reflexes, which is at least as much physiological as psychological, and characterises living tissue rather than mind. Knowledge, as we have found, is not easy to distinguish from sensitivity, which is a property possessed by scientific instruments. Introspection is a form of knowledge, but turns out, on examination, to be little more than a cautious interpretation of ordinary 'knowledge'. Where the philosopher's child at the Zoo says 'There is a hippopotamus over there,' the philosopher should reply: 'There is a coloured pattern of a certain shape, which may perhaps be connected with a system of external causes of the sort called a hippopotamus.' (I do not live up to this precept myself.) In saying that there is a coloured pattern, the philosopher is practising introspection in the only sense that I can attach to that term, i.e. his knowledge-reaction is to an event situated in his own brain from the standpoint of physical space, and is consciously avoiding physiological and other inference as far as possible. Events to which a knowledge-reaction of this sort occurs are 'mental'; so are, presumably, other events resembling them in certain respects. But I do not see any way of defining this wider group except by saying that mental events are events in a living brain, or, better, in a region combining sensitivity and the law of learned reactions to a marked extent. This definition has at least the merit of showing that mentality is an affair of causal laws, not of the quality of single events, and also that mentality is a matter of degree.

Perhaps it is not unnecessary to repeat, at this point, that events in the brain are not to be regarded as consisting of motions of bits of matter. Matter and motion, as we have seen, are logical constructions using events as their material, and events are therefore something quite different from matter in motion. I take it that, when we have a percept, just what we perceive (if we avoid avoidable sources of error) is an event occupying part of the region which, for physics, is occupied by the brain. In fact, perception gives us the most concrete knowledge we possess as to the stuff of the physical world, but what we perceive is part of the stuff of our brains, not part of the stuff of tables and chairs, sun, moon, and stars. Suppose we are looking at a leaf, and we see a green patch. This patch is not 'out there' where the leaf is, but is an event occupying a certain volume in our brains during the time that we see the leaf. Seeing the leaf consists of the existence, in the region occupied by our brain, of a green patch causally connected with the leaf, or rather with a series of events emanating from the place in physical space where physics places the leaf. The percept is one of this series of events, differing from the others in its effects owing to the peculiarities of the region in which it occurs – or perhaps it would be more correct to say that the different effects *are* the peculiarities of the region.

Thus 'mind' and 'mental' are merely approximate concepts, giving a convenient shorthand for certain approximate causal laws. In a completed science, the word 'mind' and the word 'matter' would both disappear, and would be replaced by causal laws concerning 'events', the only events known to us otherwise than in their mathematical and causal properties being percepts, which are events situated in the same region as a brain and having effects of a peculiar sort called 'knowledge-reactions'.

It will be seen that the view which I am advocating is neither materialism nor mentalism, but what (following a suggestion of Dr. H. M. Sheffer) we call 'neutral monism'. It is monism in the sense that it regards the world as composed of only one *kind* of stuff, namely events; but it is pluralism in the sense that it admits the existence of a great multiplicity of events, each minimal event being a logically self-subsistent entity.

There is, however, another question, not quite the same as this, namely the question as to the relations of psychology and physics. If we knew more, would psychology be absorbed in physics? or, conversely, would physics be absorbed in psychology? A man may be a materialist and yet hold that psychology is an independent science; this is the view taken by Dr. Broad in his important book on *The Mind and its Place in Nature*. He holds that a mind is a material structure, but that it has properties which could not, even theoretically, be inferred from those of its material constituents. He points out that structures very often have properties which, in the present state of our knowledge, cannot be inferred from the properties and relations of their parts. Water has many properties which we cannot infer from those of hydrogen and oxygen, even if we suppose ourselves to know the structure of the molecule of water more completely than we do as yet. Properties of a whole which cannot, even theoretically, be inferred from the properties and relations of its parts are called by Dr. Broad 'emergent' properties. Thus he holds that a mind (or brain) has properties which are 'emergent', and to this extent psychology will be independent of physics and chemistry. The 'emergent' properties of minds will only be discoverable by observation of minds, not by inference from the laws of physics and chemistry. This possibility is an important one, and it will be worth while to consider it.

Our decision to regard a unit of matter as itself not ultimate, but an assemblage of events, somewhat alters the form of our question as to 'emergent' properties. We have to ask: Is matter emergent from events? Is mind emergent from events? If the former, is mind emergent from matter, or deducible from the properties of matter, or neither? If the latter, is matter emergent from mind or deducible from the properties of mind, or neither? Of course, if neither mind nor matter is emergent from events, these latter questions do not arise.

Let us coin a word, 'chrono-geography', for the science which begins with events having space–time relations and does not assume at the outset that certain strings of them can be treated as persistent material units or as minds. Then we have to ask ourselves first: can the science of matter, as it appears in physics and chemistry, be wholly reduced to chrono-geography? If no, matter is emergent from events; if yes, it is not emergent.

Is matter emergent from events? In this present state of science it is difficult to give a decided answer to this question. The notion of matter, in modern physics, has become absorbed into the notion of energy. Eddington, in his *Mathematical Theory of Relativity*, shows that, in virtue of the laws assumed concerning events, there must be something having the observed properties of matter and energy as regards conservation. This he calls the 'Material-energy-tensor', and suggests that it is the reality which we sometimes call 'matter' and sometimes 'energy'. To this extent, matter has been shown to be not emergent. But the existence of electrons and protons (to the extent that they do exist) has not yet been deduced from the general theory of relativity, though attempts are being made and may at any moment succeed. If and when these attempts succeed, physics will cease to be in any degree independent of chrono-geography, but for the present it remains in part independent. As for chemistry, although we cannot practically reduce it all to physics, we can see how theoretically, this could be done, and I think it is safe to assume that it is not an ultimately independent science.

The question we have been asking is: Could we predict, theoretically, from the laws of events that there must be material units obeying the laws which they do in fact obey, or is this a new, logically independent, fact? In theory we might be able to prove that it is *not* independent, but it would be very difficult to prove that it *is*. The present position is, broadly speaking, that the continuous properties of the physical world can be deduced from chrono-geography, but not the discontinuous facts, viz. electrons and protons and Planck's quantum. Thus for the present materiality is practically, though perhaps not theoretically, an emergent characteristic of certain groups of events.

Is mind emergent from events? This question, as yet, can hardly be even discussed intelligently, because psychology is not a sufficiently advanced science. There are, nevertheless, some points to be noted. Chrono-geography is concerned only with the abstract mathematical properties of events, and cannot conceivably, unless it is radically transformed, prove that there are visual events, or auditory events, or events of any of the kinds that we know by perception. In this sense, psychology is certainly emergent from chrono-geography and also from physics, and it is hard to see how it can ever cease to be so. The reason for this is that our knowledge of data contains features of a qualitative sort, which cannot be deduced from the merely mathematical features of the space-time events inferred from data, and yet these abstract mathematical features are all that we can legitimately infer.

The above argument decides also that mind must be emergent from matter, if it is a material structure. No amount of physics can ever tell us all that we do in fact know about our own percepts.

We have still to ask whether we are to regard a mind as a structure of material units or not. If we do so regard it, we are, so far as mind is concerned, emergent materialists in view of what we have just decided; this is the view favoured by Dr. Broad. If we do not so regard it, we are in no sense materialists. In favour of the materialist view, there is the fact that, so far as our experience goes, minds only emerge in connection with certain physical structures, namely living bodies, and that mental development increases with a certain kind of complexity of physical structure. We cannot set against this the argument that minds have peculiar characteristics, for this is quite consistent with *emergent* materialism. If we are to refute it, it must be by finding out what sort of group of events constitutes a mind. It is time to address ourselves to this question.

What is a mind? It is obvious, to begin with, that a mind must be a group of mental events, since we have rejected the view that it is a single simple entity such as the ego was formerly supposed to be. Our first step, therefore, is to be clear as to what we mean by a 'mental' event.

We said a few pages ago that: *Mental events are events in a region combining sensitivity and the law of learned reactions to a marked extent.* For practical purposes, this means (subject to a proviso to be explained shortly) that a mental event is any event in a living brain. We explained that this does not mean that a mental event consists of matter in motion, which is what an old-fashioned physicist would regard as the sort of event that happens in a brain. Matter in motion, we have seen, is not an event in our sense, but a shorthand description of a very complicated causal process among events of a different sort. But we must say a few words in justification of our definition.

Let us consider some alternative definitions. A mental event, we might say, is one which is 'experienced'. When is an event 'experiencd'? We might say: when it has 'mnemic' effects, i.e. effects governed by the law of association. But we saw that this law applies to purely bodily events such as the contraction of the pupil, with which nothing 'mental' seems to be connected. Thus if our definition is to serve, we shall have to define 'experience' differently; we shall have to say that the mnemic effects must include something that can be called 'knowledge'. This would suggest the definition: A mental event is anything that is remembered. But this is too narrow: we only remember a small proportion of our mental events. We might have regarded 'consciousness' as the essence of mental events, but this view was examined and found inadequate in Chapter 20. Moreover, we do not want our definition to exclude the 'unconscious'.

It is clear that the primary mental events, those about which there can be no question, are percepts. But percepts have certain peculiar causal properties, notably that they give rise to knowledge-reactions, and that they are capable of having mnemic effects which are cognitions. These causal properties, however, belong to some events which are not apparently percepts. It seems that any event in the brain may have these properties. And perhaps we were too hasty in saying that the contraction of the pupil on hearing a loud noise involves nothing 'mental'. There may be other 'mental' events connected with a human body besides those belonging to the central personality. I shall come back to this possibility presently. Meanwhile, I shall adhere to the above definition of a 'mental' event, which, as we saw, makes mentality a matter of degree.

We can now return to the question: What is a mind? There may be mental events not forming part of the sort of group that we should call a 'mind', but there certainly are groups having that kind of unity that make us call them one mind. There are two marked characteristics of a mind: First, it is connected with a certain body; secondly, it has the unity of one 'experience'. The two *prima facie* diverge in cases of dual or multiple personality, but I think this is more apparent than real. These two characteristics are, one physical, the other psychological. Let us consider each in turn as a possible definition of what we mean by one 'mind'.

In the physical way, we begin by observing that every mental event known to us is also part of the history of a living body, and we define a 'mind' as the group of mental events which form part of the history of a certain living body. The definition of a living body is chemical, and the reduction of chemistry to physics is clear in theory, though in practice the mathematics is too difficult. It is so far a merely empirical fact that mnemic causation is almost exclusively associated with matter having a certain chemical structure. But the same may be said of magnetism. As yet, we cannot deduce the magnetic properties of iron from what we know of the structure of the atom of iron, but no one doubts that they could be deduced by a person with sufficient knowledge and sufficient mathematical skill. In like manner it may be assumed that mnemic causation is theoretically deducible from the structure of living matter. If we knew enough, we might be able to infer that some other possible structure would exhibit mnemic phenomena, perhaps in an even more marked degree; if so, we might be able to construct Robots who would be more intelligent than we are.

In the psychological way of defining a 'mind', it consists of all the mental events connected with a given mental event by 'experience', i.e. by mnemic causation, but this definition needs a little elaboration before it can be regarded as precise. We do not want the contraction of the pupil to count as a 'mental' event; therefore a mental event will have to be one which has mnemic effects, not merely mnemic causes. In that case, however, there cannot be a last mental event in a man's life, unless we assume that it may have mnemic effects on his body after death. Perhaps we may avoid this inconvenience by discovering the *kind* of event that usually has mnemic effects, though they may be prevented from occurring by special circumstances. Or we might maintain that death is gradual, even when it is what is called instantaneous; in that case the last events in a man's life grow progressively less mental as life ebbs. Neglecting this point, which is not very important, we shall define the 'experience' to which a given mental event belongs as all those mental events which can be reached from the given event by a mnemic causal chain, which may go backwards or forwards, or alternately first one and then the other. This may be conceived on the analogy of an engine shunting at a junction or where there are many points: any line that can be reached, by however many shuntings, will count as part of the same experience.

We cannot be sure that all the mental events connected with one body are connected by links of mnemic causation with each other, and therefore we cannot be sure that our two definitions of one 'mind' give the same result. In cases of multiple personality, some at least of the usual mnemic effects, notably recollection, are absent in the life of one personality when they have occurred in the life of the other. But probably both personalities are connected by mnemic chains with events which occurred before the dissociation took place, so that there would be only one mind according to our definition. But there are other possibilities which must be considered. It may be that each cell in the body has its own mental life, and that only selections from these mental lives go to make up the life which we regard as ours. The 'unconscious' might be the mental lives of subordinate parts of the body, having occasional mnemic effects which we can notice, but in the main separate from the life of which we are 'conscious'. If so, the mental events connected with one body will be more numerous than the events making up its central 'mind'. These, however, are only speculative possibilities.

I spoke a moment ago of the life of which we are 'conscious', and perhaps the reader has been wondering why I have not made more use of the notion of 'consciousness'. The reason is that I regard it as only one kind of mnemic effect, and not one entitled to a special place. To say that I am 'conscious' of an event is to say that I recollect it, at any rate for a short time after it has happened. To say that I recollect an event is to say that a certain event is occurring in me now which is connected by mnemic causation with the event recollected, and is of the sort that we call a 'cognition' of that event. But events which I do not recollect may have mnemic effects upon me. This is the case, not only where we have Freudian suppression, but in all habits which were learnt long ago and have now become automatic, such as writing and speaking. The emphasis upon consciousness has made a mystery of the 'unconscious', which ought to be in no way surprising.

It does not much matter which of our two definitions of a 'mind' we adopt. Let us, provisionally, adopt the first definition, so that a mind is all the mental events which form part of the history of a certain living body, or perhaps we should rather say a living brain.

We can now tackle the question which is to decide whether we are emergent materialists or not, namely:

Is a mind a structure of material units?

I think it is clear that the answer to this question is in the negative. Even if a mind consists of all the events in a brain, it does not consist of bundles of these events grouped as physics groups them, i.e. it does not lump together all the events that make up one piece of matter in the brain, and then all the events that make up another, and so on. Mnemic causation is what concerns us most in studying mind, but this seems to demand a recourse to physics, if we assume, as seems plausible, that mental mnemic causation is due to effects upon the brain. This question, however, is still an open one. If mnemic causation is ultimate, mind is emergent. If not, the question is more difficult. As we saw earlier, there certainly is knowledge in psychology which cannot ever form part of physics. But as this point is important, I shall repeat the argument in different terms.

The difference between physics and psychology is analogous to that between a postman's knowledge of letters and the knowledge of a recipient of letters. The postman knows the movements of many letters, the recipient knows the contents of a few. We may regard the light and sound waves that go about the world as letters of which the physicist may know the destination; some few of them are addressed to human beings, and when read give psychological knowledge. Of course the analogy is not perfect, because the letters with which the physicist deals are continually changing during their journeys, as if they were written in fading ink, which, also, was not quite dry all the time, but occasionally got smudged with rain. However, the analogy may pass if not pressed.

It would be possible without altering the detail of previous discussions except that of Chapter 25, to give a different turn to the argument, and make matter a structure composed of mental units. I am not quite sure that this is the wrong view. It arises not unnaturally from the argument as to data contained in Chapter 25. We saw that all data are mental events in the narrowest and strictest sense, since they are percepts. Consequently all verification of causal laws consists in the occurrence of expected percepts. Consequently any inference beyond percepts (actual or possible) is incapable of being empirically tested. We shall therefore be prudent if we regard the non-mental events of physics as mere auxiliary concepts, not assumed to have any reality, but only introduced to simplify the laws of percepts. Thus matter will be a construction built out of percepts, and our metaphysic will be essentially that of Berkeley. If there are no non-mental events, causal laws will be very odd; for example, a hidden dictaphone may record a conversation although it did not exist at the time, since no one was perceiving it. But although this seems odd, it is not logically impossible. And it must be conceded that it enables us to interpret physics with a smaller amount of dubious inductive and analogical inference than is required if we admit non-mental events.

In spite of the logical merits of this view, I cannot bring myself to accept it, though I am not sure that my reasons for disliking it are any better than Dr. Johnson's. I find myself constitutionally incapable of believing that the sun would not exist on a day when he was everywhere hidden by clouds, or that the meat in a pie springs into existence at the moment when the pie is opened. I know the logical answer to such objections and *quâ logician* I think the answer a good one. The logical argument, however, does not even tend to show that there are *not* non-mental events; it only tends to show that we have no right to feel sure of their existence. For my part, I find myself in fact believing in them in spite of all that can be said to persuade me that I ought to feel doubtful.

There is an argument, of a sort, against the view we are considering. I have been assuming that we admit the existence of other people and their perceptions, but question only the inference from perceptions to events of a different kind. Now there is no good reason why we should not carry our logical caution a step further. I cannot verify a theory by means of another man's perceptions, but only by means of my own. Therefore the laws of physics can only be verified by me in so far as they lead to predictions of *my* percepts. If then, I refuse to admit non-mental events because they are not verifiable, I ought to refuse to admit mental events in every one except myself, on the same ground. Thus I am reduced to what is called 'solipsism', i.e. the theory that I alone exist. This is a view which is hard to refute, but still harder to believe. I once received a letter from a philospher who professed to be a solipsist, but was surprised that there were no others! Yet this philosopher was by way of believing that no one else existed. This shows that solipsism is not really believed even by those who think they are convinced of its truth.

We may go a step further. The past can only be verified indirectly, by means of its effects in the future; therefore the type of logical caution we have been considering should lead us to abstain from asserting that the past really occurred: we ought to regard it as consisting of auxiliary concepts convenient in stating the laws applicable to the future. And since the future, though verifiable if and when it occurs, is as yet unverified, we ought to suspend judgment about the future also. If we are not willing to go so far as this, there seems no reason to draw the line at the precise point where it was drawn by Berkeley. On these grounds I feel no shame in admitting the existence of non-mental events such as the laws of physics lead us to infer. Nevertheless, it is important to realise that other views are tenable.

Chapter 27

Man's Place in the Universe

In this final chapter, I propose to recapitulate the main conclusions at which we have arrived, and then to say a few words on the subject of Man's relation to the universe in so far as philosophy has anything to teach on this subject without extraneous help.

Popular metaphysics divides the known world into mind and matter, and a human being into soul and body. Some – the materialists – have said that matter alone is real and mind is an illusion. Many – the idealists in the technical sense, or mentalists, as Dr. Broad more appropriately calls them – have taken the opposite view, that mind alone is real and matter is an illusion. The view which I have suggested is that both mind and matter are structures composed of a more primitive stuff which is neither mental nor material. This view, called 'neutral monism', is suggested in Mach's *Analysis of Sensations,* developed in William James's *Essays in Radical Empiricism,* and advocated by John Dewey, as well as by Professor R. B. Perry and other American realists. The use of the word 'neutral' in this way is due to Dr. H. M. Sheffer[1], of Harvard, who is one of the ablest logicians of our time.

Since man is the instrument of his own knowledge, it is necessary to study him as an instrument before we can appraise the value of what our senses seem to tell us concerning the world. In Part I we studied man, within the framework of common-sense beliefs, just as we might study clocks or thermometers, as an instrument sensitive to certain features of the environment, since sensitiveness to the environment is obviously an indispensable condition for knowledge about it.

In Part II we advanced to the study of the physical world. We found that matter, in modern science, has lost its solidity and substantiality; it has become a mere ghost haunting the scenes of its former splendours. In pursuit of something that could be treated as substantial, physicists analysed ordinary matter into molecules, molecules into atoms, atoms into electrons and protons. There, for a few years, analysis found a resting-place. But now electrons and protons

[1] See Holt's *Concept of Consciousness,* preface.

themselves are dissolved into systems of radiations by Heisenberg, and into systems of waves by Schrödinger – the two theories amount mathematically to much the same thing. And these are not wild metaphysical speculations; they are sober mathematical calculations, accepted by the great majority of experts.

Another department of theoretical physics, the theory of relativity, has philosophical consequences which are, if possible, even more important. The substitution of space–time for space and time has made the category of substance less applicable than formerly, since the essence of substance was persistence through time, and there is now no one cosmic time. The result of this is to turn the physical world into a four-dimensional continuum of events, instead of a series of three-dimensional states of a world composed of persistent bits of matter. A second important feature of relativity-theory is the abolition of force, particularly gravitational force, and the substitution of differential causal laws having to do only with the neighbourhood of an event, not with an influence exerted from a distance, such as gravitation formerly seemed to be.

The modern study of the atom has had two consequences which have considerably changed the philosophical bearing of physics. On the one hand, it appears that there are discontinuous changes in nature, occasions when there is a sudden jump from one state to another without passing through the intermediate states. (Schrödinger, it is true, questions the need for assuming discontinuity; but so far his opinion has not prevailed.) On the other hand, the course of nature is not so definitely determined by the physical laws at present known as it was formerly thought to be. We cannot predict when a discontinuous change will take place in a given atom, though we can predict statistical averages. It can no longer be said that, given the laws of physics and the relevant facts about the environment, the future history of an atom can theoretically be calculated from its present condition. It may be that this is merely due to the insufficiency of our knowledge, but we cannot be sure that this is the case. As things stand at present, the physical world is not so rigidly deterministic as it has been believed to be during the last 250 years. And in various directions what formerly appeared as laws governing each separate atom are now found to be only averages attributable in part to the laws of chance.

From these questions concerning the physical world in itself, we were led to others concerning the causation of our perceptions, which are the data upon which our scientific knowledge of physics is based. We saw that a long causal chain always intervenes between an external event and the event in us which we regard as perception of the external event. We cannot therefore suppose that the external event is exactly what we see or hear; it can, at best, resemble the percept only in certain structural respects. This fact has caused considerable confusion in philosophy, partly because philosophers tried to think better of perception than it deserves, partly because they failed to have clear ideas on the subject of space. It is customary to treat space as a characteristic of matter as opposed to mind, but this is only true of *physical* space. There is also *perceptual* space, which is that in which what we know immediately through the senses is situated. This space cannot be identified with that of physics. From the standpoint of physical space, all our percepts are in our heads; but in perceptual space our percept of our hand is outside our percept of our head. The failure to keep physical and perceptual space distinct has been a source of great confusion in philosophy.

In Part III we resumed the study of man, but now as he appears to himself, not only as he is known to an external observer. We decided, contrary to the view of the behaviourists, that there are important facts which cannot be known except when the observer and observed are the same person. The datum in perception, we decided, is a private fact which can only be known directly to the percipient; it is a datum for physics and psychology equally, and must be regarded as both physical and mental. We decided later that there are inductive grounds, giving probability but not certainty, in favour of the view that perceptions are causally connected with events which the percipient does not experience, which may belong only to the physical world.

The behaviour of human beings is distinguished from that of inanimate matter by what are called 'mnemic' phenomena, i.e. by a certain kind of effect of past occurrences. This kind of effect is exemplified in memory, in learning, in the intelligent use of words, and in every kind of knowledge. But we cannot, on this ground, erect an absolute barrier between mind and matter. In the first place, inanimate matter, to some slight extent, shows analogous behaviour – e.g. if you unroll a roll of paper, it will roll itself up again. In the second place, we find that living bodies display mnemic phenomena to exactly the same extent to which minds display them. In the third place, if we are to avoid what I have called 'mnemic' causation, which involves action at a distance in time, we must say that mnemic phenomena in mental events are due to the modification of the body by past events. That is to say, the set of events which constitutes one man's experience is not causally self-sufficient, but is dependent upon causal laws involving events which he cannot experience.

On the other hand, our knowledge of the physical world is purely abstract: we know certain logical characteristics of its structure, but nothing of its intrinsic character. There is nothing in physics to prove that the intrinsic character of the physical world differs, in this or that respect, from that of the mental world. Thus from both ends, both by the analysis of physics and by the analysis of psychology, we find that mental and physical events form one causal whole, which is not known to consist of two different sorts. At present, we know the laws of the physical world better than those of the mental world, but that may change. We know the intrinsic character of the mental world to some extent, but we know absolutely nothing of the intrinsic character of the physical world. And in view of the nature of the inferences upon which our knowledge of physics rests, it seems scarcely possible that we should ever know more than abstract laws about matter.

In Part IV we considered what philosophy has to say about the universe. The function of philosophy, according to the view advocated in this volume, is somewhat different from that which has been assigned to it by a large and influential school. Take, e.g. Kant's antinomies. He argues (1) that space must be infinite, (2) that space cannot be infinite; and he deduces that space is subjective. The non-Euclideans refuted the argument that it must be infinite, and Georg Cantor refuted the argument that it cannot be. Formerly, *a priori* logic was used to prove that various hypotheses which looked possible were impossible, leaving only one possibility, which philosophy therefore pronounced true. Now, *a priori* logic is used to prove the exact contrary, namely, that hypotheses which looked impossible are possible. Whereas logic was formerly counsel for the prosecution, it is now counsel for the defence. The result is that many more hypotheses are at large than was formerly the case. Formerly, to revert to the instance of space, it appeared that experience left only one kind of space to logic, and logic showed this one kind to be impossible. Now, logic presents many kinds of space as possible apart from experience, and experience only partially decides between them. Thus, while our knowledge of what is has become less than it was formerly supposed to be, our knowledge of what may be is enormously increased. Instead of being shut in within narrow walls, of which every nook and cranny could be explored, we find ourselves in an open world of free possibilities, where much remains unknown because there is so much to know. The attempt to prescribe to the universe by means of *a priori* principles has broken down; logic, instead of being, as formerly, a bar to possibilities, has become the great liberator of the imagination, presenting innumerable alternatives which are closed to unreflective common sense, and leaving to experience the task of deciding, where decision is possible, between the many worlds which logic offers for our choice.

Philosophical knowledge, if what we have been saying is correct, does not differ essentially from scientific knowledge; there is no special source of wisdom which is open to philosophy but not to science, and the results obtained by philosophy are not radically different from those reached in science. Philosophy is distinguished from science only by being more critical and more general. But when I say that philosophy is critical, I do not mean that it attempts to criticise knowledge from outside, for that would be impossible: I mean only that it examines the various parts of our supposed knowledge to see whether they are mutually consistent and whether the inferences employed are such as seem valid to a careful scrutiny. The criticism aimed at is not that which, without reason, determines to reject, but that which considers each piece of apparent knowledge on its merits, and retains whatever still appears to be knowledge when this consideration is completed. That some risk of error remains must be admitted, since human beings are fallible. Philosophy may claim justly that it diminishes the risk of error, and that in some cases it renders the risk so small as to be practically negligible. To do more than this is not possible in a world where mistakes must occur; and more than this no prudent advocate of philosophy would claim to have performed.

I want to end with a few words about man's place in the universe. It has been customary to demand of a philosopher that he should show that the world is good in certain respects. I cannot admit any duty of this sort. One might as well demand of an accountant that he should show a satisfactory balance-sheet. It is just as bad to be fraudulently optimistic in philosophy as in money matters. If the world is good, by all means let us know it; but if not, let us know that. In any case, the question of the goodness or badness of the world is one for science rather than for philosophy. We shall call the world good if it has certain characteristics that we desire. In the past philosophy professed to be able to prove that the world had such characteristics, but it is now fairly evident that the proofs were invalid. It does not, of course, follow that the world does not have the characteristics in question; it follows only that philosophy cannot decide the problem. Take for example the problem of personal immortality. You may believe this on the ground of revealed religion, but that is a ground which lies outside philosophy. You may believe it on the ground of the phenomena investigated by psychical research, but that is science, not philosophy. In former days, you could believe it on a philosophical ground, namely, that the soul is a substance and all substances are indestructible. You will find this argument, sometimes more or less disguised, in many philosophers. But the notion of substance, in the sense of a permanent entity with changing states, is no longer applicable to the world. It may happen, as with the electron, that a string of events are so interconnected causally that it is practically convenient to regard them as forming one entity, but where this happens it is a scientific fact, not a metaphysical necessity. The whole question of personal immortality, therefore lies outside philosophy, and is to be decided, if at all, either by science or by revealed religion.

I will take up another matter in regard to which what I have said may have been disappointing to some readers. It is sometimes thought that philosophy ought to aim at encouraging a good life. Now, of course, I admit that it should have this effect, but I do not admit that it should have this as a conscious purpose. To begin with, when we embark upon the study of philosophy we ought not to assume that we already know for certain what the good life is: philosophy may conceivably modify our views as to what is good, in which case it will seem to the non-philosophical to have had a bad moral effect. That, however, is a secondary point. The essential thing is that philosophy is part of the pursuit of knowledge, and that we cannot limit this pursuit by insisting that the knowledge obtained shall be such as we should have thought edifying before we obtained it. I think it could be maintained with truth that *all* knowledge is edifying, provided we have a right conception of edification. When this appears to be not the case, it is because we have moral standards based upon ignorance. It may happen by good fortune that a moral standard based upon ignorance is right, but if so knowledge will not destroy it; if knowledge can destroy it, it must be wrong. The conscious purpose of philosophy, therefore, ought to be solely to *understand* the world as well as possible, not to establish this or that proposition which is thought morally desirable. Those who embark upon philosophy must be prepared to question all their preconceptions, ethical as well as scientific; if they have a determination never to surrender certain philosophic beliefs, they are not in the frame of mind in which philosophy can be profitably pursued.

But although philosophy ought not to have a moral purpose, it ought to have certain good moral effects. Any disinterested pursuit of knowledge teaches us the limits of our power, which is salutary; at the same time, in proportion as we succeed in achieving knowledge, it teaches the limits of our impotence, which is equally desirable. And philosophical knowledge, or rather philosophical thought, has certain special merits not belonging in an equal degree to other intellectual pursuits. By its generality it enables us to see human passions in their just proportions, and to realise the absurdity of many quarrels between individuals, classes, and nations. Philosophy comes as near as possible for human beings to that large, impartial contemplation of the universe as a whole which raises us for the moment above our purely personal destiny. There is a certain asceticism of the intellect which is good as a part of life, though it cannot be the whole so long as we have to remain animals engaged in the struggle for existence. The asceticism of the intellect requires that, while we are engaged in the pursuit of knowledge, we shall repress all other desires for the sake of the desire to know. While we are philosophising, the wish to prove that the world is good, or that the dogmas of this or that sect are true, must count as weaknesses of the flesh – they are temptations to be thrust on one side. But we obtain in return something of the joy which the mystic experiences in harmony with the will of God. This joy philosophy can give, but only to those who are willing to follow it to the end, through all its arduous uncertainties.

The world presented for our belief by a philosophy based upon modern science is in many ways less alien to ourselves than the world of matter as conceived in former centuries. The events that happen in our minds are part of the course of nature, and we do not know that the events which happen elsewhere are of a totally different kind. The physical world, so far as science can show at present, is perhaps less rigidly determined by causal laws than it was thought to be; one might, more or less fancifully, attribute even to the atom a kind of limited free will. There is no need to think of ourselves as powerless and small in the grip of vast cosmic forces. All measurement is conventional, and it would be possible to devise a perfectly serviceable system of measurement according to which a man would be larger than the sun. No doubt there are limits to our power, and it is good that we should recognise the fact. But we cannot say what the limits are, except in a quite abstract way, such as that we cannot create energy. From the point of view of human life, it is not important to be able to *create* energy; what is important is to be able to direct energy into this or that channel, and this we can do more and more as our knowledge of science increases. Since men first began to think, the forces of nature have oppressed them; earthquakes, floods, pestilences, and famines have filled them with terror. Now at last, thanks to science, mankind are discovering how to avoid much of the suffering that such events have hitherto entailed. The mood in which, as it seems to me, the modern man should face the universe is one of quiet self-respect. The universe as known to science is not in itself either friendly or hostile to man, but it can be made to act as a friend if approached with patient knowledge. Where the universe is concerned, knowledge is the one thing needful. Man, alone of living things, has shown himself capable of the knowledge required to give him a certain mastery over his environment. The dangers to man in the future, or at least in any measurable future, come, not from nature, but from man himself. Will he use his power wisely? Or will he turn the energy liberated from the struggle with nature into struggles with his fellow-men? History, science, and philosophy all make us aware of the great collective achievements of mankind. It would be well if every civilised human being had a sense of these achievements and a realisation of the possibility of greater things to come, with the indifference which must result as regards the petty squabbles upon which the passions of individuals and nations are wastefully squandered.

Philosophy should make us know the ends of life, and the elements in life that have value on their own account. However our freedom may be limited in the causal sphere, we need admit no limitations to our freedom in the sphere of values: what we judge good on its own account we may continue to judge good, without regard to anything but our own feeling. Philosophy cannot itself determine the ends of life, but it can free us from the tyranny of prejudice and from distortions due to a narrow view. Love, beauty, knowledge, and joy of life: these things retain their lustre however wide our purview. And if philosophy can help us to feel the value of these things, it will have played its part in man's collective work of bringing light into a world of darkness.

Index

HISTORY OF WESTERN PHILOSOPHY

Philosophers, Bertrand Russell writes, are both effects and causes: effects of their social circumstances and of the politics and institutions of their time; causes (if they are fortunate) of beliefs which mould the politics and institutions of later ages. In most histories of philosophy, each philosopher appears in a vacuum; his opinions are set forth unrelated except, at most, to those of earlier philosophers. In his *History of Western Philosophy*, Russell tries to exhibit each philosopher as an outcome of his *milieu*, a man in whom were crystallised and concentrated thoughts and feelings which, in a vague and diffused form, were common to the community of which he was a part. By taking a wide view Russell gives unity to his subject and brings out the relations that one philosopher has to another of a different period.

'It is certain of a very wide audience, and is, in my opinion, just the kind of thing people ought to have to make them understand the past . . . It may be one of the most valuable books of our time.'

G. M. Trevelyan

'Bertrand Russell's remarkable book is, so far as I am aware, the first attempt to present a history of Western philosophy in relation to its social and economic background. As such, and also as a brilliantly written exposé of changing philosophical doctrines, it should be widely read.'

Sir Julian Huxley

'A survey of Western philosophy in relation to its environment, of such sweep and acuteness, alive in every nerve . . . a masterpiece of intellectual energy . . . the Socrates of our time.'

A. L. Rowse

THE AUTOBIOGRAPHY OF BERTRAND RUSSELL

'Three passions, simple but overwhelmingly strong, have governed my life : the longing for love, the search for knowledge, and unbearable pity for the suffering of mankind. These passions, like great winds, have blown me hither and thither . . . over a deep ocean of anguish, reaching to the very verge of despair.'

Thinker, philosopher, mathematician, educational innovator and experimenter, champion of intellectual, social and sexual freedom, campaigner for peace and for civil and human rights, Bertrand Russell's life was one of incredible variety and richness. In keeping with his character and beliefs, his life-story is told with vigour, disarming charm and total frankness. His childhood was bitterly lonely but unusually rich in experience. His adult-life was spent grappling both with his own beliefs and the problems of the universe and mankind, and the pursuit of love and permanent happiness which resulted in no less than five marriages. The many storms and episodes of his life are recalled with the vivid freshness and clarity which characterised all Russell's writing and which make this perhaps the most moving literary self-portrait of the twentieth century.

'Among the most glittering literary products of the decade.'

Bernard Levin

'These pages are by turns hilarious and deeply moving, sharp and beautiful . . . something better than a book in a million'.

Michael Foot

'A marvel of intelligence, lucidity and wit; a marvel of undeviating concern for his fellow humans.'

Philip Toynbee